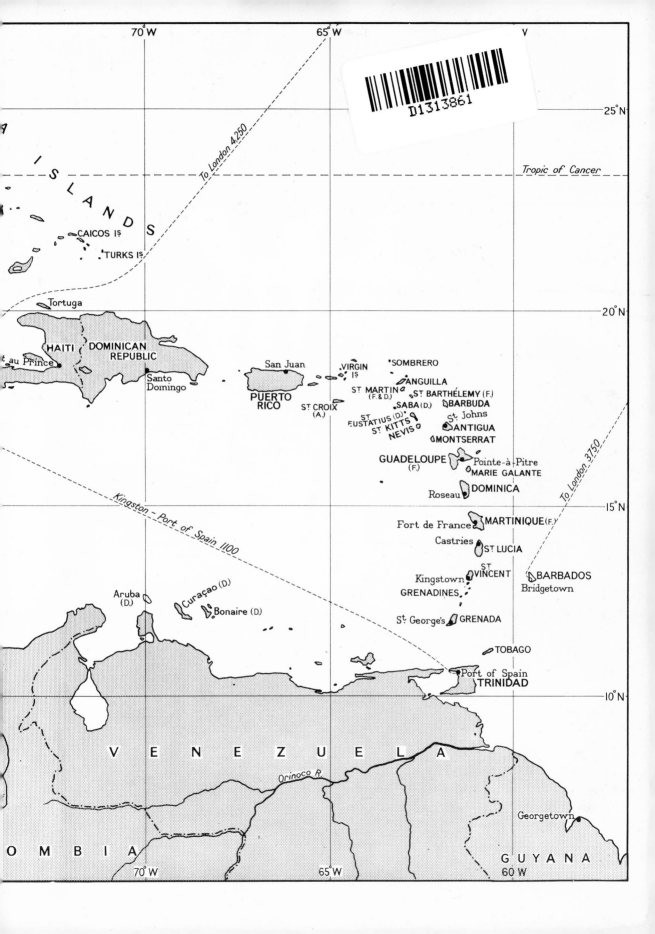

70° W

65° W

V

To London 4.250

25° N

Tropic of Cancer

ISLANDS

CAICOS IS

TURKS IS

Tortuga

20° N

HAITI

DOMINICAN REPUBLIC

t au Prince

Santo Domingo

San Juan

VIRGIN IS

SOMBRERO

ANGUILLA

St MARTIN (F. & D.)

St BARTHÉLEMY (F.)

PUERTO RICO

ST CROIX (A.)

SABA (D.)

BARBUDA

ST EUSTATIUS (D.)

St KITTS

NEVIS

St Johns

ANTIGUA

MONTSERRAT

GUADELOUPE (F.)

Pointe-à-Pitre

MARIE GALANTE

To London 3750

Roseau

DOMINICA

15° N

Kingston – Port of Spain 1100

Fort de France

MARTINIQUE (F.)

Castries

St LUCIA

Kingstown

St VINCENT

BARBADOS

GRENADINES

Bridgetown

Aruba (D.)

Curaçao (D.)

Bonaire (D.)

St George's

GRENADA

TOBAGO

Port of Spain

TRINIDAD

10° N

V E N E Z U E L A

Orinoco R.

Georgetown

O M B I A

70° W

65° W

60° W

G U Y A N A

CARIBBEAN LANDS

a geography of the West Indies

JOHN MACPHERSON

B.SC.(HONS) LOND., DIP.ED., F.R.G.S.

LONGMANS

LONGMANS, GREEN AND CO LTD
48 Grosvenor Street, London W.1

*Associated companies, branches and representatives
throughout the world*

Cartography by
John Callow, B.A., F.R.G.S.

*Printed in Great Britain by
Jarrold & Sons Ltd, Norwich*

Contents

Introduction

This book deals with the way we live and make a living in the West Indies, and explains some of the contributing factors. These factors are of two kinds. First there are the physical factors of topography, climate and mineral wealth which decree the ultimate possibilities. Thus sugar cane, oranges, jute and tea can all be grown in the West Indian climate, whereas wheat and apples cannot. Secondly, out of the possibilities provided by nature, men —moved by the desire for gain or the need to subsist—have made their selections. Thus sugar cane and oranges have been grown on a large scale here, whereas jute and tea have not. So we see that the ways by which we make a living in the West Indies are influenced both by physical and by historical factors, and both therefore play an important part in this book. The former are dealt with in general in Chapters 1, 2, and 3 and in detail in the regional chapters; the latter in Chapter 4 and also in the regional chapters.

At any time in history, men's selections have been limited by their skills. New skills have led to new achievements and to the moulding of new landscapes. Two examples of this are the rise of the sugar industry in the Lesser Antilles in the 1640s and the development of Jamaican bauxite in the 1950s. Of course, just because skills exist does not mean that everyone can, or will, make use of them. Throughout the region it is commonplace to see the same physical environment used in different ways—as, for instance, a highly mechanized sugar estate lying beside un-mechanized small holdings.

Though differences in resources and the use of resources are easy to discern between one place and another, and between one territory and another, we must not overlook the similarities that also exist, though they may perhaps be more obvious to the visitor to the West Indies or to the West Indian living abroad than to those of us who live in the region. But the very fact that we immediately recognize a fellow West Indian wherever we meet one is evidence of this regional similarity. These matters are fascinating and endless sources of topics for discussion, and opportunities for discussing them and for making geographical comparisons and contrasts abound throughout the book.

The boundaries of the Caribbean region have never been clearly established and this book does not attempt to define them. It deals in detail with the West Indian islands and with Belize and Guyana, and pays less attention to other mainland territories bordering the Caribbean. In other words it concentrates on those areas covered by examination syllabuses of G.C.E. (O) Level. However, the book may also be used by (A) Level candidates and teachers' college students,* though they will wish to do further reading about the Central American and some South American republics, and about the territory in which they live.

Useful supplementary sources of current information on the West Indies are to be found in the *Economic Surveys* published by Barclays Bank, in the C.O.I. *Fact Sheets*, and in articles in the journal *Social and Economic Studies* issued by the University of the West Indies.

The author wishes to express his gratitude and thanks to all those people in so many territories who so willingly gave advice, supplied information, and helped in so many other ways in the preparation of this book.

*Abbreviations used for the various examining authorities quoted in this book are:

A.E.B.(O). Associated Examining Board (Ordinary Level).
C.S.C. Cambridge School Certificate.
C.H.S.C. Cambridge Higher School Certificate.
J.C.E. Jamaica Certificate of Education.
J.T.C. Jamaica Training Colleges Examination.
L.G.C.E.(O) University of London General Certificate of Education (Ordinary Level).
O.C.S.E.B.(O) Oxford and Cambridge Schools Examination Board (Ordinary Level).

ACKNOWLEDGMENTS We are grateful to the Ministry of Education in Jamaica for permission to reproduce questions from the Jamaica Local Examination, Jamaica Certificate of Education and Jamaica Training Colleges Examination, and the University of London, Oxford and Cambridge Local Examinations Syndicate for questions from past papers.

v

In the West Indies, where changes are taking place so rapidly (the rate of economic growth of Jamaica in the late 1950s was the third fastest in the world) and where such things as the building of a new road and the opening, or closing, of a factory have a measurable effect on the economy of the territory in which they happen, it is necessary for us to keep our knowledge of developments in the region up to date. To help students to keep abreast of these changes a new edition of this book has been prepared only four years after its first printing. The opportunity has also been taken to include new illustrations, to modify some of the maps, and to take account of recent political changes. Thus the old political groupings of the Windward Islands and the Leeward Islands no longer exist. Most of these islands have become the *West Indian Associated States*, but because Montserrat has chosen not to join them the term *Commonwealth Eastern Caribbean Territories* has been used throughout this book when they are all being referred to. In addition, British Guiana has become *Guyana*, and British Honduras is in process of becoming *Belize*. Students should note that to simplify matters the new names have been used throughout the book, even when reference is being made to the territories as they were in the old colonial days.

CURRENCY

In this book all references to "dollars" refer to the West Indian dollar (worth 4*s*. 2*d*.). Other currencies in use in the region (e.g. Jamaica) are pounds (worth 20*s*.), Belize dollars (worth 5*s*.) and Bahamian dollars (equivalent to United States dollars, that is about 7*s*). These currencies have been converted to West Indian dollars in the text and the statistical tables so that direct comparisons can be made.

Front Cover: Petit Piton seen from the fishermen's beach at Soufrière, St Lucia. Anne Bolt.
Back Cover: Loading sugar at St. Kitts. Anne Bolt.

Illustrations

CHAPTER ONE

The Formation of the West Indies

The oldest rocks of the Caribbean region are those of the Guiana Highlands which lie to the south of the West Indies. These rocks are of Pre-Cambrian Age and thus belong to the oldest group of rocks in the world, a group that was formed during the immense period of earth history (probably about four-fifths of the total) which drew towards a close when the first primitive forms of life came into being. Other rocks of similar age outcrop in Central America, for example in the Maya Mountains of Belize. The rocks of the West Indies themselves, as can be seen from Table 1b, are relatively much younger, the oldest dating from about the middle of the Mesozoic Era.

THE MOUNTAIN-BUILDING PERIODS

The great series of earth movements that formed these rocks into mountain chains fall into two main episodes. In the first, which began about seventy million years ago towards the end of the Cretaceous Period and lasted into Eocene times, the volcano-studded backbone of Mexico and Central America appeared. Two branches of these mountains extended eastwards, one to what is now Jamaica, and the other

by way of southern Cuba, Hispaniola and Puerto Rico to the Virgin Islands. In the south the Caribbean Coastal Range was uplifted. It stretched from what today are Colombia and Venezuela to Trinidad and possibly Barbados.

Even more striking than these mountain chains was the huge trench created by the downfold. If you look at the endpaper map at the back of this book you can trace its path. The part of it that begins near Central America and passes between Cuba and Jamaica—called the Bartlett Trough—is in places over 20,000 feet below sea level. North of Puerto Rico and the Virgin Islands is the Brownson Trough which goes down even farther. It is, in fact, the deepest part of the Atlantic Ocean. If Mount Everest were submerged in it, its summit would not appear above the surface of the sea. From there the downfold continues along the outer side of the arc of eastern Caribbean islands to Trinidad.

This activity was followed in Upper Eocene and in Oligocene times by a quieter period when much of this land was submerged beneath the sea and great thicknesses of marine sediments—mainly limestones

1a. Evidence of past vulcanicity—Grand Etang, a crater lake in Grenada. Other examples of volcanic scenery are shown in plates 8p, 8u, and 8ll.

1b. Geological Eras	Geological Periods		Age (years)	Development of Life	Major Caribbean Events
CENOZOIC ERA	Quaternary Period	Recent	20,000	First men	Coral reefs, coastal plains, active volcanoes, terraces
		Pleistocene	— 2 m.		
	Tertiary Period	Pliocene			Jamaica bauxite
		Miocene	— 25 m.	Higher mammals ⎫	Alpine uplift Creation of volcanic Lesser Antilles and folded mountains in Greater Antilles
		Oligocene		Warm-blooded animals first became common ⎬	Trinidad oil
		Eocene	— 50 m.	⎭	Limestone deposited Submergence Erosion
MESOZOIC ERA	Cretaceous		— 100 m.	Extinction of most reptiles, Birds First flowering plants Flying reptiles	Central and South American and Caribbean mountain chains first formed
	Jurassic				
	Triassic			First primitive mammals Dinosaurs	Oldest identifiable rocks in the West Indies
PALAEOZOIC ERA	Permian		— 200 m.	Reptiles common Primitive reptiles and insects common	
	Carboniferous			Swamp forests (now coal)	
	Devonian		— 300 m.	First amphibians First land plants Lung fishes (first air-breathers)	
	Silurian				
	Ordovician			First fish-like creatures with backbones	
	Cambrian		— 400 m.	Sea plants and marine animals with hard shells became common	
PROTEROZOIC and ARCHAEOZOIC	Pre-Cambrian		— 500 m.	First forms of primitive life	Guiana Highlands Maya Mountains

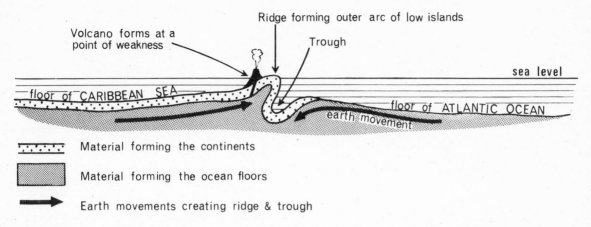

c. A simplified diagram showing how the Eastern Caribbean islands are believed to have been formed.

—were deposited. Volcanic activity died down and ne series of volcanic islands including Anguilla, St Martin, St Barthélemy, Antigua, Désirade, Marie Galante and the eastern part of Guadeloupe were laned down by the sea and buried beneath sediments, ever again becoming active.

The second great mountain-building episode took lace in late Miocene and early Pliocene times. Like he first it was part of a tremendous world-wide pheaval and it produced such great folded mountain systems as the Alps, Himalayas, Rockies and Andes. In the West Indies some parts were uplifted, thers thrown down and there was another outburst f volcanic activity. It was at this time that the olcanic islands of the Lesser Antilles began to be uilt up on the inner side of a great curving ridge which had been formed during the first period of nountain building and which reached up to and in laces rose above the surface of the sea. These islands f the inner arc, which stretch from Saba in the north o Grenada in the south, are much higher than those n the outer arc, lying on the crest of the ridge itself. Guadeloupe shows the contrast most clearly, the western volcanic half being nearly 5,000 feet high, whereas the eastern limestone portion is very low.

OLCANOES

Two or three of the volcanoes in the Lesser Antilles re still intermittently active and in historic times ave caused much damage and loss of life. La

Soufrière in Guadeloupe destroyed cultivated land in 1797. The St Vincent Soufrière erupted in 1812 and again on May 7, 1902, when it devastated nearly a third of the island and caused some 2,000 deaths. The very next day Mt Pelée in Martinique also erupted and utterly destroyed the town of St Pierre. In several other islands, notably Montserrat, Nevis, Redonda, St Lucia and Dominica, dying vulcanicity is shown by the presence of boiling sulphur springs. This accounts for the frequency of the name *soufrière* in the Lesser Antilles.

EARTHQUAKES

Earthquakes, like eruptions, are a sign that the Earth's crust is still under strain. Several centres of earthquake activity exist in the Caribbean area. One of them lies in the vicinity of the Anegada Trough, a fault which forms the only deep-water channel between the Caribbean Sea and the Atlantic Ocean. Others lie in the Bartlett Trough and elsewhere.

Most of the Caribbean lands have suffered severely from earthquakes at one time or another. The capitals of Guatemala and El Salvador were destroyed in 1917 and 1918. Jamaica had a shock of such intensity in 1692 that most of Port Royal disappeared beneath the sea, and in 1907 Kingston was destroyed. A relatively small earthquake in Jamaica in 1957 caused over £500,000 worth of damage. Some of the Lesser Antilles suffered considerable damage in 1843, the Virgin Islands in 1867. Port-au-Prince was destroyed twice in twenty years in the eighteenth century and Cap Haïtien was destroyed in 1842.

RECENT CHANGES

Evidence in the landscape of uplift in recent geological time is provided by terraces, which are areas of flat ground lying between steep slopes. On parts of the coasts of Dominica, Tortuga and St Vincent, for instance, are found, just above the present shorelines, narrow platforms of rock which have been planed-off by the action of the waves and then uplifted. The raised coral terraces found in Jamaica, Barbados and elsewhere are somewhat similar.

More common than either of these are river terraces which are the remnants of river flood-plains left higher up the sides of a valley when the river itself is forced to cut down with renewed vigour, usually because the land has been raised. River terraces occur in Jamaica, Hispaniola, Trinidad and elsewhere.

In the few thousand years that have elapsed since the last Ice Age ended new land has come into being in ways that are possible only in the tropics. Firstly, new coastal lands have been added where mangroves have trapped mud and sand carried by waves between their roots. Secondly, cays have grown up where sand has been blown and washed on top of coral reefs.

Corals are tiny, carnivorous animals that extract calcium carbonate from the surrounding sea water in order to build protective shells for themselves. These shells remain when the corals die. In time, as new corals grow on old ones, a reef is formed. There are four types of reefs, all of which occur within the

1d. Evidence of past folding, and of much subsequent erosion—the Jamaican Blue Mountains.

region. *Fringing reefs*, the most common type, either touch the coast or are separated from it by only a narrow stretch of shallow water. *Barrier reefs*, which occur off the coasts of Belize and Andros, lie several miles offshore and are separated from the land by water a hundred and more feet deep. *Bank reefs* are those which have been built on a broad, shallow submarine platform and are unattached to any mainland. Bermuda and many of the Bahamas are of this type. Some of the Bahamas, however, are *atolls*, that is, coral islands surrounded by deep water.

In the West Indies rain, rivers and to a lesser extent the sea are constantly at work moulding the landscape into new forms. In volcanic areas there is

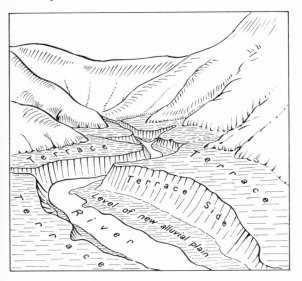

1e. One type of river terrace.

a great contrast between the regular cones of active volcanoes, the ridges and ravines of recently extinct volcanoes and the rounded, low hills and wide alluvial plains of older areas. Limestone areas, which tend to begin as plateaux, have been riddled with caves and sink-holes until in places the rock has been worn into steep-sided cone-shaped hills and deep intervening pits.

Marine erosion is less severe. For one thing the small tidal range limits the area exposed to wave attack. For another, many of the coasts are sheltered by coral reefs which also provide a ready source of beach material.

THINGS TO DO

1. Find out the conditions that are necessary for the growth of coral reefs.
2. Find evidence of erosion in the district where you live.
3. Find out what relationships there are between
   (*a*) gradient and agriculture
   (*b*) soils and agriculture
   in the district where you live.

QUESTIONS

1. Show how the islands of the Caribbean are related structurally to the mainland of Central and South America. C.H.S.C. 1955.
2. Write an essay on the way in which volcanic activity and earth movements have affected the surface features of the West Indies. L.G.C.E. (O). 1966.

CHAPTER TWO

Caribbean Climate

A TEMPERATURE

Seasonal Changes

The most outstanding feature of the climate of this region, which extends for 1,500 miles from the Bahamas to Guyana and for 2,000 miles from Barbados to Central America, is the remarkable uniformity of its high temperature, not only from place to place but also from month to month. The hottest months, with average temperatures just above 80°F., are those immediately following the passage of the overhead midday sun. The coolest months are those when the sun is south of the equator, but even then average temperatures seldom fall below 75°F. Diagram 2a shows the relationship between the overhead midday sun and the average temperatures of three places in different latitudes.

This small annual temperature range, one of the distinguishing features of the *Tropical Marine* climate, is due only in part to the constantly high angle of the sun's midday rays. A stronger influence is the Atlantic, which, like all oceans, has such a slow response to heating and cooling that its temperature varies but little from one season to another. This equability is imparted to the Trade winds, which in turn exert a moderating influence on the temperatures of the Caribbean lands as they blow over them throughout the year. Many houses are designed to make the most of the cooling effect of the Trade winds, or of day and night breezes.

Day and Night Changes

Throughout the Caribbean lands there is a greater diurnal range than there is between the mean temperatures of the hottest and coldest months. Day temperatures can exceed 90°F., even occasionally in the cooler months. Night temperatures regularly fall to 70°F. in the Lesser Antilles and to 65°F. in the Greater Antilles, where in exceptional conditions they may drop to 55°F. even in the lowlands. The sea varies much less: its surface temperature is nearly always between 80°F. and 82°F.

The Effect of Height

The last and most important factor governing local temperature is height. Temperature falls by about 1°F. for every 300 feet of ascent, so only in the lowest areas is there no relief from the heat. From this point of view it is unfortunate that the largest

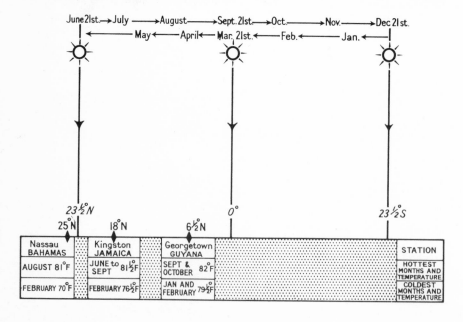

2a. *The monthly progress of the overhead midday sun. It travels through 94° of latitude in 52 weeks. Work out on what dates it is directly above the place where you live.*

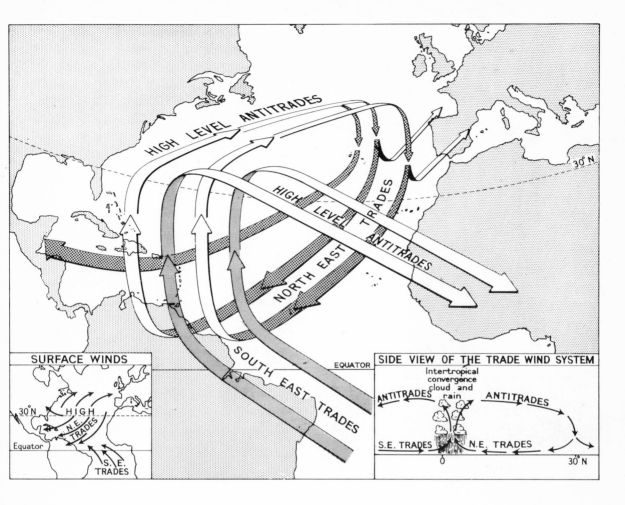

2b and 2c. Trade winds and the Intertropical Convergence.

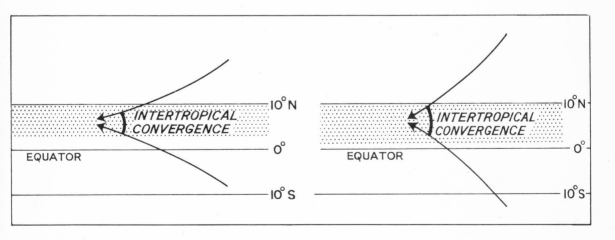

2d. The fact that the Trade winds are strongest and most regular during the dry season was used to advantage in former times when windmills were built on many sugar estates to operate cane-crushing machinery—cane being reaped and crushed in the dry months.

B PRESSURE, WINDS AND RAINFALL

The most important pressure system affecting the West Indies is the North Atlantic *high* which extends from the Azores to Bermuda. Owing to the Earth's rotation the winds blowing out of this system are deflected in a clockwise direction so that near Africa they blow as northerly winds and near the equator they are almost due east. However, as they blow from the north-east for most of their journey they are known as the *North-East* Trade winds. A similar high-pressure system over the South Atlantic gives rise to the *South-East* Trades.

In the old sailing-ship days the Trades had a marked influence on sea routes and on naval strategy in the Caribbean. Voyages from west to east could take five to ten times as long as those from east to west. An easterly situation was therefore both economically and strategically valuable. Thus Barbados became an important *entrepôt* for the southern Caribbean, and Antigua was the chief naval base for the whole region. With the coming of steamships the influence of the Trade winds declined. However, it still exists to some extent, being shown, for instance, in the east to west alignment of most West Indian airstrips.

Though the Trade winds are moisture-laden they are not normally rain-bearing and the most typical Caribbean weather conditions are blue skies dotted with white puffs of small cumulus clouds. Nevertheless, Trade wind humidity is so high (70% to 90%) that only a small disturbing factor is required to produce heavy showers. Among the most important of these factors are a slight fall of atmospheric pressure (such as occurs throughout the region in the summer months), the passage of even a weak low-pressure system, and any interruption of the winds by land. It is very difficult to predict when and where the showers will fall. It is common in the West Indies to stand only a few yards away from a heavy rainstorm and yet remain dry.

The Circulation of the Winds

The zone where the North-East and South-East Trade winds meet, near the equator, is called the *Intertropical Convergence Zone*. On coming into contact these two wind systems force each other to rise and a colossal updraught of air is produced. The sea beneath is left becalmed—a calm known to sailors as

towns in Caribbean lands are all ports. However, in some islands, notably Jamaica and Haiti, suburbs have been built in the foothills where people can live in comparatively cool surroundings.

In the Greater Antilles some of the highest peaks are subject to occasional frosts and there are large areas of highland where conditions are more suitable for the cultivation of citrus, coffee and temperate fruits and vegetables than for sugar cane, bananas, cocoa and coconuts.

2e. *Fine weather; blue skies dotted with white puffs of small cumulus clouds off the coast of Nevis.*

the "doldrums". As the air rises it is cooled and the water vapour it contains condenses to form huge rain-bearing cumulus clouds. Rain comes in the form of showers. If the angle of convergence of the Trade winds is small these showers are usually light, but if the angle is large they are frequent and heavy and are often associated with thunderstorms.

After ascending vertically for several thousand feet the two airstreams turn, as shown in Diagram 2b, and blow back towards the tropics. The presence of these high-level winds, called the *Antitrades*, is often indicated by thin, white, feathery strands of cirrus clouds composed of ice crystals. The fact that the Antitrades blow in exactly the opposite direction from the Trade winds has occasionally been shown when, after a volcanic eruption in the Caribbean, ashes and dust have fallen many miles north-east of the volcano. Barbados had a heavy fall of ash after the eruption of the St Vincent Soufrière in 1812. Jamaica once received some from Cosiguina in Guatemala. As the Trade winds blow constantly *from* the north-east, the only possible explanation of these incidents is that the ash rose high enough to enter the Antitrades and was carried north-eastwards by them.

When the Antitrades reach approximately 30° North and South, they sink back to earth again and form the Trade winds, so the whole circulation is repeated. It is not a closed system, however, for some of the descending air blows out to join the Westerlies and in return some air from the Westerlies joins the Trades. Similarly there is some merging of the air in the two Trade-wind systems. In addition, other winds at times blow into the region from the neighbouring land masses.

C RAINFALL

As we have seen, the Trade winds, though humid, are not necessarily rainy unless some rain-producing factor is present. Such factors are diverse, spasmodic, unreliable and often only of local significance. It therefore follows that rainfall varies from one place to another and that the rainfall of one year may bear no resemblance to that of the year before or the year

2f. *Showery weather; rain-bearing cumulus clouds building up off Port Antonio on the north coast of Jamaica.*

after. There are, nevertheless, certain characteristics shared by all Caribbean countries. For one thing, rain usually falls in very heavy showers. This is typical of tropical as opposed to temperate lands. For another, the Caribbean has one season—summer— which is rainy and another which is fairly dry. This is a distinguishing feature of the *Tropical Marine* climate. Monsoon countries, though similar, have a much more pronounced contrast between the wet and the dry seasons.

In spite of the fact that rain may come at any time of year, drought is a serious problem in the West Indies. A long drought lasting for several successive months is a risk everywhere, not only in the low-lying dry islands. It can wither food crops and cause great distress in rural areas. It can reduce the sugar output of such islands as Barbados and Antigua by half.

As the rain-producing factors vary in importance in different parts of the Caribbean, the region has been subdivided into three zones: the Southern Caribbean, the Greater Antilles, and the Eastern Caribbean.

The Rainfall of the Southern Caribbean

The two high-pressure belts, one over the North and the other over the South Atlantic, shift a few degrees north and south following the passage of the over-head sun. The equatorial rain belt produced by the convergence of the North-East and South-East Trades also moves north and south. It reaches its most southerly point, the equator, in January. During May the rain belt begins to move northwards and by July and August it is between 8°N, and 9°N. In the remaining months of the year it retreats slowly back to the equator. Lands lying in these latitudes get their heaviest rainfall while it is overhead or nearly over-head. Thus Georgetown, 6½°N, has May, June and December as its rainiest months and has a marked dry period from August to November. Port of Spain, 10½°N, has its heaviest rain from June to November.

The Rainfall of the Greater Antilles

The size of the Greater Antilles and the height of their mountains are both factors sufficient to produce rainfall.

Rainfall and Relief

In order to cross the mountains of the Greater Antilles, the Trade winds are forced to rise. In doing so they are cooled, and this tends to produce rain. Clouds not only commonly blanket the mountains themselves, but, as shown in Diagram 2g, extend a considerable distance to windward and a short dis-tance to leeward of them. One of the best examples of this is found in Jamaica, where the Blue Mountains stand athwart the North-East Trades. Port Antonio, a town on the north-east coast, has 126 inches, and the mountains themselves have over 200 inches of rain a year. Kingston, on the southern side, has only 30 inches a year and is said to be in "rain shadow".

Some of the Lesser Antilles are high enough to produce occasional relief rain but not high enough to cause rain-clouds to form very far to the windward of the mountains. Their windward and leeward coasts therefore display less of a contrast than do those of the Greater Antilles.

Convectional Rainfall

Convectional rainfall occurs in the Greater Antilles because of the size of each of the islands. Land has a quick response to heating and cooling influences, and soon after sunrise the temperature of these large islands rises rapidly. By mid-morning the air above the land is sufficiently hot for it to rise, and powerful convection currents are set up. As the air rises it gets cooler and the moisture it contains condenses to form cumulus clouds. If the air is very moist, these clouds grow and spread across the sky so that by afternoon they may cast large shadows over the land. In conse-quence the upward currents of air lose strength and heavy showers may fall from the clouds. Convectional showers of this kind are heaviest and most frequent in the months when the air is most humid. They are sometimes accompanied by thunder. Usually by evening the clouds disperse and the nights are clear and cool except over the sea, where it is often cloudy and occasionally rainy, especially just before dawn.

During the days a powerful sea breeze blows inland to replace the rising air. At night, on the other hand, when the land is at a lower temperature than the sea, the cool air over the land sinks and blows off-shore as a land breeze. Thus, over the coastal plains of the Greater Antilles the normal Trade wind system is

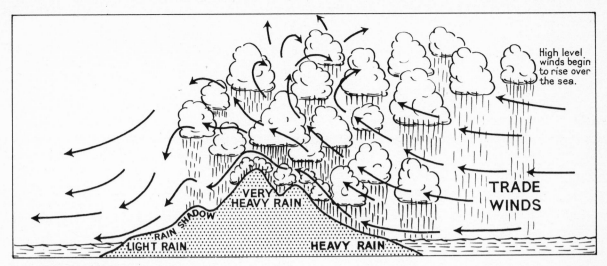

2g. *Relief Rainfall.*
Above: Showers falling over an island large enough and mountainous enough to force high-level winds to rise long before they reach it, so that showers fall over the sea and the windward coast as well as on the mountains themselves.
Below: Sometimes the showers which form over a smaller, lower island drift downwind and fall mainly on the leeward slopes. Often lines of cumulus clouds extend for many miles to the leeward of the hill summits where they form.

interrupted and replaced by this day and night alternation of sea and land breezes.

Relief and convectional rain are not the only types of rain in the Greater Antilles. Rain is also brought to them by northers in winter and by easterly waves and hurricanes in summer. Hurricanes may bring exceptionally heavy rain.

The Rainfall of the Eastern Caribbean

The islands of the Lesser Antilles are small and therefore receive little convectional rain. Some rise high enough to have relief rain and there is a great contrast between those islands which are mountainous and wet and those which are low and dry.

When describing climate it should be noted that in the West Indies a month is said to be *wet* if its rainfall is over 4 inches, and *moist* if it is between 2½ inches and 4 inches. Evaporation is so rapid and the Trade winds have such a drying effect that a month with under 2½ inches is said to be *dry* unless it follows a wet month (in which case it can be called moist).

Here is an example:

Grand Turk, Turks Islands

2·6	1·8	1·2	1·3	2·2	1·9	1·9	1·7	3·1	4·4	5·0	2·4
M	D	D	D	D	D	D	D	M	W	W	M

(Total 29·5)

W=Wet   M=Moist   D=Dry

Castries, St Lucia   (figures in inches)

J	F	M	A	M	J	J	A	S	O	N	D
5·4	4·0	3·6	3·5	5·7	9·2	9·3	10·2	9·3	9·6	8·9	7·4
W	W	M	M	W	W	W	W	W	W	W	W

(Total 86·1)

2h. *The average monthly rainfall of two contrasting islands.*

11

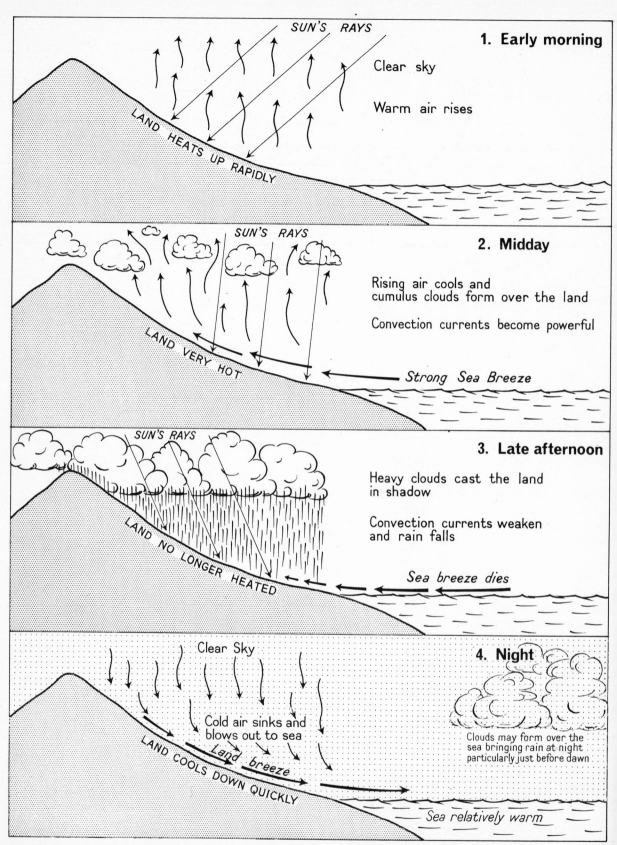

1. Early morning

SUN'S RAYS

Clear sky

Warm air rises

LAND HEATS UP RAPIDLY

2. Midday

SUN'S RAYS

Rising air cools and cumulus clouds form over the land

Convection currents become powerful

LAND VERY HOT

Strong Sea Breeze

3. Late afternoon

SUN'S RAYS

Heavy clouds cast the land in shadow

Convection currents weaken and rain falls

LAND NO LONGER HEATED

Sea breeze dies

4. Night

Clear Sky

Cold air sinks and blows out to sea

Land breeze

LAND COOLS DOWN QUICKLY

Clouds may form over the sea bringing rain at night particularly just before dawn

Sea relatively warm

2i. The development of land and sea breezes and of convectional showers throughout a day on one of the larger islands.

Among the most important rain-producing factors in this region are *easterly waves*. These are troughs of low atmospheric pressure which form in the Trade winds to the north of the Intertropical Convergence Zone. The axis of a typical easterly wave points roughly in a north to south direction and moves slowly westwards at about 10 or 12 miles per hour. Ahead of the axis, that is on its western side, the weather is fine and the skies are unusually clear. But behind it the winds tend to blow slightly south of east and to rise upwards from the ground. Here overcast or rainy weather is the rule. It may last from a few hours up to several days.

As easterly waves are most common between the months of June and November, when they appear on an average every five days, this is the rainy season for the Lesser Antilles. Some of them extend as far north as the tropic of Cancer and pass over the Greater Antilles and the Bahamas, adding to the rainfall there.

Hurricanes and Northers

Hurricanes

Occasionally a very active easterly wave over the North Atlantic Ocean develops into a hurricane. As a result of factors which are not all fully explained, a powerful upward air current is set up, creating an almost circular low-pressure system. If this is far enough from the equator (that is, north of $10°N$) the winds drawn in to replace the rising air are deflected by the force of the Earth's rotation so that they spiral inwards in an anticlockwise direction, as shown in Diagram 2j. Once the hurricane is born, wind speeds soon reach 75 miles an hour and occasional gusts near the centre may reach 200 miles an hour. The centre itself is calm. The energy needed to keep the storm going is believed to be provided by the warmth of the sea over which it passes and by the latent heat released as the water vapour in the air condenses into raindrops.

In contrast to the terrific speed of their winds the storms themselves move slowly, averaging 10 to 12 miles per hour. They may even remain stationary for a day or so. The slower they pass over a country, the longer they have to inflict damage there.

At first hurricanes are very small, perhaps no more than 5 miles across, but as they travel they grow, so that they may eventually have a diameter of over 600 miles. At this stage the calm storm centre is as much as 25 miles across. The course is unpredictable, though most of the storms originating over the Atlantic travel in a westerly direction into the Caribbean and then curve northwards. Those developing over the other two centres of origin—the southern Caribbean and the Gulf of Mexico—usually travel northwards from the outset. The commoner hurricane tracks are shown in Diagram 2m.

An as yet unexplained feature of the hurricanes which originate over the Atlantic Ocean is the way in which two of them form at about the same time and in much the same place and follow one another in close succession on similar tracks. Territories lying in their path are faced with special dangers. For one thing they have had too little time to recover from the damage caused by the first hurricane to be prepared for the next. For another, the soil is so saturated with the rain brought by the first hurricane that it can absorb none of the rain brought by the second, and the destruction caused by flooding and landslides is exceptionally severe.

Hurricanes usually die out quickly when they leave the tropics or cross the mainland of North or Central America. A few, however, sweep along the east coast of the United States and bring gales and floods as far north as New England.

The first indication of an approaching hurricane is the long, slow swell at sea. Next, feathery cirrus clouds appear high in the sky. Soon it seems as though a veil of cloud has been drawn across the sun and at sunrise and sunset the sky is bright red. The air is calm, sultry and oppressive. As the storm comes nearer there are fitful gusts of wind and showers of rain. Wind speeds increase rapidly and the sky is quickly covered with low black rain clouds. The rain pours down and the gale grows in violence until, if the storm centre passes overhead, there is a short period of calm broken by a few sharp gusts of wind. Suddenly, with little or no warning, the winds reappear, blowing from the opposite direction. As the storm recedes the winds gradually drop, but the rain can continue for several more days.

The destructiveness of hurricanes has been recorded from the earliest days of West Indian history. Columbus weathered at least three. One of the worst

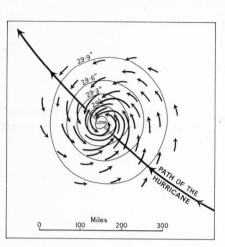

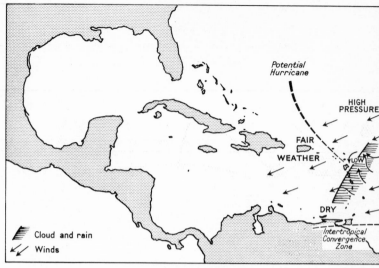

2j. *A well-developed hurricane.*

2k. *The birth of a hurricane from an easterly wave.*

2l. *Hurricane Alma (1966) north-east of the Yucatan peninsula. This photograph was taken from an American weather satellite.*

years of all was 1780 when hurricanes destroyed a Spanish, a French and an English fleet in the Caribbean and took a toll on sea and land of 20,000 lives. Today such tragedies are rare for, with satellites and special aircraft reporting the progress of each hurricane, ships have enough warning to keep well away from them. On land, though these warnings are valuable in saving lives, they cannot prevent the force of the wind, the torrential rain and sometimes an accompanying "tidal" wave from destroying crops and buildings worth millions of dollars each year. For example, in October 1963 hurricane Flora struck Tobago, Haiti and Cuba—where one town recorded over 90 inches of rain. Its outlying winds and rain caused considerable damage in Grenada, the Dominican Republic, Jamaica, and the Bahamas. Altogether about 2½ million people suffered in one way or another, and over 7,000 were killed. Fortunately these are days of international co-operation, and several organizations sent relief to the stricken areas. For instance, UNICEF (the United Nations Children's Fund) provided special help for children and gave vitamins to hospitals and vehicles to health centres, thus preventing further suffering.

No island in the Caribbean can be considered entirely free from danger. Trinidad, normally outside the hurricane belt, had a freak storm in 1933 which destroyed coconut plantations and oil installations in the south of the island. Barbados, storm free for the

14

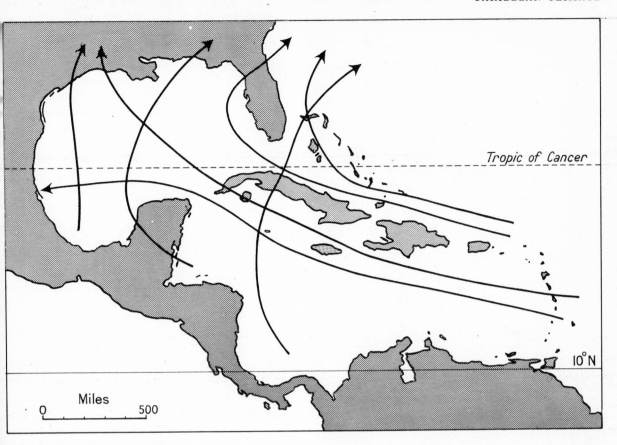

2m. Common hurricane tracks.

first half of the century, suffered in 1955 from a hurricane which went on to wreck Grenada.

The official hurricane season in the Caribbean lasts from June to November, during which time about eight hurricanes can be expected to develop. Not all of these will be severe, nor will they necessarily touch land. August and September are the months of the most numerous and most violent storms.

Northers

Northers are winds which periodically blow out from the cold interior plains of North America in winter. They bring squalls, low temperatures, dull skies and rain to Mexico, the northern part of Central America, Cuba and Jamaica. These winds, which can last for several days at a time, are strong enough to damage and destroy such crops as bananas and cocoa, especially on exposed northward facing slopes. In travelling over the sea the winds warm up and lose their strength so that those northers which reach as far as the southern Caribbean are not destructive, bringing only a wide belt of cloudy skies and sometimes rain.

CLIMATE AND AGRICULTURE IN THE WEST INDIES

Temperatures throughout the West Indies are very favourable for agriculture. There are no elevations where it is too cold for crops to be grown, though many mountains are too misty, too rainy and too steep to make cultivation worth while. There is no winter to slow up plant growth, and some crops— like bananas—bear throughout the year and are of particular value to the small farmer as they provide him with a steady income. Quick-growing crops, such as rice and vegetables, may be planted and reaped more than once a year.

The amount of rainfall has a great deal to do with

15

2n. *Hurricane damage—Belize.*

Until it was known that disease was caused by germs the climate was commonly blamed for ill health in the tropics. Evidence of this can be seen in the word "malaria" which means "bad air". But in fact climate affects health only in an indirect way. For instance, the absence of severe frost in the West Indies encourages the growth and multiplication of disease bearing organisms in man, animals and plants. On the other hand the plentiful sunshine destroys many of these organisms and now that we are able to control such diseases as yellow fever, cholera, typhoid, yaws and malaria, the West Indies are rightly regarded as health resorts for visitors from other countries.

There are varying beliefs about the psychological effect of the West Indian climate but it does seem that on some days the temperature and humidity are high enough to affect people's work. In order to make conditions more comfortable and to increase output, some businesses and offices are air-conditioned.

A more complex chain of events arising from the tropical climate affects the food supply and in turn the health of many people in the West Indies. Heavy rains remove most of the minerals from the soils and both grass and crops are thereby impoverished. Where grass does grow its quality is usually poor and it cannot support as many animals as the grass of temperate countries. As a result the West Indies can produce only a fraction of their requirements of animal products. Imports are expensive and beyond the means of many people who therefore exist largely on a diet of vegetables and sugar. Unfortunately, again because of the climate, these foods are generally deficient in minerals and proteins. Indeed it has been stated that throughout the West Indies the poorer people live on diets that are inadequate, providing neither sufficient energy for long periods of manual work nor proper protection against disease.

THINGS TO DO

1. By keeping daily weather records find out:
   (a) The highest and lowest temperatures that occur for each month.
   (b) The longest period over which there is no rain.
2. From whatever information is available and from your general knowledge make your own forecast of tomorrow's weather. Try to predict maximum

the type of crop grown. Thus in the Lesser Antilles such tree crops as cocoa, coconuts, nutmegs and citrus are exported from the rainy, mountainous islands, whereas the lower, drier islands tend to specialize in sugar cane.

The chief climatic hazards are drought and hurricanes. Sugar cane stands up relatively well to both (in any case most has been harvested before the beginning of the hurricane season), and this is one reason for its success in the West Indies. Bananas suffer very badly in hurricanes, but recovery is swift because new plants come into bearing within a year. Tree crops are worst affected and their output may be reduced for years afterwards.

and minimum temperatures, wind speed and direction, and the sky condition (cloudiness) at various times of day.

Later, look back at your forecast. Which of your predictions were reasonably accurate? Which were not? Why can you always expect some to be better than others?

3. Draw a chart to show the relationship between the rainy and dry seasons and the planting and harvesting of the crops grown in the vicinity of your home or school.

4. Convert the rainfall figures given in diagram 2h into bar-graphs like those shown in 5g, 6i, 7c, 15d and 17e.

5. The percentage frequency of hurricanes is as follows:

May	June	July	Aug.	Sept.	Oct.	Nov.
1	6	7	22	32	26	6

Show these figures in a diagram of your own devising.

QUESTIONS

1. By reference to specific examples describe the climate of the Caribbean region under the headings: (a) temperature; (b) rainfall; (c) winds. O.C.S.E.B.(O). 1965.

2. What parts of the world have a Tropical Marine climate? What are its chief characteristics? How can it be distinguished from (a) Equatorial, (b) Tropical Monsoon, (c) Warm Temperate Eastern Margin types of climate?

3. (a) Name *three* types of rainfall, and describe the way in which *one* type is caused.
(b) Describe and account for the distribution of rainfall in *one* of: the Bahamas, Guyana, Jamaica. L.G.C.E.(O). 1966.

4. Naming your home district,
(a) State clearly its main climatic features.
(b) With the aid of graphs or diagrams, describe the seasonal changes in the weather during the year. L.G.C.E.(O). 1965.

5. Hurricanes in the Caribbean area can cause widespread damage to forests and crops.
(a) State what you understand by "hurricanes". Explain how they occur in the area.
(b) Describe and explain briefly the other ways in which specific crops have occasionally failed. A.E.B.(O). 1966.

CHAPTER THREE

Vegetation and Soils

Forest formerly covered the greater part of the West Indies. Because of the variety of soils and climatic conditions, in its natural state it varied considerably in character from place to place. The cutting of forests by man and the introduction of many foreign species (e.g. logwood in Jamaica, marabú in Cuba and fruit trees everywhere) have greatly changed the make up of West Indian forest vegetation.

Along rocky or sandy coasts it is common to see sea grapes and other bushes bent low and permanently gnarled or flattened on top by the strong salty breeze. In other places there are swamps—*mangrove swamps* wherever the water is salt or brackish, but filled with other plants where it is fresh. Mangrove trees, of which there are several kinds, are able to grow in or near salt water and are an important element of West Indian coastal vegetation. Having tenacious root systems they help to protect low lying coastal areas from erosion by the sea, and may even promote the extension of land by accumulating soil about their roots. Coconut palms grow well in the sand along the shore, as they are not harmed by the sea air. They are a useful source of food and other materials. These palms, however, are almost always planted; they do not form natural forests. Unfortunately, in some places (e.g. Grand Cayman) they have nearly been wiped out by disease in recent years and other areas (e.g. Jamaica) are also suffering.

In the plains behind the coasts of Caribbean islands the type of vegetation depends mainly on the amount of rainfall, which, as we saw in Chapter Two, varies greatly from one place to another.

In areas where there is a prolonged seasonal drought each year—that is, usually on the leeward side of an island—there is *semi-deciduous woodland*. Some of the trees, which are mostly short and often

3a. Coastal vegetation adapted to the wind and salt spray.

3b. Tropical rain-forest (Guyana).

Compare these two types of vegetation and the conditions that give rise to them.

3c. Cactus thorn scrub (Antigua).

thorny, shed their leaves in the dry months. Burning and shifting cultivation have turned large areas of this woodland into scrub and thicket.

In a very few dry areas, notably the Cul de Sac plain of southern Hispaniola, the eastern tip of Cuba and part of the southern coastlands of Puerto Rico and Jamaica there is *cactus thorn scrub*. Cacti have long roots and tiny, spiny leaves specially adapted to withstand aridity.

On the other hand in the wettest lowland areas where conditions are most favourable for plant growth, *tropical rain-forest* occurs. This forest has been cleared from most of the inhabited areas but fine examples still exist in Guyana and parts of Central America, and some small stands remain in Trinidad and the Lesser Antilles. The rain forest contains a great variety of tall, evergreen, broad-leaved trees, some of which rise to a height of 120

feet and more. Lianas and epiphytes are common.

This tall forest merges gradually with increasing elevation into *montane forest*. Here the trees are somewhat smaller than in the lowland rain-forest and are more thickly covered with epiphytes such as orchids, bromeliads (wild pines), ferns and mosses. Tree ferns are common, particularly in areas which have been cleared at one time or another. Some kinds of trees occur that are absent or rare in the lowlands, for example the nearly pure stands of pitch pine which cover large parts of the interior mountain ranges of Hispaniola. Elsewhere the undisturbed montane forest consists of a complex mixture of trees and shrubs. It contains even more species than the lowland rain-forest, sometimes over a hundred to the acre. Thus the total woody flora of the West Indies is very rich, containing in all thousands of species. Many of these, however, are restricted to particular localities or islands, for example the pine barrens which exist on some of the low-lying islands of the Bahamas.

On exposed ridges and high peaks amidst the drifting clouds, where temperatures are rather low and the air is always saturated with moisture, *elfin woodland* grows. This vegetation is so called because the densely growing trees are stunted and twisted into strange contorted shapes that appear ghost-like in the mist. Their gnarled and dripping limbs are swathed with lichens and draped with tangled masses of sodden moss. Embedded in the moss grow many tiny epiphytic orchids and ferns belonging to species never found except under such conditions.

All forests are affected by soil conditions as well as by moisture and temperature. For instance, the Lesser Antillean lowland rain-forest grows farther up the slopes of young volcanoes (where the soils are new and rich in minerals) than of old, eroded volcanic areas where the soil is poorer. Again, the vegetation in limestone regions differs markedly from that in shaly or igneous areas. Thus, in dry places where the porous nature of limestone increases the effect of aridity, dry *evergreen woodland* commonly occurs. It also exists on the porous white sand of Guyana.

Some species of trees and shrubs are limited to soils derived from limestone and seldom, if ever, occur elsewhere. Others cannot grow in limy soils. Many plants, on the other hand, are much more widely tolerant. The effect of salt in the soil can be

3d. Badly eroded mountain land (Jamaica). The bare slope can probably never be reclaimed. It threatens both the land above and that below.

seen in coastal areas throughout the West Indies; relatively few species of plants can grow in saline soils, and these species usually cannot grow elsewhere. A special case of a different kind occurs in some of the Lesser Antilles, where the sulphurous vapour given off from volcanic vents or fissures kills many plants, allowing to grow only those that can withstand the fumes. Examples occur in the Valley of Desolation, Dominica, and on the slopes of the Soufrière mountains in St Vincent and St Lucia. Such phenomena are absent from the Greater Antilles.

In order to collect fuel, obtain building material, and clear the land for cultivation, man has removed most of the original forest cover from the accessible parts of the West Indies. Some islands such as Antigua were cleared right up to the hill-tops by the sugar planters of the eighteenth century. If cut-over land is later abandoned, the forest may never grow back in the same way as it was before. In many areas its place is taken by fern brake or by savanna, followed later by poor scrub. In short it is true to say that the present vegetation cover of most of the West Indies is secondary in nature; that is, it has succeeded, usually in some degenerate form or other, the original so-called "natural" vegetation.

Savanna is tropical grassland which may or may not contain scattered scrub trees. Many savannas in the West Indies have been made by man and are maintained by annual fires; indeed the name "Burnt Savanna" occurs in numerous places. In a few other parts of the region savannas are the result of natural conditions. In the interior of Guyana the long dry season is too severe for forest growth and savanna occurs instead, except along the banks of rivers. Soils are the determining factor in Barbuda—the only island in the Lesser Antilles to possess a natural savanna. Here, a few inches below the surface, lies a layer of dense clay which tree-roots cannot penetrate. Moreover, this clay bed is impervious to water. As a result the thin overlying soil becomes waterlogged during the rains but dries out completely afterwards. Such conditions effectively prevent trees from growing, so the vegetation consists chiefly of drought-resistant grasses and water-tolerant sedges. In Trinidad and the Greater Antilles savannas are more common, and the word appears in several place-names, for example, Savanna-la-Mar in Jamaica and Sabana Grande in Puerto Rico. In these islands vannas are usually the result of a combination of climatic, soil and human factors. They occur in lowland areas and at higher elevations.

Reckless clearing of steep slopes has caused disastrous soil erosion in many areas, for example, the Scotland district of Barbados and the Yallahs Valley in Jamaica. In many countries laws have been passed in recent years to prohibit the clearing of certain forest reserves, and some of the worst eroded land is being reforested. This policy is important not only to prevent further erosion but also to protect water-supplies. It is noticeable, for instance, that in Dominica—where much of the forest still exists—the rivers and streams are clearer and fluctuate less in volume than those in other territories. Elsewhere in the West Indies the typical peasant practice of burning a patch of forest, cultivating a small holding for two or three years and, after exhausting the soil, moving on to destroy another patch in the same manner, is still much too common.

Another serious and widespread problem is the decline of soil fertility especially on the slopes and hills where, as we have just seen, the peasant cultivator often "mines" the soil, robbing it of its fertility and replacing little or nothing by way of manure. It is perhaps fair to note that the soils themselves are seldom very fertile even before this disastrous treatment. The heavy showers of warm rain dissolve most of the minerals present in the soil and carry them, together with much organic matter, deep into the ground where they can be reached only by the roots of trees and shrubs. This explains why most of the Caribbean lands were originally clothed with forests and not with grass. The lush appearance of these forests gave the impression that the soils supporting them were rich. In fact, except for certain favoured areas—for example, the rich lowlands of Cuba and the volcanic soils of some of the small islands—they are not. If forests are cleared, they are unable to re-establish themselves in their original form. Grass is usually poor and food crops are often deficient in minerals and proteins. The topsoil, although easily worked, is exhausted after a few years' cropping.

The situation is better on the whole in lowland areas, where soils are generally deeper, where erosion and excessive "leaching" (dissolving and carrying away of minerals, etc.) are less common, and where fertilizing and other good soil management practices are often more readily appreciated as being sound investments.

THINGS TO DO

1. Debate this topic: "Governments should have the power to prevent a landowner from allowing serious soil erosion to occur on his own property."
2. Discuss the following statement. "It has been repeatedly said that British Guiana and British Honduras (Guyana and Belize) have vast reserves of undeveloped wealth in the form of land now under forest. This illusion arises from supposing that land which bears a dense covering of tall trees could continuously bear good agricultural crops. In fact, the two territories must be regarded as plain examples of big forests of which none but forestry use can be made." (West Indian Royal Commission Report, 1945.)

QUESTIONS

1. What parts of the territory in which you live are preserved in forest? Why has this been done?
2. What use is made of local timber in the territory in which you live? What types of lumber are imported and for what purposes? What is the annual cost of these imports?

3e. This is better. Trees stop the gullies from growing. Grass barriers planted along the contours help to stop the soil on the cultivated land from being washed away. What measures do you know of for preventing soil erosion in the territory in which you live?

CHAPTER FOUR

The Settlement and Development of the West Indies

DISCOVERY

In the late summer of 1492, Columbus and about a hundred men set sail from Spain in three small ships in search of a new trade route to the rich lands of south-east Asia. Basing his calculations on mistaken beliefs about the size of the world, Columbus expected to arrive there after only 2,500 miles of westward sailing—a gross under-estimate, the true distance being nearer to 11,000 miles. He called first at the Canary Islands and then, helped by the favourable Trade winds, crossed the Atlantic in thirty-six days and landed on one of the Bahamas, which he believed to be part of the East Indies. Guided by some of the "Indians" he met there, he sailed south until he reached Cuba. Then turning east he sailed along the north coast of Hispaniola where his biggest ship ran aground on a reef and had to be abandoned. When Columbus set out for home, he was unable to take all of its crew with him and forty men were left behind in a small fort built on the shore—the first European settlers in the West Indies.

In the following year Columbus set forth from Spain again, this time with a fleet of seventeen ships and over 1,200 men. Taking a more southerly course than before, he reached Dominica and then sailed to Puerto Rico and Hispaniola where he found that his garrison had been killed by the Arawaks. Columbus spent the next two years organizing the construction of a small township near by and in leading forays into the interior of the island in search of gold. He made one short cruise in 1494 when he explored most of the southern coast of Cuba and circumnavigated Jamaica.

Meanwhile, the Treaty of Tordesillas had been signed by Spain and Portugal and confirmed by the Pope. This agreement gave Spain the right to exploit all newly discovered lands west of a line 370 leagues west of the Cape Verde Islands—that is, about longitude 50° W. This explains why Brazil was colonized by Portugal and why Barbados (59° 30′ W), though discovered by a Portuguese navigator in 1536, was never claimed or settled by that country.

Columbus travelled twice more to the Caribbean. On his third voyage he discovered Trinidad and on his fourth he explored much of the Central American coast.

Though he had failed in his original intention, Columbus had accomplished much for Spain. He had discovered a new world, the wealth from which was soon to make Spain the richest and most powerful nation in Europe. He had established the best sailing-ship routes to the Caribbean, using the Trade winds on the way out and the Westerlies on the way back again. He had also found two previously unknown peoples—the Arawaks and the Caribs.

ARAWAKS AND CARIBS

Partly because the resources of the islands were so meagre, both of these peoples were very primitive. There were no cows, pigs, sheep, goats or horses in the West Indies, so it was impossible to make a living by herding. The diet was based on fish and cassava, so most of the people lived near the sea, and the interior forests were left undisturbed. There were not enough useful plants to support an advanced agricultural economy or to maintain more than village life. Precious metals were also scarce: the few gold ornaments the Spaniards found in the possession of the Arawaks were the accumulation of generations. Moreover, cut off as they were from any contact with the outside world, the Arawaks and Caribs had never learned to trade and there were no ports or cities. Thus, unlike the people of India and other eastern countries, the Arawaks and Caribs had neither the means nor the desire to become traders as the Spaniards originally hoped.

Of the two peoples, the Arawaks were more easily overcome. They were made to work to support the early Spanish settlements in the Greater Antilles and to find all the gold they could, but within fifty years nearly all of them had perished. Some had been killed in battle, others had died in slavery, but most had died of various European diseases to which they succumbed in vast numbers.

The Caribs, who inhabited the Lesser Antilles, were more warlike people. They fought fiercely for their freedom and prevented Europeans from colonizing the more mountainous islands for a long time. In Grenada their resistance was broken by the French in 1651. Those in St Vincent came to terms with the British in 1773, but few survived the eruption of Soufrière in 1812, and most of their descendants were killed by the next outburst in 1902.

The 1960 census listed only 1,265 people of Amerindian and Carib descent in St Vincent, 395 in Dominica and 150 in St Lucia. Thus, of the countries dealt with in this book, only Belize and Guyana have significant numbers of Amerindian inhabitants today.

SPAIN'S CHALLENGERS

Since the Spaniards had discovered the great riches of gold, gems and silver in Central and South America, they concentrated their energies there, neglecting the small islands altogether and using the larger ones chiefly as cattle ranches.

Other European nations, especially the Netherlands, France and England, seized their chance to challenge the Spanish claim to the monopoly of the New World. They traded wherever they could, they established settlements wherever they could and they allowed and even encouraged their seamen to plunder the Spaniards wherever they could.

There were innumerable harbours where pirates and buccaneers could hide, revictual and careen their ships and where they could lie in wait for the Spanish treasure fleets. The buccaneers were at times even powerful enough to assault Spanish towns, so the Spaniards chose defensible sites for their towns and

a. Sixteenth-century fortifications built by the Spanish to protect San Juan harbour.

fortified them. Santo Domingo in Hispaniola, Havana in Cuba and San Juan in Puerto Rico were the most important bases in the islands, and Veracruz, Porto Bello and Cartagena were amongst the most important on the mainland. With the exception of Veracruz, which is in Mexico, these places are shown on the endpaper map at the front of the book.

One of the Spanish rules was that no other nation could trade with her Caribbean possessions unless given permission to do so. As permission was hard to obtain, certain venturers towards the end of the sixteenth century took the risk of trading illicitly with the Spanish colonies. Their cargoes of manufactured goods, clothes, wine and slaves were so eagerly sought after that large Dutch, French and English companies were formed to handle West Indian trade and colonization.

Colonizing began in the small islands farthest from the Spanish centre of interest. The English successfully occupied Bermuda in 1612, St Kitts in 1624, and Barbados a year later. Nevis, Antigua, Montserrat, certain of the Bahamas, Anguilla and Barbuda followed in quick succession. The French landed on St Kitts shortly after the English, and for some years the two nations shared the island. The French also took St Barthélemy, Guadeloupe, Marie Galante and Martinique, and shared St Martin with the Dutch. The Dutch seized Saba and St Eustatius in the northern Caribbean, and Curaçao, Bonaire and Aruba in the south and began the settlement of the Guianas. The first of the Greater Antilles fell in 1655 when an English expedition captured Jamaica. From Jamaica a few settlers ventured to the Central American coast. This settlement persisted, in spite of Spanish opposition, to become Belize. French colonists, in league with the buccaneers of Tortuga, settled in the western part of Hispaniola and in 1697 the Spaniards were forced to cede this part of the island to them. It became the French colony of St Domingue. However, Spain held on to most of her possessions and it was not until the nineteenth century, when one by one they broke away to become independent republics, that Spain lost her power in the New World.

AGRICULTURE AND SETTLEMENT IN THE YOUNG BRITISH COLONIES

The first settlers in the British West Indian islands established small farms, some 5 to 30 acres in size, on which they grew tobacco, ginger, indigo and cotton for export, and maize, cassava and vegetables for themselves. The emphasis was on export crops rather than foodstuffs, and from the outset the colonies imported such provisions as flour, salted meat and fish as well as manufactured goods. This pattern still exists, though the output of local foodstuffs and industrial products is growing, often with special government support.

In the early days of colonization the labourers were mostly people who left the British Isles to work as indentured servants in the fields for a few years, after which they were paid a small sum of money and were allowed to clear and cultivate land of their own. Some people went voluntarily but, as the supply of volunteers dwindled, others were sent from prison or were transported after rebellion. A few were even kidnapped.

For a time tobacco was the most profitable export, but it was not long before it was unable to compete with the better quality leaf produced in large quantities in Virginia in North America. So in the 1640s, when the colonists learned a successful method of extracting sugar from sugar cane, the crop was an immediate success. Sugar was very profitable because of the great demand for it in Europe and North America; a demand which continued to expand as these two markets grew into great commercial and industrial communities. Sugar cane was well suited to the temperature, the rainfall, and the rainy and dry seasons of the West Indies. It withstood droughts better than most crops, and reaping was usually completed before the onset of the hurricane season. Moreover, because cane could not be grown far outside the tropics, there was little fear of competition from other areas. Sugar therefore replaced tobacco as the chief export and soon became the only product of importance in the Lesser Antilles.

The change of crop resulted in a change in the type of farming, for it was found that cane was more suited to large than to small holdings and to planters with plenty of money to begin with rather than to those who started out with nothing. The main reason for this was that, as cane had to be manufactured into sugar as soon as it was cut, each farmer had to have manufacturing equipment of his own and buildings to house it in. These things were costly and were only worth while if the property was large enough to

supply a lot of cane and earn a lot of money. In addition those farmers who could afford to pay several thousand pounds for an estate could find enough money or credit to tide them through bad years. Small farmers could not, and after such disasters as a succession of droughts, hurricanes, losses at sea, or a fall in the price of sugar they were forced to sell out to their richer neighbours. Thus the land fell into the hands of a few rich planters who were then in a position to make enormous profits if they managed their properties well.

Many unskilled labourers were needed in the cane fields, but few were available. The supply from Britain was dwindling, and those who had served their indentures preferred to join those who had sold their properties and were emigrating, rather than stay and work in the fields. Within forty years of the first colonies being founded in the Lesser Antilles thousands of settlers had left again to look for a better life. Some went to Jamaica after its capture in 1655. Others went to America and elsewhere.

It was to supply the growing demand for field workers that slavery grew to such a volume. There developed a "triangle of trade". Ships setting out from British ports carried cloth and other cheap manufactured goods to the coast of West Africa. There they were exchanged for slaves, who were transported to the West Indies where they were either sold to planters or transferred to other ships for sale to the Spaniards. Some ports, notably Kingston, had a very large trade with the Spanish colonies. On the return voyage to Britain the ships carried sugar and other tropical produce. A secondary trade grew up between the West Indies and the North American colonies. Sugar and molasses were the chief exports and flour, salt fish and some manufactures were bought in exchange.

It is not known how many African slaves were brought to the Caribbean and to North, Central and South America from the time the Spaniards began the traffic in the early sixteenth century to the time when it was stopped in the nineteenth century, but it must have been several million. There were about 700,000 slaves living in the British West Indies alone at the time of their emancipation in 1834. By then they outnumbered the whites by seven to one. Today their descendants form the majority of the people in nearly every Commonwealth Caribbean country.

TRADE AND RIVALRY IN THE CARIBBEAN

Just at the time when the British West Indies were beginning to export sugar and were becoming commercially important, that is, about 1650, the British enacted a number of laws designed to link the colonies more securely to Britain and keep any profits out of foreign hands. Based on the Spanish idea of monopoly, these laws obliged the British West Indies to trade only with Britain or with other British colonies. All their goods had to be carried in British or colonial-built ships. In return the colonists were given a protected market in Britain, their sugar being charged much less duty than sugar from elsewhere. However, this applied only to unrefined sugar. Britain imposed such high duties on refined sugar that it could not be made profitably in the colonies.

This is still the case. The small quantity of refined sugar made in the Commonwealth Caribbean territories today is sold only in the territories themselves. It cannot easily compete with sugar produced by refineries built near to the market. They have the advantage of being able to import raw sugar from countries in different parts of the world and keep operating all through the year. Also they are better placed to make the various types and grades of sugar which sell best in that market, and package them to suit their customers.

The laws Britain imposed on shipping were resented by other nations. The Dutch, who were the chief traders in the Caribbean in the early seventeenth century, were the first to suffer, and soon they were at war with Britain. The Dutch thereafter lost much of their influence in the Caribbean, though their islands of St Eustatius and Curaçao continued to act as important free ports where ships of all nationalities would call to buy wine, slaves, European manufactures and American goods. From then on, Britain's chief rival was France, often allied with Spain. The French colonists in Martinique, Guadeloupe and St Domingue not only produced more sugar than the British colonies but sold it much more cheaply and so built up a considerable trade with North America, which was legally a British market. As the West Indies became increasingly valuable, so the conflicts over the islands became increasingly fierce. Raids were carried out to devastate plantations, destroy sugar works and capture slaves in order to reduce the enemy's sugar output for years to come. Those islands of the Lesser Antilles that were weak enough to be easily captured and rich enough to be worth taking changed ownership several times with the result that their development was retarded.

THE END OF WEST INDIAN PROSPERITY

Though each of the sugar colonies reached the peak of its prosperity at a different time, the last half of the eighteenth century saw them all at about their richest. They were rightly described as being "the jewels in the English crown", as they brought more money to Britain than did any other part of the world. A century later, however, all had changed. The output of sugar had dwindled in most colonies and had ceased altogether in some.

The underlying cause of this decline was the high cost of British West Indian sugar. This resulted in part from the high duties which Parliament was persuaded to charge on sugar entering Britain from sources outside the British West Indies. Safeguarded in this way from competition, the planters had no incentive to improve their estates. They kept large numbers of slaves who, being unpaid, knew no incentive for work except force. This was inefficient because the workers were naturally reluctant to do more than they had to, and because about one man in twelve was needed as a supervisor and did no productive work. None of the slaves had a skilled job. The few who worked in the factories were semi-skilled; the vast majority in the fields were entirely unskilled and used only the simplest tools. Unskilled labour and primitive equipment resulted—as it always does—in low productivity. Labour-saving methods were not unknown, but they were disregarded by the planters because their main concern was to find ways of keeping their slaves occupied for as much of the year as possible. Nothing could have been less suited to sugar—a seasonal crop which pays the best returns to those who plant and reap it quickly. Yields were therefore low and prices high.

Another factor in the decline was the over-dependence on sugar and the lack of alternative exports or even of foodstuffs for local consumption. Any fall in the price of sugar or rise in the price of imports was a severe blow to all the estates and was ruinous to the weaker ones.

As for the planters themselves, they often preferred

to spend their income on lavish living rather than on improving their estates. When times were bad they maintained their way of life by borrowing from British merchants and then paying high rates of interest. Money therefore flowed out of the West Indies, not into them. Many of the estate-owners lived in England and seldom if ever visited the West Indies. They left their properties in the hands of managers who had little interest in efficient farming and every opportunity to be dishonest.

In spite of these weaknesses the British West Indies enjoyed a final short period of prosperity at the end of the eighteenth century when the slaves in St Domingue successfully revolted and set up the independent state of Haiti. Sugar exports suddenly ceased from what had been the world's largest producer, and so the American and European markets were open to British West Indian sugar for a few more years. However, the latter market was lost when in 1804 war broke out between France and Britain, and Napoleon closed the European ports to British shipping. In order to maintain the supply of sugar on the continent, Napoleon encouraged the cultivation of sugar beet. Sugar production was no longer confined to the tropics and cane sugar never regained its former importance.

The emancipation of the slaves in the British West Indies in 1834 created further problems for the sugar industry. The freed men resented the way the planters had bitterly resisted Emancipation, and the period of apprenticeship designed to encourage them to remain as paid labourers on the estates was not successful. Wherever they could, they left to settle on small holdings of their own. This was most common in Jamaica, Guyana and Trinidad, where plenty of un-used land was still available. It was least common in such small, densely peopled islands as St Kitts, Antigua and Barbados, where there was no such choice and life had to go on much as before.

For some years after Emancipation Britain continued to charge much lower duties on colonial sugar than on sugar from other countries. Unfortunately for the British West Indies this policy was short-lived. Large manufacturing towns were springing up in Britain and as factory workers in them were paid very low wages they had to have cheap foodstuffs. In the years following 1846 the duties on non-colonial sugar were gradually reduced until there was no difference in treatment between colonial and non colonial imports. British West Indian sugar was no longer protected. As we have seen, it was expensive and it could not easily compete on equal terms with slave-grown sugar from such rapidly developing territories as Cuba and Brazil. Many estates were sold at a fraction of their original cost. Many others could not find purchasers at any price.

In spite of the difficulty of making much money from cane, it was not easy to find anything to replace it. Cane cultivation had been so successful for so long that it had absorbed all West Indian capital, interest and skill. Little was known about other tropical crops which in any case were less able to withstand hurricanes, diseases and droughts. Some islands did begin to develop alternative or subsidiary crops but the chances of success were slim. Nutmegs and mace in Grenada, vanilla and limes in Dominica, arrowroot in St Vincent, cocoa in Trinidad and Grenada, coffee and sea-island cotton in several islands, and bananas in Jamaica were the few major successes out of a vast number of experiments.

The greatest efforts were still directed towards improving the sugar industry. Profits could still be made in favoured areas provided there were enough workers to handle the crop. Some places, such as Barbados, had enough estate workers. Others, such as Antigua, Tobago, and Nevis, started a share-cropping system. Still others, such as Grenada, Trinidad and Guyana were short of labour, and so in the 1840s a new wave of immigration began. Some people moved from the densely populated parts of the region to the sparsely settled areas. Others came from Africa, Madeira and China, but by far the largest number came from India. Nearly half a million Indians arrived in the West Indies in the following eighty years, coming mainly to the Guianas and Trinidad. They were employed for a few years as indentured labourers and could return home when their contracts expired. Some did so, but the majority chose to remain on the estates or to settle on small holdings of their own. Their descendants form the majority of the population in Guyana, the second largest group in Trinidad, and small proportions of the populations of other islands. They are particularly associated with the cultivation of sugar cane and rice.

Once assured of a labour supply the estate-owners

could set about improving the methods of cultivating and processing their cane. Ploughs became common in the West Indies for the first time. New varieties of better yielding cane were planted. Steam-driven machinery was installed in a few of the bigger factories and gradually the dependence on water and wind power dwindled. The quality of the sugar was much improved by boiling it at a relatively low temperature in vacuum pans. Where centrifugals were installed, dry crystals were extracted which could be sent overseas in cheap sacks instead of in the costly hogsheads required to carry the wet sugar made previously.

These improvements were under way on some estates, notably in Guyana and Trinidad, when the industry received the greatest set-back of all. Towards the end of the nineteenth century the governments of some European countries subsidized their exports of beet sugar so that it was cheaper than cane sugar. It sold so well that by 1893 cane sugar formed little more than a quarter of Britain's sugar imports. Only the sales of British West Indian sugar in America at this time saved the industry from complete ruin.

4b. Vacuum pans in a modern sugar factory (St Kitts).

THE WEST INDIES IN THE TWENTIETH CENTURY

A slow and intermittent recovery of the British West Indian sugar industry began at the turn of the present century when the governments of those countries most concerned in the sugar trade agreed to abolish the subsidy on beet sugar exports. Sales of British West Indian sugar in Britain increased a little, and a new and expanding market for sugar and molasses was found in Canada. However, at about the same time the United States imposed high duties on British West Indian sugar in order to encourage production in Cuba, Puerto Rico and the Philippines.

During the First World War between 1914 and 1918 Britain was cut off from her sources of beet sugar, and the market for British West Indian cane sugar improved considerably. In fact, the output from the Caribbean, particularly from Cuba, soared at this time, and soon after the war ended more sugar was being produced than the world could consume and prices fell to very low levels. Tariff preferences in Britain and Canada enabled the British West Indian sugar industry to survive but at a cost of low wages and deplorable conditions for the

workers. The first real sign of relief came in 1937 when the International Sugar Agreement was established to regulate exports and maintain a basic price for sugar. Two years later the Second World War broke out and the Agreement was unable to operate properly until 1945. In 1951, when world production was known to be stabilized, the Commonwealth Sugar Agreement was signed. This provided the British West Indies with a basic export quota of 900,000 tons of sugar a year. Of this, 640,000 tons are purchased at a special price designed to be reasonably remunerative to efficient producers. This price is negotiated between representatives of the British and Commonwealth governments each year. Apart from a few brief periods it has been considerably above the world market price at which the remainder of the British West Indian output is sold to Britain and Canada, where it receives a tariff preference.

A recent modification of the negotiated price sugar scheme has been the payment of a special extra sum to underdeveloped sugar producing countries. This is of particular benefit to the Commonwealth Caribbean territories.

The basic quotas for the individual territories are as follows:

	Overall Quota	Negotiated Price Quota
Antigua	tons 32,000	tons 24,500
Barbados	163,000	126,000
Guyana	225,000	153,000
Jamaica	270,000	180,000
St Kitts	40,900	29,500
St Lucia	11,250	8,000
Trinidad	157,850	119,000
	900,000	640,000

4c. Sugar export quotas.

Two territories not originally included on the list are Belize with an overall export quota of 25,000 tons, of which 18,000 are purchased at the negotiated price, and St Vincent with an overall quota of 1,500 tons, of which 1,050 tons would be bought at the negotiated price if the island produced it.

4d. Improvements in loading sugar have matched improvements in production. Georgetown, Guyana, is one of the places in the West Indies where it is bulk-loaded directly into ships' holds.

The quotas of any of these territories may be increased if for any reason British or Canadian requirements are not met. Thus if a hurricane in Barbados or a strike in Australia or a drought in Britain reduces sugar supplies, Jamaica or St Kitts may be called on to make up the deficit if they are able to do so.

To take a specific example to show the quantity of sugar exported and the range of sugar prices, in 196... Jamaica sold Britain about 223,000 tons of sugar at the negotiated price of £43 ($206) a ton and a further 19,000 tons at about £20 ($96) a ton. Canada bought 103,400 tons at £22. 8s. ($107) a ton. The United States—sharing out its former Cuban quota among many other countries—bought 79,000 tons at £42. 14... ($205) a ton.[1]

Throughout the century the tendency in most Caribbean countries has been to reduce the cost of producing sugar by concentrating the output in large central factories capable of processing at least a quarter of a million tons of cane in a season. As the cost of setting up one of these factories is about $10 million, they are owned not by individuals but by companies, often controlled from overseas. The

[1] See note on currencies, page vi.

are set in the midst of wide expanses of cane fields, most of which usually belong to the company that owns the factory. The remainder of the land may belong to other estates or to cane farmers.

Several square miles of flat land are required to grow enough cane to support a central factory. In some of the smaller and most mountainous islands this is not available and sugar production has ceased. The most recent islands to stop production have been St Lucia and St Vincent. In Grenada there is barely enough flat land and the industry barely survives. On the other hand Antigua, St Kitts, Jamaica, Guyana and Trinidad are all able to support large factories. Barbados is a special case; the provision of employment there is so important that relatively small factories continue to process the crop.

Large-scale agriculture in the West Indies presents many problems. One is that farm work is not well paid and has no prestige. This explains why workers prefer to reap crops in America, or even in another West Indian territory, rather than in the place where they live. Another is that there are still large tracts of land lying unused or ineffectively used. A third is that more mechanization is needed if sugar estates are to improve their efficiency, but people are reluctant to accept it for fear of unemployment.

The bulk of the export crops other than sugar and the foodstuffs consumed locally are grown on small holdings which, in all, amount to two-thirds of the cultivated land in the Commonwealth Caribbean territories. Some small farmers are fairly well off, but the great majority live in poor conditions on tiny plots of land which they cultivate in a primitive and inefficient way. Improving their living conditions, their methods of cultivation and their crop yields are among the biggest problems facing West Indian governments today. Some of the most useful forms of help are the provision of proper titles to the land, the establishment of land settlements, the granting of loans for development, the formation of co-operative and other organizations to assist in producing and marketing crops, and the provision of plants, seeds and fertilizers at little cost.

A problem of a different kind is that the British and American markets for West Indian agricultural products are saturated. Britain and America are developed countries and any rise in the standard of living there does not result in the consumption of

much more food; the people have enough to eat already. Thus the present consumption of sugar in Britain (112 lbs. per person per year) and in the United States (96 lbs.) is unlikely to increase much. And at the other extreme, countries like Nigeria— where the sugar consumption is only 4 lbs. per person per year—are not potential markets because they are not rich enough to increase their imports of food.

Though the lack of an expanding market for agricultural products has proved to be a big handicap to the economic progress of the West Indies, an even bigger one has been the rapid rise of population in recent years. This is no longer the result of immigration but is due in part to a high birth-rate and in part to a sharp reduction of the death-rate. The actual increase since 1921 is shown in the following table:

	1921	1946	1960
Antigua	29,800	41,800	54,400
Montserrat	12,100	14,300	12,200
St Kitts-Nevis	38,200	46,250	56,700
Barbados	156,300	192,800	232,100
Jamaica	858,100	1,290,000	1,606,600
Dominica	37,000	47,700	59,500
Grenada	66,300	72,400	88,600
St Lucia	51,500	70,000	86,200
St Vincent	44,500	61,700	80,000
Trinidad and Tobago	365,900	558,400	825,700
Guyana	307,400	376,100	558,800
Belize	43,300	59,150	90,400
	2,010,400	2,830,600	3,751,200

4e. *Population figures since 1921.*

This increase has taken place in spite of the emigration of many thousands of West Indians to other parts of the world in search of better conditions. Early in the century they went to Panama to help to construct the canal, to the Central American republics to work on the giant banana plantations there and to Cuba and the Dominican Republic to work in the cane fields. Since then they have gone to the oil industries of Venezuela, Curaçao and Aruba and to the goldfields of French Guiana. They have been employed as agricultural labourers in the United States. More recently, since these outlets have been closed or restricted, they have gone to the United Kingdom. In 1961, the last year before restrictions were imposed there too, 66,300 West Indians emigrated to Britain, bringing the total number living there to about 250,000. The money sent by emigrants to relatives and friends forms a useful source of income in all the islands and is a substantial contribution to the economy of some of the smaller ones.

Emigration, however, is a mixed blessing as it also tends to attract the more enterprising and the more skilled workers who are not the people who can most easily be spared; it is in no sense a substitute for economic development.

The effect of the rising population has been felt in agricultural districts where small farmers have had to divide their holdings between so many dependants that they are no longer capable of fully supporting the people. The result has been a migration from the countryside to the towns, which have grown in size very rapidly and which contain large numbers of unemployed people who live in sub-human conditions.

Each territory is dominated by one town—the chief port. This has come about because the West Indies are very dependent on overseas trade and because there is rarely more than one harbour that can accommodate large steamships. Moreover, the territories are compact enough for a single port to be able to distribute imported goods quickly and cheaply to all districts by road and, in some cases by railway. The chief port has also become the capital and the chief commercial, shopping, manufacturing educational and entertainment centre of each territory.

If the standard of living of a country is to rise, its economic development must proceed faster than the rise of population. It is clear that in the West Indies considerable development is necessary even to maintain standards. This is very difficult to do where resources are so meagre. Agriculture is restricted by steep slopes, poor soils and drought to small portions of most territories. The proportion of arable land ranges from the outstandingly high figure of 60% of the total land area in Barbados to a low of 14% in Dominica, with an average for all the islands of 27%. The full facts are shown in diagram 4f.

If the land has its limitations, so also has the sea. The Caribbean is not rich in fish and may never be able to supply even local demands. What of the two remaining primary industries—forestry and mining? Large-scale forestry is restricted to Guyana and Belize, and in any case forestry cannot maintain an advanced economy. Large deposits of minerals appear to be limited to petroleum in Trinidad and bauxite in Jamaica and Guyana, yet these two minerals account for half the exports from the Commonwealth Caribbean territories when the refined petroleum and alumina made from them are included.

Some of the most valuable ways in which development is being undertaken in the West Indies are:

1. The establishment of new industries to create employment, reduce imports of manufactured goods, and—in some cases—to increase exports. Among the recently established heavy industries are alumina production in Jamaica, Guyana, and St Croix, oil refining (from imported crude petroleum) in Jamaica, Puerto Rico, and Antigua, and cement in Jamaica, Puerto Rico, Trinidad, and Grand Bahama. Light industries are growing in number and variety in most territories—particularly in Puerto Rico, Jamaica, and Trinidad—often being supported by tax holidays and by restrictions or heavy duties on competing imports. Trinidad in particular has established assembly plants

4f. Percentage of land in the Commonwealth Caribbean islands used for various purposes.

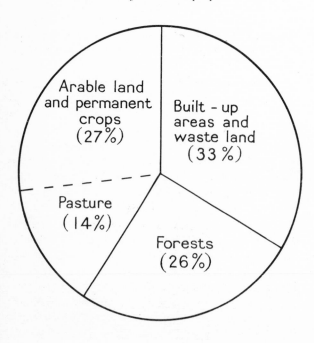

Arable land and permanent crops (27%)

Built - up areas and waste land (33%)

Pasture (14%)

Forests (26%)

for imported machine parts. For example, several makes of motor vehicles are assembled there. Puerto Rico, and to a lesser extent Jamaica, have developed light industries and assembly plants making such things as garments, sports goods and electronic equipment solely for export.

The need for increased exports can be seen from the following table:

Territory	Value of Imports 1958	Value of Exports 1958	Approximate Value of Exports per head of Population
	$000	$000	$ (=4/2)
Antigua	13,440	5,700	98
Montserrat	1,520	377	25
St Kitts, Nevis and Anguilla	11,360	9,430	160
Barbados	73,390	40,430	170
Jamaica	310,370	223,340	134
Dominica	8,760	6,700	100
Grenada	10,930	8,350	90
St Lucia	9,034	4,459	53
St Vincent	10,690	5,570	70
Trinidad and Tobago	412,490	393,540	500
Guyana	116,390	97,710	180
Belize	22,220	10,900	122

4g. Table of imports and exports.

When considering these figures, it should be remembered that:

(i) The Table does not take into account "invisible" exports, such as the earnings from tourism and investments by West Indians in other countries, or the money sent home by West Indian emigrants.
(ii) A significant proportion of the crops grown in these territories is not exported but is sold locally. Foodstuffs are grown largely by peasants who think more in terms of their local market than of overseas markets.

2. The provision of facilities for the growing number of American tourists. Those who come on Caribbean cruises call at such ports as Nassau, Kingston and Curaçao where a wide variety of duty-free goods is on sale to them. Those who travel by air usually come to spend a vacation. Their contribution to the economy of the West Indies is particularly valuable. A tourist couple staying at a luxury hotel spends on accommodation alone as much money in five days as an acre of good estate cane earns in a year. They are believed to spend an almost equal amount on purchases to take home with them.

The Bahamas receive so many visitors that they have developed a more purely tourist economy than any other country in the world. A million visitors are expected to visit the islands in 1970. In Jamaica in 1965 the estimated earnings from tourism were worth almost a third as much as the exports. In Barbados and Antigua tourism is in some years more valuable than sugar. Here and elsewhere the earnings are rising year by year.

3. In these days of international co-operation, assistance is coming to the Commonwealth Caribbean territories from various sources; in particular from the governments of the United States, Britain, and Canada, from private foundations, and from the United Nations and its Specialized Agencies. Examples of such assistance are the provision of low-interest loans for large projects from the World Bank and of technical experts—such as those from the Food and Agricultural Organization who are developing Caribbean fisheries and those from the World Health Organization who are eradicating malaria and other diseases.

4h. *"New skills have led . . . to the moulding of new landscapes." Tourists play golf beside the ruins of an old Jamaican sugar mill on land which was once under cane. What changes of land use do you know of in the district in which you live?*

New Industries

4i. Garments   *4j. Textiles*
4k. Edible oil   *4l. Tyres*

What industries employ women mostly, and men mostly?

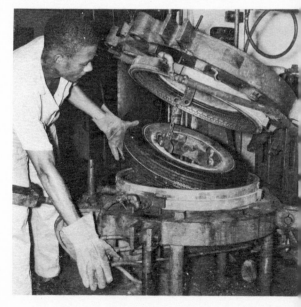

The fact that the West Indies receives such aid suggests that they are among the world's under-developed nations, but this is not entirely true. One indication of relative prosperity is given by the figures for *per capita* income (that is the total income of a country for a year divided by the number of people living there). These show that the world's richest country was the United States with a figure of $4,700 in the early 1960s. That for India was $118. The Commonwealth Caribbean territories lay well between these extremes. Trinidad had the highest *per capita* income, $1,100; Jamaica had $620; and St Vincent had the lowest, $280. Other examples to show where we stand in the world are Japan, $640; Spain, $540; and Ghana, $234.[1]

Another indication is given by the number of automobiles in use. Again at the summit is America which, with 69 million cars on the roads in the early 1960s, has one car for every $2\frac{3}{4}$ inhabitants. Puerto Rico had one for every 13 people; Trinidad and Tobago one for every 17; Jamaica one for every 30; and Haiti one for every 664.

[1] For currencies, see page vi.

4m. More crops are sold in local markets than in foreign ones.

4n. What goods are on sale here? What others can you list?

4o. *A tourist hotel in Jamaica. In some places land that is valueless for agriculture and mining can still bring rich returns. What other examples can you think of?*

4p. *An example of UNESCO assistance—the Engineering Faculty building at the University of the West Indies in Trinidad.*

THINGS TO DO

1. Pay a visit to any fortifications guarding a town. Draw a sketch-map to show their position in relation to the town they were meant to protect. What advantage was taken of natural landscape features in building the fortifications?

2. Find place-names in Jamaica and Trinidad that show evidence of settlement by people of different nationalities in each island.

3. Draw a sketch-map to show how winds affected West Indian shipping routes and the siting of ports in the days of sailing-ships.

4. Work out from Table 4e on page 29 the percentage increase of population in each territory between 1921 and 1946 and between 1946 and 1960.

5. Draw a diagram to show the comparative populations of the territories in these years.

6. Find out the best conditions for the cultivation of sugar cane. What are the chief problems facing cane growers in the territory in which you live?

7. Make lists of the manufacturing industries operating in the territory in which you live and in one other territory under these headings:
   (a) local materials for local markets;
   (b) local materials for overseas markets;
   (c) overseas materials for local markets;
   (d) overseas materials for overseas markets.

8. With information obtained from travel agencies or from the air companies themselves, draw a sketch-map to show the chief air routes to the Caribbean and within the West Indies. Show also the distances covered by these routes and the time it takes to travel by air to the major towns in other countries.

9. Using material obtained from census or electoral districts, draw a large map to show the distribution of population in the district in which you live.

QUESTIONS

1. In what ways do you think the West Indies can take the best advantage of their position relative to North, Central and South America?

2. If you were asked to show an English geographer the major features of geographical interest in the neighbourhood of your home or school, what would you show him and why? C.H.S.C. 1954.

3. The development of industries is one of the solutions of over-population in the West Indies. What are the conditions necessary for this development and how far can the West Indies fulfil them? J.T.C. 1952.

4. Since 1920, the population of the West Indies has approximately doubled to its present size of 3 millions.
   (a) Where are the most densely populated areas?
   (b) What problems have arisen owing to this large increase of population and what steps are being taken to solve them? O.C.S.E.B.(O) 1965.

CHAPTER FIVE

Jamaica

Area: 4,411 square miles; population (1966): about 1,811,000; density of population: 410 per square mile

THE CAPTURE OF JAMAICA AND ITS EARLY DEVELOPMENT

In 1655 a force of 2,500 men in a large fleet of ships set out from England under orders from Cromwell to seize any Spanish West Indian possession which could be used as a base for the conquest of all Central America. This was the first direct challenge to Spanish supremacy in the Caribbean, for up to that time the only other non-Spanish settlements in the area were confined to the smaller islands which Spain had never bothered to occupy.

The expedition touched first at Barbados, where a further 4,000 men were recruited. Most of these were dissatisfied British indentured servants glad of the opportunity to leave the colony (see page 24). After still more men had been added to their numbers as they sailed northwards through the Leeward Islands, an attempt was made to capture Hispaniola. It failed, so the leaders decided to try to take Jamaica instead, for they knew it was sparsely settled and weakly garrisoned. This time they were successful, though the Spaniards with the aid of their freed slaves, the *Maroons*, and with occasional reinforcements from Cuba were able to fight on in the hills for five years before they were finally overcome. Even then the Maroons did not submit and, as their numbers were continually reinforced by escaped slaves, they resisted conquest. Some of their descendants remain to this day, living in semi-isolation in the hills in the interior of the island.

Throughout the century and a half of Spanish occupation Jamaica was poorly developed. Manual labour was scarce, for the original Arawak population—estimated at 60,000—quickly died out, and few African slaves were imported. In any case the Spaniards never paid much attention to the island. Only a very small area was cultivated and most of the settlers made their living by rearing cattle, horses and pigs on the savannas. They sent their products to Europe and the mainland of Central America. Hides and tallow were most in demand and much of the meat was wasted.

Under the British, things changed rapidly. The island's strategic position in the heart of the Spanish Empire was immediately exploited by the buccaneers, who soon turned Port Royal into a treasure-chest of Spanish booty. For the first thirty years or so, while the new colony needed their protection, the buccaneers were given official encouragement. Once it was secure they were suppressed. Soon afterwards Port Royal, still one of the largest, richest and most riotous ports in the Caribbean, was almost entirely destroyed by an earthquake in 1692, much of it disappearing beneath the sea. Port Royal was used as a naval base throughout the eighteenth century, but its other functions were transferred to Kingston, which grew up on the opposite side of the same harbour. Kingston rapidly became one of the chief centres of trade in the Caribbean. In the mid eighteenth century it was declared a free port. Slaves, foodstuffs, cloth, ironware and other manufactured goods were landed there, transferred to smaller ships and taken to many other parts of the Caribbean. The Spanish colonists, in need of all these things, were glad to buy them in spite of their Government's laws declaring such trade to be illegal.

But the greatest profits were made by the estate-owners and those engaged in the sugar trade. Simply because of its size Jamaica was destined to become the richest British West Indian colony. Within a few years of the conquest former soldiers and buccaneers, unsuccessful colonists from Barbados and the Leeward Islands hoping for better fortune in Jamaica, and immigrants from Britain had acquired huge properties. Using African slave labour they saw their estates spread quickly over the lowlands. At the beginning of the nineteenth century a thousand were in operation, producing about 100,000 tons of sugar

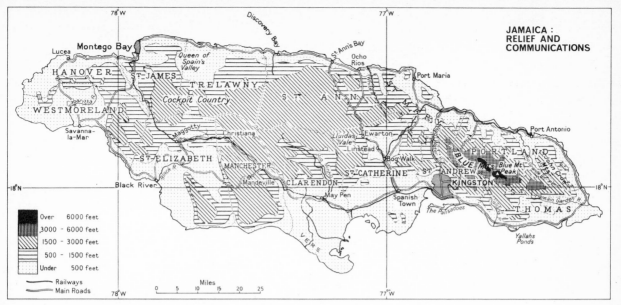

5a. What relationships are there between relief and communications?

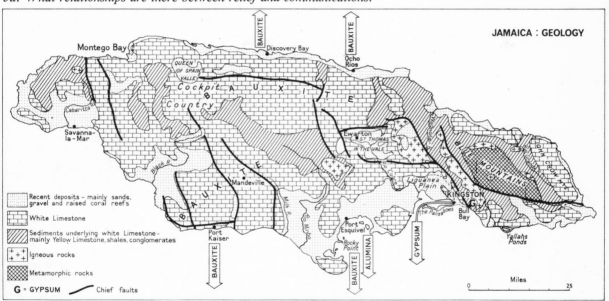

5b. What relationships are there between the geology and relief of Jamaica?

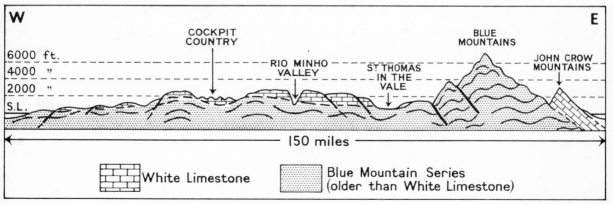

5c. Sketch section across Jamaica to show the geology.

a year. By this time coffee was important too, and for a while Jamaica was England's richest overseas possession. What happened to alter this position we shall learn later.

THE LAND

Jamaica, with an area of 4,411 square miles, is the third largest Caribbean island. In fact, it is bigger than all the other Commonwealth Caribbean islands put together, and has just over half the total population.

Jamaica may be divided into three structural regions:

(i) The eastern part is composed of many different igneous, sedimentary and metamorphic rocks which were folded and uplifted in Cretaceous times. Since then they have been severely eroded by many rivers, of which the largest are the Yallahs, Plantain Garden, Wagwater and Rio Grande, so that today the landscape is one of sharp-crested ridges and deep, twisting valleys. Standing in the midst is the highest range of all, the Blue Mountains, where Blue Mountain Peak rises to 7,402 feet. (See the photograph on page 4.)

(ii) Most of the rest of the island is capped by thick layers of Tertiary white limestone. In the centre and west this has been uplifted in stages to form several distinct plateau surfaces, though they have been considerably broken up by block faulting.

As limestone is soluble in water containing weak acids, it is eroded in a characteristic way. The result is called *karst* scenery, named after a district in Yugoslavia where the process has been studied most closely. All the typical *karst* features occur in Jamaica. Streams seldom remain on the surface for long but disappear underground to flow through a maze of caverns, reappearing only in the deeper basins or at the edge of the limestone. Enormous quantities of limestone have been dissolved away and in places, as shown in Diagram 5c, the underlying rocks have been exposed. Where limestone still remains, as it does over at least half the island, the landscape varies from place to place. The Cockpit

5d. This rolling limestone upland is typical of large parts of Central Jamaica.
What is the land being used for? Why?

Country is so broken up into deep, circular arenas and huge rocky buttresses that it is almost impenetrable and is therefore sparsely populated. Elsewhere erosion has produced a rolling upland countryside of rounded hills and hollows. Here conditions are better, though much of the land has had to be left in pasture and scattered clumps of trees. In general, poor soils and the difficulty of obtaining water make cultivation difficult. Dense agricultural settlement exists only where deep, rich soils have been deposited in large solution-basins. The biggest of these are the Rio Minho Valley, the Black River Valley in St Elizabeth, St Thomas in the Vale round the town of Linstead, the Queen of Spain's Valley near Montego Bay, and the Cabaritta Valley near Savanna-la-Mar. There are many more smaller ones.

Though it is not good for cultivation, limestone has other uses. It is a good stone for building and for road-making. More important, over much of its surface there lies a red clay containing bauxite, now being worked by several large mining companies.

(iii) Surrounding the highlands is a narrow coastal plain interrupted occasionally by spurs of highland reaching down to the sea. The largest lowland area is the southern plain which extends westwards from Kingston into the parish of Clarendon.

Along most of the western and northern shores the land descends sharply to narrow coral terraces which provide evidence of recent small uplifts. Elsewhere the plains are composed of mixed alluvial clays, sands and pebbles. Along parts of the coast the sea has deposited beach material in the form of spits and bars; for example, Palisadoes, and the bar enclosing Yallahs ponds.

MINERALS

Bauxite is by far the most important mineral occurring in Jamaica. It exists as a layer varying in thickness over about a thousand square miles of the Tertiary white limestone in the western two-thirds of the island. The best deposits lie in shallow basins at heights above 1,000 feet. Its origin is unknown. One suggestion is that it resulted from the tropical weathering of vast quantities of limestone over millions of years. But this leaves unsolved the question of how the rock—which is almost pure calcium carbonate—produced a deposit rich in alumina. Another theory is that the bauxite came from the older volcanic rocks in the island which do contain aluminium silicate. If this is the true source, the question is how the mineral came to be deposited in such quantities on top of the limestone.

Though the existence of the bauxite had been known for some years beforehand, it was not until the demand for aluminium mounted sharply in the Second World War that tests were made to see if it was worth mining. Samples sent abroad for analysis indicated that its composition differed from the ores worked in America and from those imported by that country from the Guianas. For one thing, its alumina content was lower. Thus it was discovered that 6 tons of Jamaican bauxite were needed to make 1 ton of aluminium, compared with only 4 tons of the ore mined in Guyana. Because of this and other differences it was impossible to extract the alumina economically in any of the factories existing at that time. However, this disadvantage was more than offset by certain favourable factors. Firstly, Jamaican reserves were enormous, estimated at over 500 million tons. Secondly, being a soft rock lying on the surface not far from the sea, it was readily accessible and easily worked. Drilling and blasting were unnecessary. Thirdly, as the deposits lay only 1,000 miles from the Gulf Coast ports, transport costs were low, and in war-time ships could be guarded by aircraft throughout their voyage to America. Soon after the war, Canadian and American companies built the special plants needed to extract alumina from Jamaican bauxite, purchased large properties in the island and began operations. The amount of bauxite mined rose rapidly from 400,000 tons in 1952 to 5,722,000 tons in 1958 and reached 8,500,000 tons in 1965.

Mining is carried out by open-pit methods, so no miners work underground. The topsoil is cleared from a few acres and the underlying bauxite is removed with huge mechanical shovels. A single deposit 50 acres in extent may yield over 5 million tons. The American firms dry their ore in rotating ovens and take it to storage sheds at Port Kaiser, Ocho Rios, Discovery Bay, and Rocky Point, where it is shipped to their alumina plants in the United States. Jamaican bauxite exports, which totalled over 7 million tons in 1965, are by far the largest in the world. The Canadian firm does not export any bauxite but extracts all its alumina locally at two plants, one near Mandeville and the other near

5e. The alumina factory near Mandeville is set in a hollow in the limestone plateau.

Ewarton, which have a combined capacity of about a million tons a year. Here the ore is ground into fine particles and dumped into tanks of hot caustic soda solution under high pressure. This process dissolves alumina (that is aluminium oxide), while the unwanted residue—consisting mainly of iron oxide and silica—settles to the bottom and is strained off and dumped. The alumina is then reprecipitated from solution and heated to 2,000°F. in rotary kilns. It emerges as a white powder resembling table salt. About 2½ tons of dry bauxite are needed to make a ton of alumina. The output, which totalled 768,300 tons in 1964, is taken by rail to Port Esquivel and shipped to Kitimat in British Columbia and to Scandinavia, where it is converted into aluminium. The metal itself is not made in Jamaica as the process requires large quantities of cheap electricity. This is obtained from hydro-electricity at Kitimat and in Scandinavia. In the southern United States it is generated from oil and natural gas.

Though all the bauxite and alumina development is in foreign hands, the Jamaican Government receives money from royalties and from income tax. In addition over 6,000 employees, nearly all of whom are Jamaicans, are earning wages considerably better than those paid to agricultural workers. Bauxite has thus brought prosperity to parts of Jamaica that were previously depressed agricultural districts.

On the southern slopes of the mountains behind Bull Bay a few miles east of Kingston there is a deposit of several million tons of gypsum. Over 200,000 tons of it are quarried each year. Some is used in the local cement industry and the manufacture of other building materials. The remainder is taken to the eastern end of Kingston harbour to await export to the United States.

Other minerals present in Jamaica include marble and silica, and ores of copper, lead, zinc, manganese and iron. Some of these are worked in small quantities. For instance, silica sand found near Black River is made into glass. Bat guano, found in caves in limestone areas, is used locally as fertilizer as it is rich in phosphates. Petroleum has been sought for, but so far none has been found.

CLIMATE

Temperature

As in the other Caribbean islands the monthly temperature-range is small. Thus in Kingston the difference between the hottest month, July (81.4°F.) and the coolest, January (75.8°F.) is less than 6°F. The diurnal range is somewhat greater (15°F. to 20°F.), though owing to the moderating influence of the sea it is rare for day temperatures on the plains to exceed 91°F. or to fall below 60°F. at night.

Highland temperatures are 10°F. to 20°F. lower than these, and the summits of the Blue Mountains have been known to have occasional light frosts in winter.

Rainfall

The chief features of Caribbean rainfall have been dealt with in Chapter Two. In Jamaica the rainy season begins at about the end of April and reaches a maximum in September, October and November with a somewhat drier intervening period in June. Several factors combine to produce the summer maximum. Firstly, as the convection currents are strongest in the hot months, the heaviest showers occur then. Thunder often accompanies afternoon downpours. Secondly, this is the period when the *Inter-Tropical Convergence Zone* is farthest north and rain-bearing easterly waves, moving along its northern boundary, sometimes cross the island. Thirdly, this is the hurricane season. Though hurricanes strike Jamaica on an average only once in seven or eight years, they bring such heavy rain when they strike or pass nearby that average monthly rainfall figures are affected.

In the colder months convection currents are weaker and the air is less humid, so showers are fewer, lighter and shorter. The tendency to drought is partly offset by occasional *northers* blowing out from North America in winter. They bring with them cool,

40

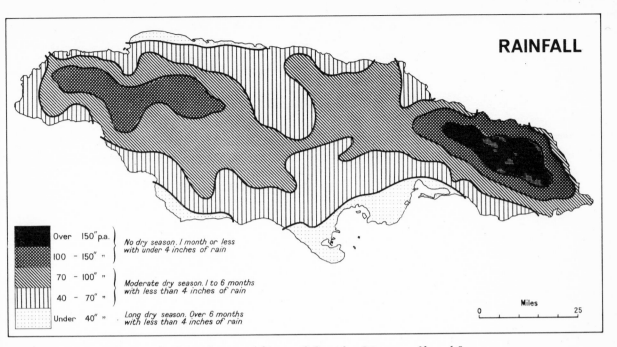

RAINFALL

Over 150" p.a. }
100 - 150" "   } No dry season. I month or less with under 4 inches of rain
70 - 100" " }
40 - 70" "   } Moderate dry season. I to 6 months with less than 4 inches of rain
Under 40" " } Long dry season. Over 6 months with less than 4 inches of rain

Miles
0   25

5f. What factors influence the facts shown on this map? See also Diagrams 2h and 5g.

damp conditions lasting sometimes for several days.

As the prevailing winds blow from the north and east, the northward and eastward-facing parts of Jamaica receive more rain than the south. The Blue Mountains exert a marked influence on rainfall distribution in eastern Jamaica. Their summits, usually enveloped in cloud, have over 200 inches of rain a year. The north-east coast has over 100 inches, but the south-east coast and the Liguanea Plain are cast in rain shadow and parts have less than 35 inches. Thus the largest lowland has the least rain and irrigation is necessary if crops are to be grown successfully. The most recent irrigation work has been carried out in mid-Clarendon where 12,000 acres now obtain water from underground wells. Altogether about 50,000 acres are irrigated in Jamaica, sugar cane, citrus, rice and bananas benefiting most. The south-east also has the longest and most severe dry season. Streams flowing down the southern slopes of the Blue Mountains are reduced to mere trickles of water most of the time and may dry up altogether.

5g. Average monthly rainfall of Port Antonio (top) and Kingston (bottom).
Describe the rainfall of both places using the method given on page 13.

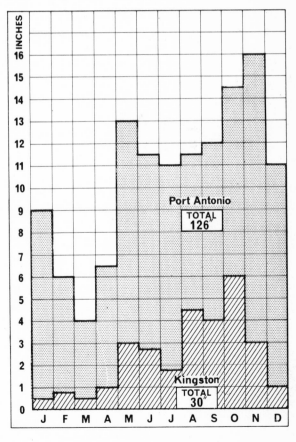

Port Antonio
TOTAL 126"

Kingston
TOTAL 30"

INCHES

J F M A M J J A S O N D

41

LAND USE

Diagram 5h reveals the high proportion of unproductive land in Jamaica. The mountainous nature of the country—half of which lies above 1,000 feet—the steep, rocky slopes and the large tracts of poor, thin soils are the chief natural factors accounting for this. But in addition much harm has been done by man. Over large areas forests have been cut for lumber, burned for charcoal and cleared for cultivation, thus exposing the land to rapid tropical weathering. Plantations established in unsuitable areas in the prosperous days of slavery now lie "ruinate", or provide a few squatting tenants with a meagre subsistence. In some of these areas soil erosion has become so serious that land is now very difficult to reclaim. Nevertheless attempts are being made to do so. Two areas to which particular attention has been given are the Yallahs Valley leading southwards from the Blue Mountains to the coast and a somewhat larger area around Christiana in the centre of Jamaica. More recently, attention has been directed to the protection of badly eroded watersheds all over the island—especially to the reforestation of sharp-crested ridges separating deep valleys.

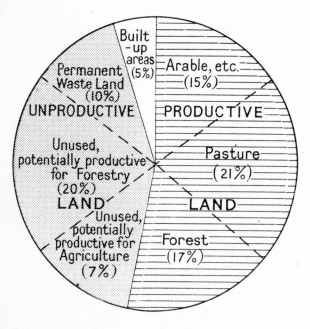

5h. *The proportions of Productive Land, Unproductive Land and Built-up Areas in Jamaica.*

LAND HOLDINGS

In the slave days the Jamaican lowlands were occupied by large sugar estates and cattle pens while the hills were mostly left in forest and bush. After Emancipation the majority of the freed slaves left the estates and cleared small subsistence holdings for themselves in the hills. These two contrasting types of land tenure—estates and peasant holdings—still exist, and so Jamaican properties are usually either very large or very small. Thus 38% of all land is taken up by 300 properties of 500 acres and over. At the other end of the scale, 71% of the farms are under 5 acres in size; an area which is generally agreed to be much too small to support a family. These tiny farms take up 12% of the area.

THE CROPS

Sugar

Reasons for the rapid decline in British West Indian sugar output in the first half of the nineteenth century have been given in Chapter Four. It remains to be said that Jamaica, the world's largest producer in the early part of the century, suffered more severely than any other colony. The high proportion of absentee owners, their extravagance, their failure to improve cultivation and processing methods in times of prosperity, the cultivation of unsuitable land, the dependence on slave labour which largely abandoned the estates after emancipation, together with changing British economic policy led to the collapse of the industry. This lasted for a century. Indeed the output of 100,000 tons of sugar in 1805 was not surpassed until 1937. Since then production has risen greatly. Under the Commonwealth Sugar Agreement of 1951 Jamaica was allocated an overall quota of 270,000 tons. This figure, plus an extra 50,000 tons needed for local consumption, was reached in 1953. Two years later the total output was almost 400,000 tons. Jamaica had little difficulty in disposing of the surplus, as she was allowed to make up the quotas not filled by other Commonwealth territories. However, in order to prevent the island from producing a lot more sugar than can be sold, estate expansion is being controlled and most of the fluctuations in the area under cane are caused by cane farmers. The output in 1965 was 506,000 tons, of which 424,000 tons were exported.

Cane fields occupy about 35% of the arable land. By comparing Maps 5a and 5i it can be seen that the cane is grown chiefly on the lowlands. Here stand the seventeen factories operating today. One of them, Frome, in the western part of the island, is the largest in the Commonwealth Caribbean. Another, Monymusk, which stands on the irrigated plains of Vere in southern Clarendon, is almost as big and is the only one producing refined white sugar. Most of the white sugar is sold locally, though a little goes to other territories.

In addition to sugar Jamaica produces about 4 million gallons of rum a year and some molasses.

Bananas

Though the banana was introduced into Jamaica by the Spaniards in the sixteenth century, it was not until the middle of the nineteenth century that American schooners, calling at north shore ports, began to take small quantities of the fruit back with them to the United States. They sold so well that American companies were formed to handle the trade, and regular shipments began in the 1880s. This was fortunate for Jamaica, for at that time many of the peasants were finding it hard to support themselves on their own small farms and they welcomed the opportunity to earn a regular income from bananas. At that time, too, the Jamaican sugar industry, unable to compete with subsidized European beet sugar, was in its most depressed state. By 1900 banana exports had become more valuable than sugar, and they remained so, apart from a few years, until the Second World War. The peak year was 1937, when Jamaica exported nearly 27 million stems, twice as many as any other country in the world. By this time the United Kingdom had become the chief purchaser and a large fleet of fast, refrigerated banana boats was operating between Jamaica and Britain.

Banana production in the period between the two world wars would have been considerably greater had it not been for Panama disease. Not only did this fungus damage or kill the plants, but it infected the soil so that bananas could not again be grown on the spot for years. Several estates went out of production altogether. Output was maintained only by bringing into use steep hill-slopes unsuited to cultivation and only bearing for a few years. In 1936 a second disease

5i. A fine stem of bananas. How much would one like this weigh?

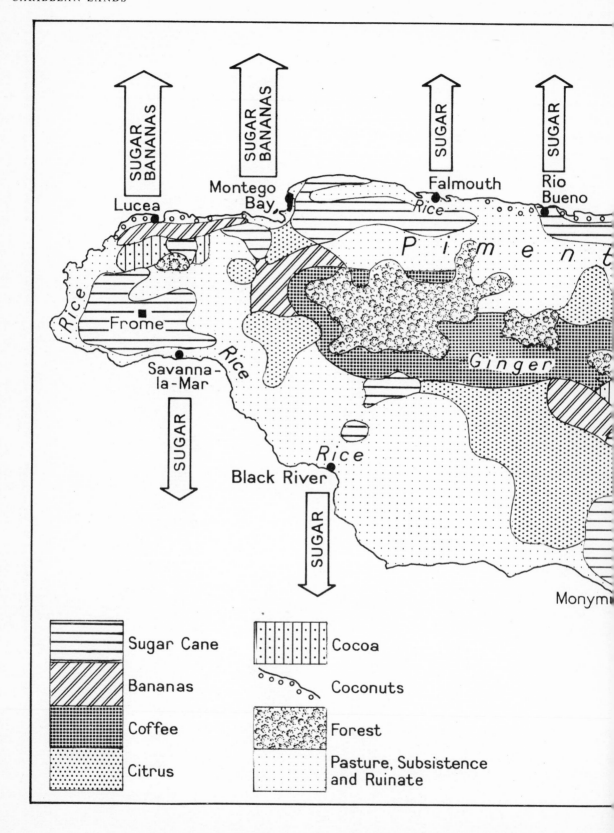

SUGAR
BANANAS

SUGAR
BANANAS

SUGAR

SUGAR

Lucea

Montego
Bay

Falmouth

Rio
Bueno

Rice

P i m e n t

Rice

Frome

Rice

Ginger

Savanna-
la-Mar

Rice

SUGAR

Rice

Black River

SUGAR

Monym

Sugar Cane

Cocoa

Bananas

Coconuts

Coffee

Forest

Citrus

Pasture, Subsistence
and Ruinate

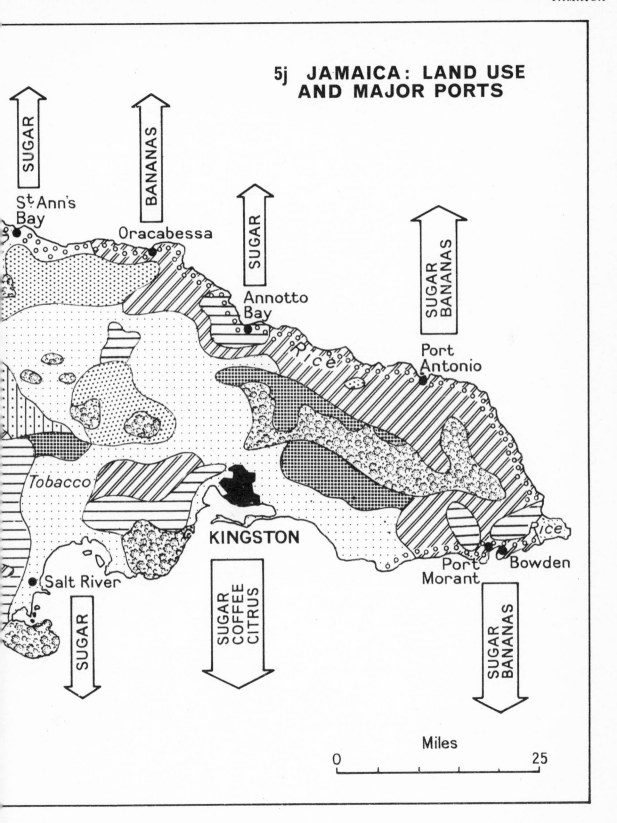

5j JAMAICA: LAND USE AND MAJOR PORTS

SUGAR

BANANAS

St Ann's Bay

Oracabessa

SUGAR

Annotto Bay

Rice

SUGAR BANANAS

Port Antonio

Tobacco

KINGSTON

Salt River

Rice

Port Morant

Bowden

SUGAR

SUGAR COFFEE CITRUS

SUGAR BANANAS

Miles

0   25

—leaf spot—appeared, and soon afterwards in 1939 the Second World War began. During the war few ships could be spared for such luxuries as bananas, and in the worst year of all, 1943, only 289,000 stems were exported. The industry was preserved only because the British Ministry of Food undertook to purchase all bananas fit for export, even though they could not be shipped.

After the war there was a fairly rapid recovery in spite of Panama disease, but in 1951 a severe hurricane destroyed millions of plants. The government then helped farmers to plant a new variety of banana which was immune to the disease. This type—the Lacatan—now makes up over 80% of the exports.

Bananas are grown on about 20% of the arable land. The bulk of the output comes from estates and small holdings in the valleys and on the foothills near the northern and eastern coasts, but some are grown on estates in drier areas where irrigation is used to supplement rainfall. The estates have the advantage that they can afford to tend the bananas carefully, which is necessary if Lacatans are to bear well. They are very susceptible to leaf spot disease, which can only be controlled by regular spraying. They are easily damaged, so they have to be packed in plastic bags or in padded boxes and handled gently if they are to arrive in Britain in good condition. As Jamaican bananas have to compete with those from the Canary Islands, the Cameroons and several of the Commonwealth Eastern Caribbean territories, only the best can be accepted for export. Many small farmers, especially those in the hills, have found these conditions too exacting and have given up growing bananas for export. In the late 1950s and early 1960s exports remained fairly steady at between 10 and 11 million stems a year. In 1965 they rose to just over 15 million, some being sold in Western Europe as well as in Britain. But as usually happens with agriculture, the rise in quantity resulted in a fall of price, and the marketing of bananas is another problem for Jamaica to solve. Between 4 and 5 million stems are consumed annually in the island itself.

Bananas are especially valuable as they bring the growers a steady income throughout the year. In addition they provide good shade for young cocoa and coffee plants before they begin to bear, and grow well with coconuts—a common combination in Jamaica.

Coffee

Jamaican coffee, first grown in the eighteenth century, soon found a ready market in Europe. One type, Blue Mountain coffee, came to be considered among the best in the world. Output rose rapidly and in 1814, the peak year, over 15,000 tons were exported. This prosperity was short-lived, for coffee was a plantation crop and soon after the slaves were emancipated the industry collapsed. Some of the land was taken over by small holders but they allowed the land, the trees and the methods of production to deteriorate so that for the next hundred years exports averaged less than 4,000 tons a year. Times were bad, for as both quantity and quality fell, so did the price. Moreover, throughout this period soil erosion went unchecked, proceeding so far that some old coffee lands will never again be productive.

Coffee is of particular value as it grows well in hilly districts unsuited to other crops. Since the war much work has been done to improve the industry. Several million young plants have been given to farmers prepared to look after them properly. A number of pulperies have been built throughout the island to process the crop. During the picking season, which lasts from August to March, ripe cherry-red berries are taken to the pulperies where they are unloaded into water tanks. The best berries sink, whereas immature ones and waste matter float on the surface and are easily removed. While the berries are still under water, a machine removes the pulp surrounding the beans. The beans are then sent to a factory in Kingston where they are dried, either artificially, using hot air, or by spreading them on a large barbecue in the sun. A few days later they are fed into a hulling machine which strips the parchment and the underlying silver skin off the beans and polishes them. Finally the beans are graded according to size, the largest and best being carefully inspected before they are packed into sacks for export. This "washed coffee", as it is called, is exported to several countries including the United Kingdom, Italy and Germany. Some of the coffee, especially that sent to the United States and Canada, is roasted prior to shipment. Some is packed in vacuum-sealed tins to keep it fresh for a long time, and some is made into instant coffee.

The famous Blue Mountain coffee is grown on small farms on the slopes of the Blue Mountains,

5k. Coffee in the Blue Mountains. What problems face people who live in districts as mountainous as this?

mostly between 3,000 and 5,000 feet. At these heights the cooler climate causes the berries to take longer to ripen and in consequence the beans develop more of the substances which on roasting give coffee its flavour. The beans are carefully processed at a number of pulperies in the area and exported in barrels.

Citrus

Most of the Jamaican citrus fruit is produced in a wide belt stretching from north to south across the centre of the island. Oranges and grapefruit grow best below 2,500 feet in places where rainfall is well distributed throughout the year. Limes prefer the drier areas. During the picking season, which lasts from November to April, all oranges and grapefruit for export as fresh fruit are sent to two factories where the best are selected, wrapped and carefully packed in wooden crates for shipment to Britain and New Zealand. The bulk of the crop, however, is processed at these and other factories into marmalade, concentrated orange juice, and canned citrus oils, juices and segments.

Cocoa

Cocoa, though grown in Jamaica since the earliest days of English settlement, first became important during the decline of the sugar industry in the latter half of the nineteenth century. Cocoa trees replaced cane in some areas, notably the moist sheltered valleys leading up into the Blue Mountains. Exports rose to about 3,000 tons a year in the first quarter of the present century. During this time, however, prices fell because of the remarkable expansion in Ghana—then called the Gold Coast. Few new trees were planted and, as the old ones ceased to bear, bananas were grown in their place.

51. Jamaican small farmers find it hard to market their crops. This is one means of transporting them. What others are there?

Jamaica is fortunate in being free from the diseases affecting cocoa in West Africa and Trinidad and as prices have been high since the war the Government has set about reorganizing the industry. Plants are given free of cost to growers in cocoa-growing areas and large fermentaries have been built to process the cocoa properly. Local sales, which include the cocoa used to make instant drinks and confectionery, absorb about one-third of the output. The remainder is exported.

Pimento
The dried berries of the pimento tree yield a spice which, because of its resemblance to the combined flavours of cinnamon, cloves and nutmeg, is called "allspice". Pimento thrives best amidst the pastures on the limestone highlands of the central parishes. Though it is grown a little in other parts of the Caribbean, Jamaica has an almost complete monopoly of the world's allspice trade. The leaves of the tree are also valuable as they yield pimento oil. The output—and therefore the price—fluctuates from year to year.

Ginger
Another export long associated with Jamaica is high-grade ginger. Most of it is grown by small farmers in the central hills north of Christiana where it has caused considerable soil erosion.

When the plants are dug out of the ground, the roots—shaped like a man's hand—are peeled, washed thoroughly and dried in the sun. They must be handled carefully to prevent them from breaking, for broken ginger loses its value. It is sold to Britain, Canada and America.

Tobacco
Before the war Jamaica had a considerable cigar trade with Britain. This has declined in recent years because of the high tax imposed on tobacco there. Moreover Jamaican cigars have to compete on equal terms with those from Cuba, which are usually regarded as being the best in the world.

A coarse tobacco is grown for local use, but most of the cigarettes manufactured in the island are made of Virginia tobacco or blended with imported Canadian leaf.

Sisal
Some sisal is grown on poor soils in the hills near May Pen. It is converted into rope sufficient to satisfy Jamaican requirements.

Fruit
Many tropical fruits are grown in the island, primarily for home consumption, though guava jelly and canned pineapples, mangoes and other fruits and fruit products are exported in small quantities. Strawberries grow well in the Blue Mountains, but it is difficult to carry them to Kingston for marketing.

Coconuts
Coconuts, grown mainly along the northern and eastern coasts of the island, provide enough copra to supply a fairly large industry making such products as butterine, margarine, lard, edible oil, toilet soap and laundry soap. In some years there is a small export of copra, and some fresh coconuts are sent to the United States.

THE SMALL FARMERS
Throughout the period of slavery Jamaican slaves were granted a certain amount of time to grow food crops on their own small plots of land. Thus many of them gained enough experience to be able to set up on their own after Emancipation. They acquired small holdings, especially in the hills, which they used

48

primarily for subsistence crops, though they also earned small sums from the sale of such things as bananas, cocoa, coffee, ginger and pimento. The rise of a stable, fairly prosperous peasantry was one of the most notable features of nineteenth-century Jamaica.

There have been further changes since then. For one thing, export estate-grown crops have again become prominent. For another, the increased demands of hotels and towns, especially Kingston, the construction of good roads, and the improvement of marketing and cold-storage facilities have encouraged small farmers throughout the island to earn a regular income from the sale of fruit, vegetables, and animal products. Together with an increasing number of people with larger properties they are thinking more in terms of the local market than of exports. Their products are of considerably more value than all the export crops combined. The diverse output of foodstuffs includes yams, sweet and Irish potatoes, rice, several varieties of beans, plantains, mangoes, avocado pears, breadfruit, cassava, maize, ackees and many other tropical and temperate products.

LIVESTOCK

Pastures take up a greater area than arable land in Jamaica. Many properties, including some very large ones in the central parishes, specialize in cattle rearing. Altogether there are about 300,000 cattle, that is nearly three times as many as there are in all the other Commonwealth Caribbean islands combined. In addition there are about 2 million chickens, 200,000 goats, 150,000 pigs and 10,000 sheep.

Dairying

Since the erection in 1940 of a condensed milk factory at Bog Walk, milk production in the island has more than doubled. The regular demands of the factory have encouraged small farmers to take up dairying. In addition many cane farmers make a supplementary income from milk, which is of special value to them in the out-of-crop season from July to January. Even so the supply of dairy products is not enough to meet local requirements, and there are large imports of powdered milk, butter and cheese, mainly from New Zealand.

Meat

Although about half of the 300,000 cattle in Jamaica

are reared for beef, the supply does not equal the demand. In an attempt to increase the present low output per acre efforts are being made to improve the quality of the pastures. Taking part in this development are the bauxite companies, which have enlarged and improved their cattle herds. For instance, one of them has 16,000 cattle, a livestock feed mill and a cold-storage plant. The bauxite companies have also extended their forest land, their citrus and other orchards, and have set aside some land for tenant farms.

AGRICULTURE AND EMPLOYMENT

One indication of the stage of development of a country is the proportion of the labour force employed in agriculture. By mechanizing their farming, highly developed countries have released many workers for other jobs, such as manufacturing and commerce.

Throughout the West Indies, though the proportion of agricultural workers is falling, it is still high. In the case of Jamaica 44% of the labour force was engaged in agriculture in 1943; 38% in 1960. Those in manufacturing rose in this period from 12% to 15%, and those in commerce from 8% to 10%. Mining, in spite of the size of the bauxite industry, employed less than 1% of the labour force in 1960. This shows how highly mechanized the bauxite operations are.

FORESTS

Most of the natural forest has been destroyed by man. The remainder is classified in Table 5h, page 42, as "productive". This is not altogether true, for though in some areas the forest supplies fruit, lumber or charcoal, in others it exists today only because of its inaccessibility. Even here, however, it serves the useful purpose of preventing soil erosion. For this reason most of the remaining forest is protected by the Government and in recent years the worst eroded areas have been reforested.

Local wood is used to make railway sleepers, furniture and other things, but the bulk of the lumber requirements have to be imported, mostly from Belize, some of the Central American republics and Canada. In former times logwood was valuable, but since the discovery of synthetic dyes this industry has declined. However, there is still a small export of logwood and its extracts, and of annatto and fustic which are also used to make dyestuffs.

FISHERIES

Several thousand fishermen earn an uncertain income from the fish they catch in their canoes. There are few deep-sea boats. The shallow waters and cays off the south coast are richer than the northern waters, where, outside the reef, the sea-floor shelves steeply to great depths. Some fish are also obtained from inland ponds specially stocked for the purpose.

The catch is not sufficient for local consumption and there is a large import of salt cod and other fish from Canada.

INDUSTRIES

Though a few industries were in existence before 1939, war-time shortages of manufactured goods showed the need to establish new ones. The Jamaican Government, following the lead given by Puerto Rico, therefore encouraged and protected many new industries, and Jamaica now has the widest range of manufactured products in the Commonwealth Caribbean. Most of the factories are in Kingston, where a large industrial estate has been developed on the waterfront, but some have been set up outside the capital to provide much-needed employment in the smaller towns and reduce the movement of people to Kingston.

Those industries concerned with the processing of local agricultural products employ most labour. These include sugar and its by-products, confectionery, tobacco, soap and edible oils, rice, leather, and canned goods. Other foodstuffs—notably flour, bread, biscuits and bottled beverages—rely mainly on imported raw materials. Some of the cloth and most of the clothes, boots and shoes sold in the island are made locally. Straw goods and embroidered linens are popular with tourists. Some building materials, including cement, concrete pipes, bricks, building blocks, tiles and gypsum products, are made from local raw materials. The importance of the cement industry is shown by the fact that in 1960 29% of all Jamaican dwellings were made of concrete, as against only 4% in 1943. Other manufactures, such as metal products, pharmaceuticals, gramophone records, plastic goods, paper bags and cardboard cartons, tin cans, tyres, razor blades and electrical equipment are made from imported materials. In addition, there are some factories that make clothes, undergarments, buttons, footwear, sports equipment and other goods primarily or solely for export.

An oil refinery built on the industrial estate converts crude petroleum obtained from Venezuela into gasoline and other products. These are mainly for local use, though some are exported to some Caribbean and Central American countries. Electricity for domestic, commercial, industrial and agricultural purposes is generated in diesel-powered stations, and in small hydro-electric stations on the White River, at Maggotty on the Black River, and elsewhere. Some firms, such as the bauxite companies, generate their own power.

TRADE
Exports, 1965

Chief Agricultural Exports	Per cent Value
Sugar, rum and molasses.....................	24
Bananas...................................	8
Citrus and citrus products..................	4½
Cocoa, coffee, pimento and ginger.............	2½

Chief Non-Agricultural Exports	
Bauxite	24
Alumina	23
Manufactured goods........................	7

All Other Exports	7

Bauxite and alumina exports are so large that North America is the biggest trading partner with Jamaica. In 1965 the United States took 40% of the exports and supplied 43% of the imports (chiefly machinery, manufactured goods, and foodstuffs). Canada took most of the alumina and about a quarter of the sugar (that is, 16% of the exports) and supplied flour, fish and lumber (11% of the imports). Most of the bananas, over half of the sugar, and the bulk of the fruit and fruit products went to Britain, which took 28% of the exports and supplied 24% of the imports. Crude oil from Venezuela amounted to 7% of the total imports. There are large imports of meat and butter from New Zealand and a small return trade in citrus and citrus juices. Jamaican coffee, pimento and ginger, though small, go to many countries.

A country which relies heavily on trade must always watch its "balance of payments", that is it must be careful not to spend more on imports than it earns from exports and other sources of income (such as tourism and the returns from overseas investments). To improve the balance of payments in Jamaica encouragement is being given to the development of new export industries, and certain imports are being heavily taxed. Some goods are not allowed into the country at all.

TOURISM

The diverse natural attractions of the island which Columbus called "the fairest that eyes have beheld" are the basis of a large tourist industry. Montego Bay has long been famous as a holiday resort. It is not the only one, however. Today there are luxury hotels close to many of the white sand beaches along the north shore, where bathing and fishing are excellent. Those people preferring cooler conditions stay in Mandeville and other upland towns. Most visitors travel by air, but some of the liners cruising in the Caribbean allow passengers ashore for a short time in Kingston. In 1965 about 317,000 visitors to Jamaica spent about £23 million ($110 million) there. As most of the visitors are Americans, the industry is a valuable source of U.S. dollars.

POPULATION

The population of Jamaica is almost entirely derived from four immigrant streams entering the island since its capture by the British in 1655. By far the largest number came from Africa. About a million people were landed throughout the slave period, and though some of these were sent elsewhere, at the time of Emancipation they nevertheless outnumbered the white settlers by about ten to one. Today about 96% of the population is coloured or black.

Jamaica took only a small share of the indentured Indian labourers who came to the Caribbean in the last half of the nineteenth century. Their descendants now make up about 2% of the total. In more recent years there has been a small but steady immigration of Chinese. These people, numbering some 1% of the total, are mainly engaged in shopkeeping. All other groups, including Europeans, make up only 1%.

Since the days of slavery population has risen steadily, and in recent years rapidly, in spite of considerable emigration. The first outlet for emigrants was Panama, where they worked on the canal which was begun and abandoned by the French in the 1880s and completed by the Americans between 1908 and 1914. Many Jamaicans chose to remain in Panama and a considerable number of Jamaican families are still there. Throughout this period other emigrants left for Cuba during the expansion of the sugar industry there, and for Central America—especially Costa Rica—to work on the banana estates. Between the two world wars many Jamaicans went to America. Several thousand still go there each year to help in agriculture, but they are under contract and must eventually return. In the 1950s the chief goal of emigrants was Britain where many men and women found employment in factories and on public transport in London, Liverpool, Birmingham and other big cities. In addition, West Indian women were attracted to nursing to such an extent that many British hospitals would have to close if they left. More recently, owing to British immigration restrictions, the number of Jamaicans going abroad has been much reduced. That this has affected the rate of increase of the Jamaican population can be seen by comparing the figures for 1960 and 1965.

	1960	1965
Births	69,200	69,800
Deaths	14,300	14,000
Excess of births over deaths	54,900	55,800
Net emigration	30,400	6,500
Net increase of population	24,500	49,300

The population is unevenly distributed over the island. This may be seen from Map 5n, though in fact the real contrasts are not between one parish and another but between those areas which have the resources to support dense settlement and those which do not. We have already noted the contrast between the sparsely settled limestone uplands and the densely peopled basins within them. In the Blue Mountains there is also a marked contrast between the summits and the valleys, even though many precipitous slopes have been cleared for cultivation and settlement. The coastal lowlands are densely peopled, apart from a few swampy areas.

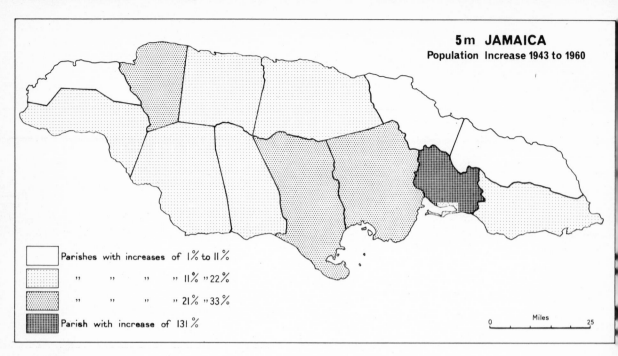

5m JAMAICA
Population Increase 1943 to 1960

Parishes with increases of 1% to 11%
    "   "   "   " 11% " 22%
    "   "   "   " 21% " 33%
Parish with increase of 131%

Miles
0 _____ 25

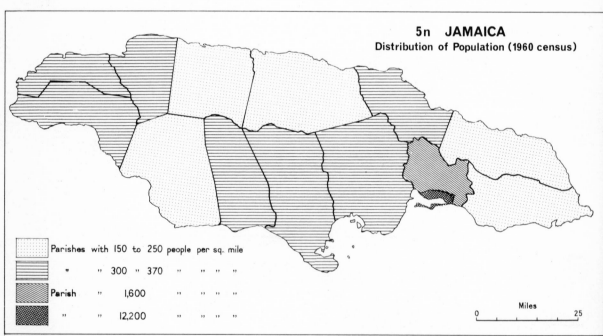

5n JAMAICA
Distribution of Population (1960 census)

Parishes with 150 to 250 people per sq. mile
    "   " 300 " 370   "   " " "
Parish   "   1,600   "   " " "
    "   "   12,200   "   " " "

Miles
0 _____ 25

THE TOWNS

Kingston, which with its suburbs contains over 400,000 people, overshadows all other towns in size. In fact, it has more than twice the population of the next thirty-five towns put together.

Founded after the destruction of Port Royal in 1692, Kingston prospered immediately. Its chief natural advantages were the large land-space available for building and the long, sheltered waterfront. It was also safe from attack, the narrow harbour entrance

5o. Kingston—with the old wharves in the foreground and the new docking facilities, the oil refinery and the industrial estate in the distance. In what direction was the camera pointing? Draw a sketch-map of the area shown.

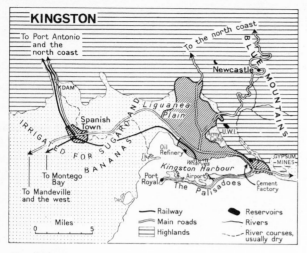

5p. Kingston.

being protected by a fort at Port Royal on the tip of Palisadoes and another on a smaller sandspit opposite. Throughout the eighteenth and early nineteenth centuries, Kingston handled a large local trade, and was the chief *entrepôt* for British exports to the Spanish colonies. For the remainder of the nineteenth century its development was retarded by the decline of Jamaican trade. Though it became the terminus of the island railway and though the capital was transferred there from Spanish Town, Kingston was not in a prosperous condition when it was badly damaged by earthquake and fire in 1907.

Since its reconstruction on more modern lines it has grown rapidly in size and importance, as it lies on the only harbour capable of docking several large ships simultaneously. It is therefore the chief port, though it does not export bananas, alumina or bauxite. It is the focus of road and rail communications and there is an airport near by. It is the main banking, industrial, business and entertainment centre. In recent years its suburbs have spread rapidly in the parish of St Andrew across the Liguanea Plain and up into the encircling foothills. This explains why the rate of increase of population in St Andrew between 1943 and 1960 was more than four times as great as that of any other parish.

Montego Bay and Port Antonio have the best harbours on the north coast. Montego Bay (24,500) has been a busy port since Spanish times. Today it exports bananas and sugar, grown on the rich agricultural land surrounding the town. As the sea is shallow, ships have to stand some distance off-shore and be loaded by lighters.

There are many hotels near by, as Montego Bay is the leading tourist resort. It has a large airport and is the terminus of one branch of the railway.

Port Antonio (10,000) grew to importance with the expansion of the banana trade. It is not as busy today as it was before the war, though it is one of the few places where banana boats can tie up alongside a wharf. There they are sheltered from northers by Navy Island, which almost encloses the harbour mouth. Port Antonio is the terminus of the other railway crossing the island from Kingston. It is the most easterly of the north shore tourist resorts.

THINGS TO DO

1. Using the following tables, draw a diagram to show (*a*) the relative value of the total Jamaican imports and exports, and (*b*) the relative value of each of the major classes of goods imported and exported.

	£000	$000
Imports, 1965 Total	105,400	505,920
Food, beverages and tobacco ...	22,000	105,600
Mineral fuels, lubricants, etc....	11,300	54,240
Chemicals	8,900	42,720
Manufactured goods	36,000	172,800
Machinery	22,800	109,440
Other imports	4,400	21,120
Exports, 1965 Total..........	74,700	358,560
Bauxite.....................	17,800	85,440
Alumina.....................	17,400	83,520
Sugar, rum and molasses	17,800	85,440
Bananas	6,100	29,280
Citrus and citrus products	3,300	15,840
Cocoa, coffee, pimento and ginger	1,900	9,120
Manufactured goods	5,400	25,920
Other exports	5,000	24,000

2. Using the following figures, draw a graph to show the rise of population in Jamaica.

Year	Population
1871	506,000
1891	639,000
1911	831,000
1921	858,000
1943	1,237,000
1960	1,610,000
1965	1,811,000

In what year do you think the population reached 1¼ million? Extend your graph and find what you think the population will be in 1975 and 1985. In what year do you think the population will reach 2½ million?

. Find out the conditions best suited to the cultivation of bananas. Draw a diagram to show the comparative banana exports of Jamaica, St Lucia, St Vincent, Grenada, and Dominica.

UESTIONS

. Describe the climates of (a) Jamaica and (b) Trinidad. Account for them and show the chief ways in which they differ. C.S.C. 1956.
. What are the main factors influencing land use in Jamaica?
. Sugar, bananas and citrus fruits are three important agricultural exports from Jamaica: (a) Locate the chief areas where these crops are grown in large quantities; (b) Give two reasons to explain why each crop is grown in the areas you mention; (c) For any two of these crops, state one problem which is at present limiting production. J.C.E. 1956.

4. Compare the farming, mining and industrial activities of Jamaica and Guyana.
5. (a) Exports from Jamaica include sugar (250,000 tons), pimento (3,000 tons), and coffee (2,000 tons).
   (i) Draw a diagram to represent these figures.
   (ii) Account briefly for the importance of sugar.
   (b) Mineral exports from Jamaica include bauxite.
   (i) Draw a map to locate the producing areas of this mineral.
   (ii) Mark and name the chief exporting ports.
   (iii) Add labelled arrows to show the destination of the mineral. L.G.C.E.(O). 1965.

HE CAYMAN ISLANDS

Grand Cayman, the largest and most important of the three Cayman Islands, lies about 200 miles north-west of Jamaica. It has an area of 76 square miles and had a population, in 1960, of 6,350. The other two islands, Little Cayman (10 square miles; population 3) and Cayman Brac (14 square miles; population ,250), lie close to each other, about 70 miles east of Grand Cayman. (See Map 13a.)

Over two-thirds of their area is low-lying mangrove swamp and otherwise useless land. Much of the remainder is scrub forest able to withstand the drought imposed by the long dry season and the porous lime-stone rock which composes the islands. Agriculture is unimportant. Cotton and sugar cane cultivation has died out, and the output of coconuts has been greatly reduced by disease. Small holders grow bananas, plantains, cassava, yams, sweet and Irish potatoes and rear some cattle for subsistence. The sea is the basis of the economy, the chief occupation being turtle fishing. As few turtles are left on the Cayman Islands themselves, most are caught hundreds of miles away on the cays near the Nicaraguan coast. They are sold primarily to make soup, the old tortoiseshell industry having declined in the face of competition from cheap plastics. Other exports are shark-skins and rope. The rope, made from palmetto, is sold all over the West Indies. A valuable source of income for the government is derived from the sale of postage stamps.

The Caymanians are expert boat-builders and sailors. Many of the young men are employed by shipping companies, and the money they send home goes far towards balancing the islands' budget. Grand Cayman has a growing tourist industry centred on George Town, the capital, which is connected by air to Jamaica and Miami. Because of its position, Grand Cayman is a refuelling stop for aeroplanes carrying freight between Miami and Central America. It enables them to reduce the amount of fuel they need to carry at the beginning of the journey and to take heavier payloads.

CHAPTER SIX

Trinidad and Tobago

Total Area: 1,978 square miles; population (1965): about 974,000

Trinidad

Area: 1,864 square miles; population (1965): 929,000; density of population: 498 per square mile

SETTLEMENT AND DEVELOPMENT

It was more than thirty years after Columbus discovered Trinidad in 1498 that the first Spaniards began to settle there. They found the island sparsely peopled by Arawak tribes, who, unlike the fierce Caribs on the islands farther north, could be made to work on the land. In spite of this, development was slow. There were no deposits of precious metals to attract settlers and those who established plantations met many set-backs. They were raided by English, French and Dutch marauders. Their chief export, cocoa, which they had found growing wild but had cultivated until they were able to supply all Spain's requirements, was struck by disease. Many settlements were abandoned, and by 1733 the number of Spaniards had fallen from several thousand to one hundred and fifty.

Recovery was slow until 1783 when Spain offered special encouragement to foreigners of the Catholic faith to settle in Trinidad. The French in particular took advantage of this offer. Some came from Canada and from those of the Lesser Antilles that had recently been acquired by Britain. Others fled to Trinidad during the revolutions in France and in Haiti. The French settlers brought coffee and new varieties of cocoa and sugar cane with them and planted cotton as well. When the British took the island in 1797, they found a belt of cultivation along most of the west coast, and scattered plantations in other coastal districts and in some of the valleys leading up into the Northern Range.

The sugar industry, which had developed when Haiti ceased to export sugar after the revolution, became increasingly important. Slaves were brought in to work in the cane fields but, because of the late start, there were only 21,000 slaves in Trinidad at the time of their emancipation in 1834. In contrast Jamaica had 311,000 and Barbados 83,000 in that year. The resulting labour shortage was accentuated by the number of freed slaves who left the estates in order to establish small holdings of their own in the unoccupied interior of the island. It was solved, after 1846, by employing indentured Indian labourers. In the seventy years that the system lasted, over 140,000 Indians went to work in Trinidad—about a third of the total who came to the Caribbean. About three out of every four stayed when their contracts expired and, as we shall see, their descendants form a large proportion of the population today. Many people have also migrated to Trinidad from the less wealthy West Indian islands, especially from the Lesser Antilles. There were 60,000 of them in 1960 and this movement is still going on today.

THE LAND

Geologically, Trinidad is not old, very little of it being earlier than the Cretaceous Period. At that time the southern Caribbean region was a great submarine trough in which great thicknesses of sediments were deposited by rivers flowing out from the ancient mass of the Guiana Highlands. At the close of the Cretaceous Period earth movements produced the folds which are now the Northern, Central and Southern Ranges, but which were then three separate islands. During the quieter period that followed, Tertiary sands and clays, and a little limestone, were deposited in the shallow seas around the islands. Then further movements occurred which lifted the whole area out of the water. In addition they exerted such pressure that they metamorphosed many of the rocks of the Northern Range.

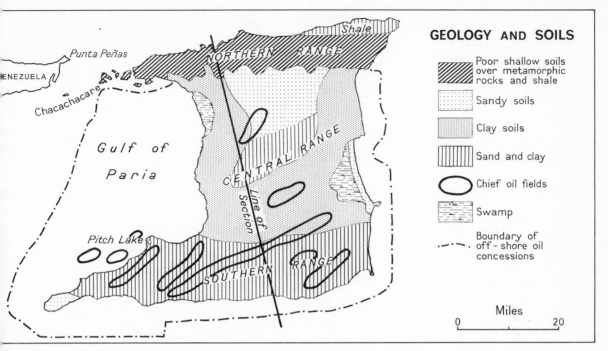

GEOLOGY AND SOILS

- Poor shallow soils over metamorphic rocks and shale
- Sandy soils
- Clay soils
- Sand and clay
- Chief oil fields
- Swamp
- Boundary of off-shore oil concessions

a. The section is drawn in Diagram 6c on page 58.

Since then there has been little change apart from the relatively small earth movement that broke Trinidad off from the South American continent some 10,000 years ago. The sea passage it created between Chacachacare, the last of a series of small islands off the north-west tip of Trinidad, and Punta Peñas in Venezuela is about 7 miles wide.

The only true mountain system in Trinidad is the Northern Range. Though the highest peaks, Cerro Aripo and El Tucuche, rise to only 3,085 and 3,072 feet respectively, which is not high by Caribbean standards, the range forms an almost complete barrier for 50 miles across the north of the island. It rises so abruptly from the north shore that there is virtually no coastal plain. Its southern flanks, however, are not quite so steep, and rivers have carved deep pouch-shaped valleys in the soft rock and deposited gravel fans where they flow out on to the Caroni Plain.

The other two upland regions are unlike the Northern Range in that they slope gradually to the plains and present no great contrast with them. The Central Range is a broad highland mass running diagonally across the island from north-east to south-west and rising to little more than 1,000 feet. The

Southern Range is lower still and is much narrower. Its highest peaks, the three Trinity Hills near the eastern end, do not quite reach 1,000 feet in height. Westwards the range decreases in altitude and ends in the low sandy peninsula of Cedros and Icacos Points.

The Caroni Plain which lies between the Northern and Central Ranges is lower and flatter in the west than in the east. It is drained by the Caroni River, which ends in a large mangrove-fringed swamp where it reaches the sea just south of Port of Spain. The undulating Naparima Plain in the south-west is drained by the Oropuche River which also ends in a swamp near the coast. In the east there is the Nariva Plain. Here Atlantic waves have built up a long sandbar which encloses the Nariva Swamp. There are plans to drain large parts of all these swamps and create valuable agricultural land.

MINERALS

Petroleum

In the Tertiary rocks of the southern part of the island, and to some extent in the underlying Cretaceous as well, there are deposits of petroleum, which, though not large, are the basis of the most valuable industry in the Commonwealth Caribbean territories.

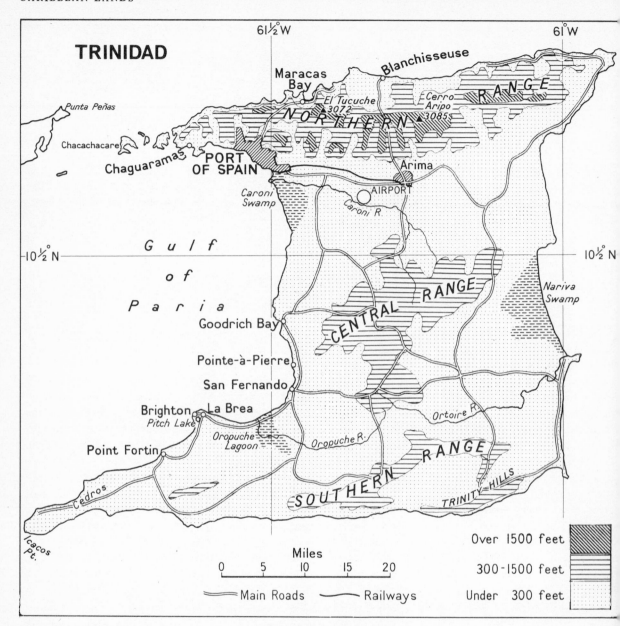

TRINIDAD

Punta Peñas

Chacachacare

Maracas Bay

Blanchisseuse

El Tucuche ▲3072

Cerro Aripo ▲3085

NORTHERN RANGE

Chaguaramas

PORT OF SPAIN

Arima

AIRPORT

Caroni Swamp

Caroni R.

—10½°N

G u l f

o f

P a r i a

Goodrich Bay

CENTRAL RANGE

Nariva Swamp

10½°N—

Pointe-à-Pierre

San Fernando

Brighton La Brea

Pitch Lake

Ortoire R.

Oropuche Lagoon

Oropuche R.

Point Fortin

SOUTHERN RANGE

TRINITY HILLS

Cedros

Icacos Pt.

Miles

| 0 | 5 | 10 | 15 | 20 |

═══ Main Roads   ── Railways

Over 1500 feet

300-1500 feet

Under 300 feet

6b. What relationships are there between relief and communications?

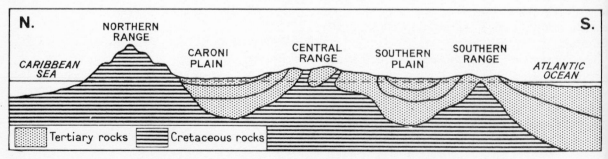

N.   S.

| NORTHERN RANGE | CARONI PLAIN | CENTRAL RANGE | SOUTHERN PLAIN | SOUTHERN RANGE | |

CARIBBEAN SEA

ATLANTIC OCEAN

▨ Tertiary rocks   ▤ Cretaceous rocks

6c. Section showing relief and geology. (The line of section is shown on map 6a on page 57.)

Unfortunately Trinidad is one of the most difficult countries in the world in which to find and produce petroleum in commercial quantities. The main reasons for this are:

(i) In many places the underground rock structures containing it have been cracked and broken so that the deposits have collected in small scattered pools. Diagram 6e shows why these deposits are difficult to locate and why a high proportion of exploratory drillings are unsuccessful.

Sometimes the petroleum has escaped altogether. A famous example of oil seeping to the surface is the Pitch Lake at La Brea. Less well known are the so-called "mud volcanoes", a number of which occur in the Southern Range. These broad, low mounds, anything from fifty feet to several hundred yards across, are formed where hydrocarbon gases escape from underground bringing up mud and traces of petroleum with them.

(ii) Petroleum deposits in Trinidad are small and so each well can tap only a limited quantity. A well in any of the Middle East oilfields may produce over a hundred times as much petroleum as one in Trinidad. The island's output is therefore relatively small. In fact, Trinidad produces only $\frac{1}{2}\%$ of the world total. That this makes the island the second largest producer in the Commonwealth only goes to show how poor the Commonwealth is in oil reserves.

(iii) In the search for petroleum, wells have been drilled to a depth of 16,000 feet and more. Others have been sunk several miles off-shore in the Gulf of Paria. Drillings of this sort cost millions of dollars and may—or may not—strike oil.

(iv) Only about half the petroleum comes up under its own pressure. The rest has to be pumped to the surface. This is a slow and costly undertaking.

(v) Trinidad produces a number of different types of crude petroleum, each of which needs separate treatment at the refineries. This also adds to the cost of production.

Commercial production in Trinidad began in 1909 with the export of 57,000 barrels. Output increased slowly to 2 million barrels in 1920 and then more rapidly to reach just over 22 million in 1940. Since then it has needed intensive drilling both on land and under the Gulf of Paria to maintain this pace and

6d. *Two resources in one place: rice on the surface of the land; petroleum underneath.*

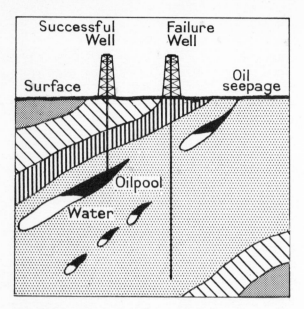

6e. *Oil deposits collected in scattered pools.*

fuel but also to generate electricity and make ammonia, sulphur, artificial fertilizers and an ever-increasing range of petro-chemicals.

Today the petroleum industry provides well-paid employment for more than 18,000 workers. It accounts for about 80% of the island's exports and provides the Government with about a third of its revenue. It is because of petroleum that Trinidad's foreign earnings are considerably greater than those of Jamaica, an island more than twice its size and with more than twice its population.

Asphalt
The world's largest source of natural asphalt is the

bring the output up to 50 million barrels in 1965.

There are about a dozen oil companies operating in Trinidad, of which the largest by far is American-owned. Besides carrying out drilling operations this company operates the largest refinery in the Commonwealth at Pointe-à-Pierre. There is another refinery at Point Fortin.

In these refineries the various chemicals which together make up crude petroleum are separated from each other. The oils produced range from light aviation spirit and gasoline down to heavy fuel oil and asphalt. Indeed more asphalt is produced from the refineries than from the Pitch Lake. Other major products are kerosene, lubricating oil, the "normal paraffins" used to make detergents, and benzene and toluene which are used in the petro-chemical industry.

To keep the refineries working economically the local supply of crude petroleum is supplemented by large imports from Venezuela and smaller amounts from Saudi Arabia and Colombia. Together these imports exceed local production. From the four shipping terminals at Pointe-à-Pierre, Point Fortin, Brighton, and La Brea refined products are sent to the United States, the United Kingdom, Brazil, the West Indies and many other countries.

The natural gas released with petroleum from many of the wells is used not only as an industrial

6f. *The Pitch Lake, showing the different consistencies of the pitch.*

Pitch Lake at La Brea. About 95 acres in extent, it lies in a shallow basin about half a mile from the Gulf of Paria. It is owned by the Government, but exports are handled by a private company.

In one or two places the pitch is soft and sticky, but over most of its surface it is hard enough to be cut into blocks. These are loaded on to light railway trucks which are hauled up the steep slope at the edge of the lake to a factory where dried asphalt, asphalt cement and other by-products are made. "Dried" or "refined" asphalt is made by heating the pitch in stills to drive off the water. It is then strained and poured into wooden barrels where, on cooling, it solidifies. By adding crude oil and other chemicals, "asphalt cement" is made. As this is more fluid than refined asphalt it is stored in iron drums. Both the barrels and the drums are made on the premises.

The products for export are taken by a cable railway to the company's pier, from which they are shipped to all parts of the world. Asphalt is constantly in demand for surfacing roads, and since 1900 over seven million tons have been removed from the Pitch Lake. At present the annual output is about 150,000 tons, of which about half is exported.

Iron Ore

Iron ore deposits, suitable for extraction, are known to exist in the Northern Range.

CLIMATE

Because Trinidad lies only 10° to 11° north of the equator its temperature range is, if anything, less than that of the islands farther north. Temperature is lowest in January when it averages 77° F. This rises to 81° F. in May just after the sun has passed overhead on its way north. For the next few months it is a little cooler, but the increased humidity in this, the rainy season, makes many of the afternoons feel uncomfortably hot, although, in fact, day temperatures rarely rise above 92° F. As the sun moves south again towards the equator, temperatures rise again and September is almost as hot as May. Relief from the heat is not so easy to find as it is in Jamaica, where the mountains are much higher and where there are considerable expanses of plateau.

As can be seen from Map 6h the heaviest rainfall occurs in the Northern Range, the crest of which is often cloud-capped. From here a belt of more than

6g. Inside the asphalt factory. What product is being poured into the barrels?

100 inches a year extends southwards along almost the whole length of the eastern side of the island. To the west the amount decreases, but not to a marked extent, for the only mountains high enough to cause rain shadow run parallel to the prevailing winds and not across their path as do the Blue Mountains of

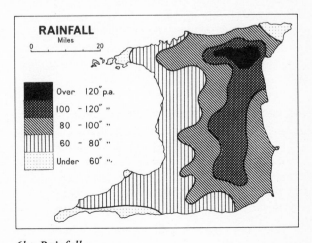

6h. Rainfall.

61

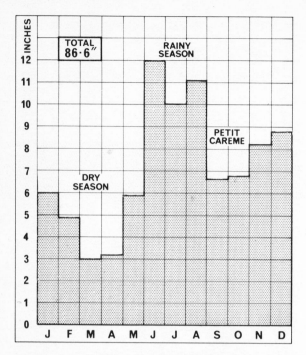

6i. Average monthly rainfall of Trinidad.

Jamaica. Only the tips of the two westward-pointing peninsulas have less than 60 inches a year.

The rainy season usually begins towards the end of May and continues until November, though a dry period called the *petit carême*[1] often occurs for one or two weeks in September or October. The driest month of all is March.

Trinidad is unique in the West Indies in that it lies south of the regular hurricane paths. Only on two or three occasions in the island's history has there been any storm damage. Thus it is less hazardous to grow tree crops such as cocoa and coconuts in Trinidad than in the other islands.

SOILS

In contrast to Barbados, where the most important factor governing soil type is the amount of rainfall, the soils of Trinidad owe their nature largely to the underlying rock. The complex geology of the island has given rise to a diversity of soils within short distances. This in turn has affected agriculture. For instance, the recent decline in cocoa has been most

[1] *Petit carême* (Fr.) = a little Lent (as though the land were fasting).

marked in areas where the soil is least suited to the crop. Some relationships between soil type and land use can be seen by comparing Maps 6a and 6k.

The rocks of the Northern Range produce a poor, shallow soil best left in forest. Where clearings have been made, soil erosion has occurred. Only the valleys are suitable for cultivation, and these have long supported cocoa.

In the Caroni Plain there is a marked contrast between the clays, which are fertile and intensively cultivated, and the larger areas of sands and gravels which are poor and of little use. The sands improve as they merge with the clays and shales of the Central Range, the clays being the best cocoa soils in the island. The silts and clays of the Naparima Plain are also very good, especially round the Oropuche lagoon. The sands and clays of the Southern Range are less fertile and are mostly forested, though the Cedros area is planted in coconuts, for which the sand there is well suited.

LAND USE

One of the most striking features of Trinidad, as seen from the air, is the way so much of it appears to be forested, especially in the highlands. In fact, as diagram 6j shows, 45% of the total land area is classified as forest and woodland, but it appears to be much more than this because of the cocoa, citrus, coffee and other tree crops grown in the country. From above, cocoa is especially hard to distinguish from the forests because it is usually grown beneath shade trees.

AGRICULTURE

Sugar

The sugar industry of Trinidad had not been in existence for long when it was beset by the problems that affected all British West Indian sugar producers in the nineteenth century (see pages 25–26). As we have seen, the labour shortage that followed the emancipation of the slaves was met by employing indentured Indian immigrants. In addition, costs were reduced by making use of many new discoveries to improve yields in both field and factory. Even so, towards the end of the century the owners of many small estates found themselves unable to compete with subsidized European beet sugar. They had to close their mills and plant other crops or sell out to ge estates which alone could survive this period of pression. The change was a rapid one. The first atral—the Usine St Madeleine—was built in 1870. irty years later almost all the sugar production s in the hands of a few firms. Cane fields, once despread throughout the island, became concen- ted around the new big factories in a belt extending wn the western side from the Caroni Plain to the opuche lagoon. Here, on flat or gently rolling land, eat expanses of cane could be planted. Here, too, e climate was most suitable.

Since then there has been an increasing concentra- n of sugar cane in this belt. Very little else is grown ere today and very little cane is grown elsewhere.

Today there are over 90,000 acres under cane; that about 20% of the agricultural land. A little more an half of this is estate land. The remainder is orked by about 11,000 cane farmers, who, because ey lack the resources of the estates, produce only out a third of the crop. All the cane is milled in x factories, the two largest of which are owned by British company which also owns the two largest ctories in Jamaica. One factory makes granulated gar for local consumption. The island's basic export uota is 157,850 tons, but Trinidad produces and ports more than this as can be seen from the llowing figures for 1965:

otal production .... 250,586 tons

xports:
  United Kingdom .... 143,529 tons
  Canada .... 47,112 tons
  United States .... 15,127 tons
  West Indies....................... 6,528 tons

ocal Sales .... 36,316 tons

Over a million gallons of rum are made each year, bout half of which is consumed locally. Rum is also ne of the chief ingredients in Angostura bitters, vhich are made only in Trinidad. Originally sold as medicine, bitters are now in use throughout the vorld to flavour cocktails. As in Jamaica, sugar-cane lcohol is used to make gin and vodka for local onsumption.

Cocoa

n the late nineteenth century many of the farmers who were forced by low prices to give up producing sugar planted cocoa in its place. Output rose rapidly

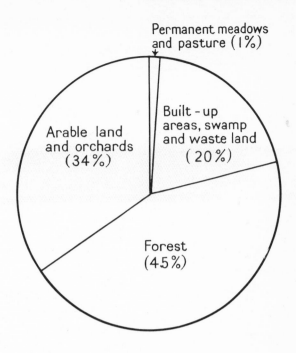

6j. *Land use in Trinidad.*

and by 1900 cocoa was no longer a minor crop but the island's leading export. This continued until 1921 when 75 million lbs. were exported, but then a decline set in. One reason for this was the remarkable increase of cocoa exports from Ghana (then called the Gold Coast). These rose from an average of 12 tons a year in the 1890s to 231,000 tons in 1926 and to 311,000 tons (that is, nearly 800 million lbs.) in 1936. As a result the price of cocoa fell sharply and it was no longer worth while to plant new trees in Trinidad. A second reason for the decline was the appearance of "witch's broom" disease which at- tacked many of the trees. The whole country was affected and some areas went out of production altogether. Cocoa exports fell to 6½ million lbs. in 1946. Sugar once again became the leading agricul- tural export, a position it has held ever since.

Since the war the Government has helped to restore the industry by setting up large propagating stations to supply farmers with young trees. At the stations, cuttings from disease-resistant and high- yielding varieties are rooted in special pots and care- fully tended until they are ready to be planted. Mainly because of this project cocoa exports reached 16 million lbs. in 1960, that is about three-fifths of

6k TRINIDAD : PRODUCTS

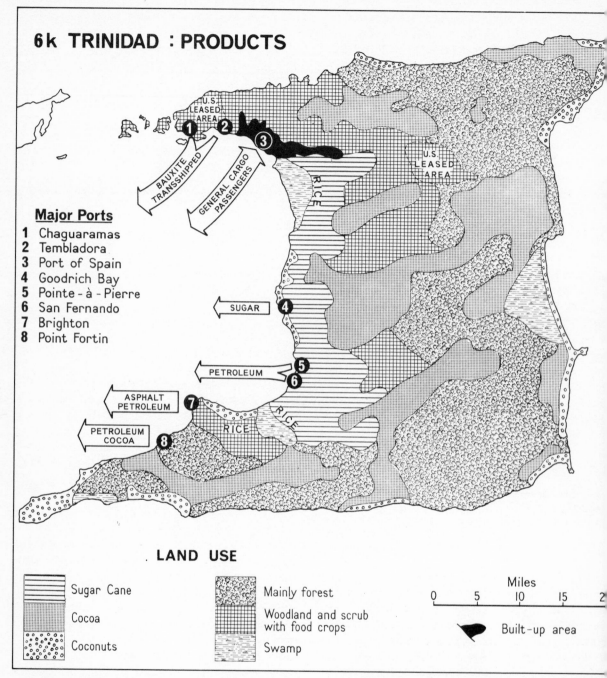

U.S. LEASED AREA

BAUXITE TRANSSHIPPED

GENERAL CARGO PASSENGERS

Major Ports

1 Chaguaramas
2 Tembladora
3 Port of Spain
4 Goodrich Bay
5 Pointe - à - Pierre
6 San Fernando
7 Brighton
8 Point Fortin

RICE

U.S. LEASED AREA

SUGAR

PETROLEUM

ASPHALT PETROLEUM

RICE

PETROLEUM COCOA

RICE

LAND USE

☰	Sugar Cane
▦	Cocoa
○○	Coconuts
∴	Mainly forest
⊞	Woodland and scrub with food crops
≈	Swamp

Miles
0   5   10   15   2[0]

Built-up area

---

the West Indian total. Since then prices have fallen and exports have declined.

Cocoa is grown on plantations and on small farms. Though it still takes up more land than sugar, the area under cocoa is less than it was before the war. Less is grown in the valleys of the Northern Range, some

of which have become built-up areas and one which, the Santa Cruz Valley, is now a big citr[us] producer. Today the greatest output comes from t[he] Central Range north-east of San Fernando.

As the price of cocoa depends partly on its qualit[y] most growers process their beans before selling the[m]

1. One of Trinidad's sugar factories. Draw a sketch-map of the area in the picture to show land use and settlement.

When the freshly picked pods have been split open, the beans, and some of the juicy pulp in which they are embedded, are collected in sweating-boxes and left to ferment for several days. The heat generated during fermentation partially cooks the beans and gives them their flavour. The beans are then dried in the sun and in some cases they are also spread on wooden floors for people to dance among them. This removes any last remaining particles of pulp and gives the beans a smooth, shiny surface. Most of the cocoa is exported to Europe and to Britain, where it is blended with less highly flavoured West African cocoa, but some is manufactured locally into chocolate and other products.

Citrus

Citrus first became important in the 1930s when many trees were planted in badly stricken cocoa areas and on some old sugar and coconut lands. Grapefruits, which form the bulk of the output, are packed in Port of Spain and exported, most going to the United Kingdom. Oranges are sent to Barbados, Guyana, Curaçao and Bermuda. Lime production has declined because of disease.

In addition, grapefruit juice and orange juice are canned for sale on the local market and abroad. A by-product, dried pulp, is used as a cattle feed.

Coffee

Coffee is another crop to become more prominent since the decline of cocoa. On the estates, which produce about half the crop, coffee trees were formerly interplanted with cocoa so as to provide shade, but there are now some pure coffee stands. The bulk of the output is of the Robusta variety, but Arabica coffee is also grown.

Coconuts

Most of Trinidad's coconuts are grown on large estates close to the sea. Copra, edible oil, margarine, glycerine, soap and soap flakes are all manufactured in the island. Some of these products, together with coir, are exported to other Caribbean territories.

Other Crops

Rice is intensively cultivated on small plots of land, mainly in the low, swampy areas of the Oropuche lagoon and on the fringes of the Caroni Swamp. It is grown in the wet season between June and December and for the rest of the year the fields are often planted in vegetables. Nearly all the rice is produced by Indian small farmers who keep most of it for their households. Many Indians with jobs such as taxi-driving, hairdressing, shopkeeping and tailoring grow an acre or so of rice as a subsidiary occupation. A small quantity of hill rice is grown in the interior. But about three-quarters of the island's supply has to be imported—mainly from Guyana—and there are plans to drain part of the Oropuche lagoon, cultivate more rice there and reduce these imports.

Tonca beans are another export. They are of use in the manufacture of perfumes and in flavouring tobacco.

Trinidad has never been a major exporter of bananas, but at times some have been shipped to the United States and to Britain.

The contrast between the area under cultivation in Trinidad and Tobago (432,000 acres) and in Jamaica (571,000 acres) is not nearly as great as the contrast in the acreages under pasture (12,000 acres in Trinidad and Tobago; 640,000 acres in Jamaica). Trinidad's

livestock industry is therefore comparatively sma For instance, it has only a quarter as many cattle Jamaica, and considerable imports of animal pr ducts, especially meat and butter, are required. As Jamaica, powdered milk has to be imported supplement the local supply received at the condens milk factory.

The supply of vegetables is also insufficient to me the demand and Port of Spain is an important mark for vegetables from near-by islands, especially Vincent and Grenada. Indeed the total food impo of Trinidad are greater than those of Jamaica, whi has more than twice the population. So in spite of t earnings from petroleum exports, Trinidad is n entirely free from a balance of payments problem.

FORESTRY

Apart from a few patches of savanna on the plains t whole of Trinidad was once forested. The rainy flan of the Northern Range were clothed with tropic evergreen forest, their summits with montane fore Evergreen seasonal forest covered most of the re of the island, with deciduous seasonal forest in t drier areas and thousands of acres of mangroves the swamps. Some of these forests remain and son have been cleared for agriculture. Much more wou have been cleared if the sugar industry had develope earlier, for in those days wood was the fuel used the factories. Territories developed before Trinida all have smaller proportions of forest. Thus Jamaic has 18% under forest, St Kitts 17%, and Barbad virtually none.

Though most of the forest in Trinidad is owned b the Government, timber is cut by a number of privat concerns which together produce about two-thirds the island's requirements. Teak, mora, mahoe, ceda cypre and mahogany are among the trees most i demand for building and for making charcoal an furniture. Mangroves provide both charcoal and ta bark. Railway sleepers and matches are also mad from local wood. There are some rubber plantation

The Forest Department is carrying out a larg replanting programme, especially with pitch pine an teak. Pitch pine has the advantage that it will gro in poor sandy soils. It is a useful softwood. Teak, on of the most beautiful hardwoods, takes many year to mature, but the constant thinning of the stand provides a certain amount every year.

m. Port of Spain. From what direction and at what time of day was the picture taken? Draw a sketch-map of the area showing the waterfront, the commercial and residential sections of the city, and the mountains. Compare this picture with Plate 5o.

FISHING

Though there are some large fishing-boats that go a considerable distance out to sea, most fish are caught from small canoes close to the coast. Others are caught in the swampy lower courses of the rivers and some are specially reared in inland ponds. All are consumed locally, but this does not meet the demand, and there is a large import of salt fish.

INDUSTRY

In addition to the industries based on the island's oil, asphalt, agricultural and forest resources, there is a wide range of other industries in Trinidad. Though many of them have been developed with Government support, they depend mainly on the availability of cheap labour, cheap power, a fair-sized local market and easy access to neighbouring countries. The industries include cement and cement products, paints, artificial fertilizers, detergents, textiles and clothing, boots, shoes and slippers, metal containers, boxes and cartons, glass bottles, pharmaceuticals, plastic goods, cigarettes, handbags, and many kinds of food and drink. In addition, some makes of cars, trucks, buses, and machines are assembled.

67

POPULATION

The population of Trinidad is perhaps the most mixed of all West Indian islands. There are still some traces of the Arawaks. There are small proportions of Europeans from many different countries, including descendants of indentured Portuguese labourers, of Chinese, Syrians, Jews and Latin Americans. But the bulk of the population is of Negro and Indian descent, the Negroes forming 40½ % and the Indians 38% of the total in 1960. In this respect Trinidad bears a closer resemblance to Guyana than to any West Indian island. As in Guyana, there is little inter-marriage between the two largest racial groups which retain certain distinct social patterns, have somewhat different diets and homes and tend to be found doing certain types of jobs and not others. The greatest distinction is in religion, and in 1960 there were 190,000 Hindus, 50,000 Moslems, 300,000 Roman Catholics, and 175,000 Anglicans in Trinidad. Racial considerations also play a part in voting in elections, though the political parties are inter-racial.

The complexity of the situation makes it hard to define. Some sociologists consider that Trinidad and the other West Indian territories are examples of "plural societies" in which the different races mix but do not combine: they live side by side but have little in common and little desire for integration. Others dispute this, believing that there is sufficient inter-racial co-operation to create a national identity and to tackle national problems.

Numbers are rapidly increasing. In 1960 the population was about 795,000. In 1965 it was about 929,000. This gave a density of 498 per square mile, which was somewhat higher than that of Jamaica. Even though Trinidad is relatively well off, it is difficult to find employment for so many people.

Map 6n shows in general terms the marked contrast between the counties with a high population density in the north-west and west of Trinidad and those with a low density in the east and south-east. Looked at in more detail we find that the forested mountainous areas are most sparsely settled. More people live in regions where tree crops are grown, the typical settlement pattern here being one of small villages strung out along the roads. In the sugar belt the villages are much larger. Many of them have East Indian names and are peopled largely by Indians who still form the bulk of the field labourers.

The most marked concentration of population extends from the capital, Port of Spain, eastward along the foot of the Northern Range. Here a number of villages, which originally grew up at the valley mouths as collecting centres for cocoa, are merging together as they grow and are losing their separate identities. The biggest of these is Arima with a population of over 11,000. There are also pockets of dense settlement in the ports, all of which are situated on the sheltered Gulf of Paria. The east coast, in contrast, is sparsely settled. The long sand-bars in some places and the rough, rocky stretches in others make it almost unapproachable from the sea.

Port of Spain has grown up at the only place in the island where there is both a sheltered deep-water harbour and easy overland communication with the main producing areas. With its suburbs and adjoining townships the city has a population of about 270,000 making it the second largest in the Commonwealth Caribbean territories. It is the capital and the commercial and banking centre of the island.

Though docking facilities are limited and large ocean-going vessels have to be served by lighters, Port of Spain is the busiest port in the Commonwealth Caribbean. It is the chief passenger port of Trinidad. It is the chief link with Tobago and the Lesser Antilles. It handles the bulk of the imports except crude petroleum. But precisely because it imports no petroleum and exports only limited quantities of petroleum, asphalt, sugar and bauxite, it handles less cargo tonnage than Pointe-à-Pierre and Point Fortin and only a little more than Brighton.

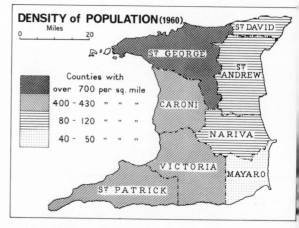

6n. Density of population.

Because Port of Spain is hemmed in by mountains
the north and swamp to the south, most of the new
suburbs are being built to the east, at the foot of the
Northern Range. The Diego Martin and Maraval
valleys have also been heavily built up.

Not far from Port of Spain are the two main bauxite
terminals of Tembladora and Chaguaramas. Here
bauxite, brought from Guyana and Surinam in small
vessels, is transhipped to large ocean-going ships for
export to the United States, Norway and Canada.
The bauxite destined for Canada has to be stored in
Trinidad throughout the winter months when the
St. Lawrence River is frozen. Partly to protect these
bauxite supplies and partly to guard the southern
approaches to the Caribbean and the Panama Canal,
the United States operates a naval base in the north-
western tip of Trinidad.

Pointe-à-Pierre, Point Fortin and Brighton deal
mainly with petroleum and petroleum products, but
they also handle a relatively small amount of cocoa
and general cargo. Goodrich Bay has facilities for
handling bulk sugar and accounts for almost the
entire sugar export.

San Fernando (40,000), the second largest town in
Trinidad, is situated about thirty miles south of the
capital. It lies at the foot and on the lower slopes of
Naparima Hill, a large block of limestone some 600
feet high which stands out boldly from the surrounding plain. It began as a small fishing village and grew
to prominence when the south-western part of
Trinidad was developed for sugar and cocoa. With
the building of good roads and a railway to Port of
Spain its importance as a port declined, though there
is still some lighterage traffic to the capital. On the
other hand its importance as a shopping centre has
increased with the development of the near-by oil
installations and the growth of population at
Pointe-à-Pierre.

COMMUNICATIONS

Main roads connect Port of Spain with most parts
of the island. Only the Northern Range provides a
major barrier and there is still no road running along
the length of the north coast. This is a handicap to the
tourist industry, for it is here that the island's best
beaches are to be found. With cheap gasoline and
plentiful supplies of asphalt to surface the roads,
Trinidad, as might be expected, has a large number

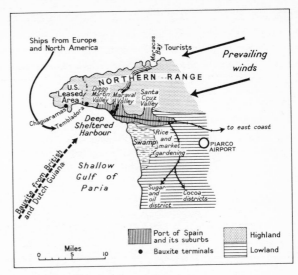

60. *The setting of Port of Spain.*

of cars. Comparative figures with certain other
countries are given on page 33. Most of the railways
which once connected the capital with the most populated sugar and cocoa growing districts and the oilfields have been closed. All that remains is a cheap
shuttle service for passengers from Port of Spain to
Arima.

Piarco airport, about 17 miles out of Port of Spain,
handles not only the local traffic but many travellers
in transit from Caribbean and South American
countries as well.

TRADE

Not only does Trinidad have a larger overseas trade
than any other Commonwealth Caribbean territory,
but with the exception of Guyana it is the only one
where the value of exports often exceeds the value of
imports. Petroleum and its by-products make up over
80% of the exports, the chief purchasing countries
being the United Kingdom, some of the Caribbean
territories and Brazil. Sugar and its by-products,
which make up 8% to 9% of the exports, are sent to
the United Kingdom and Canada. Cocoa and asphalt
sell in many different countries.

The United Kingdom is both the largest purchaser
and the largest supplier, the chief imported goods
being such manufactures as vehicles, machinery and
textiles. Venezuela is second on the list because of
Trinidad's purchases of crude oil from that country.

69

Then comes the United States, another source of varied manufactures. Canada supplies nearly all the wheat flour and some of the lumber, paper and tobacco, while Australia and New Zealand supply dairy products and meat.

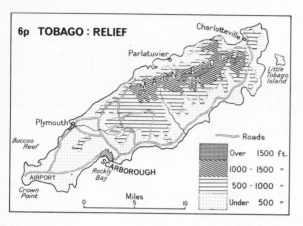

6p TOBAGO : RELIEF

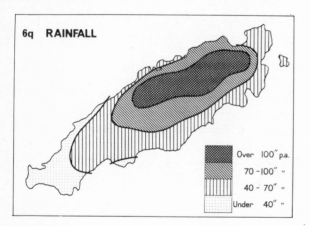

6q RAINFALL

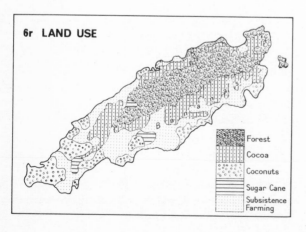

6r LAND USE

Tobago

Area: 116 square miles; population (est. 1965 45,000; density of population: 390 per square mi.

A sea passage of only 20 miles separates Tobago from the north-east tip of Trinidad. Yet this island, 2 miles long by 7½ miles wide, shows few similarities to Trinidad. In size it is like the near-by islands to the north, but it differs from them in having no recent vulcanism.

THE LAND

Running from the north-east tip south-westward for about two-thirds of the length of Tobago are the forested mountains of the Main Ridge which rise very steeply from the north coast to a maximum height of about 1,860 feet. Their gentler southern slopes are deeply indented by valleys which run down to a narrow but fertile coastal plain. Though the northern slopes of the Main Ridge are made of metamorphic rocks similar to those of the Northern Range of Trinidad, the mountains are mainly composed of igneous material. This rock, which covers over half the area of the island, weathers easily to produce the most fertile soils in Tobago.

The south-western part of the island is very different. With the exception of a few small hills in the centre this area is made of a series of flat coral terraces nowhere more than 150 feet high, giving the landscape an appearance rather like that of Barbados.

RAINFALL

Rainfall is heaviest on the summits and northern slopes of the Main Ridge, where in places it exceeds 150 inches a year. It decreases towards the south and south-west which is in rain shadow and has under 50 inches a year. In the south-west the low rainfall and the porous nature of the coral rock makes the provision of water for coconuts and livestock a problem, particularly in the dry months—February, March and April.

DEVELOPMENT

During the sixteenth and seventeenth centuries the prized sugar, cotton and indigo plantations of Tobago were the cause of repeated disputes between the English, French and Dutch, and the island changed hands more often than any other in the Caribbean. By the beginning of the nineteenth century sugar was by far the most important crop and the island was prosperous. But a decline set in which was intensified when the island's 11,000 slaves were freed in 1838 and a severe hurricane struck Tobago in 1847. Some sugar estates struggled on for a while by introducing the *metayer* system under which men were allowed to cultivate small plots of the estate land provided they sent their canes to the estate-owner, who extracted the sugar and took half the crop. This could do no more than postpone the collapse made inevitable by falling sugar prices in Britain and the lack of sufficient suitable lowland in Tobago to support a large central factory. One by one the small mills ceased to operate, and many cane fields reverted to bush. By 1886 the island's exports were worth only a tenth of those of 1839. Two years later, economic distress forced Tobago to amalgamate with the near-by richer and more powerful colony of Trinidad.

With the decline of sugar, new crops had to be established. Many estates, notably those on the wind-ward side, gave out allotments to peasants, who in return for tending young cocoa plants were allowed to grow their own food crops until the trees came into bearing. Cocoa was also planted by immigrants from Grenada, attracted to Tobago by the sale of Crown Lands there. Today cocoa is the outstanding cash crop. It occupies about a third of the cultivated land and in 1956 nearly 2 million lbs. were exported.

Estates on the leeward side also used the allotment system to increase their production of coconuts, which now take up more land than cocoa, though they are not as valuable. Other estates, particularly those in the centre of the island, sold or leased their land to small farmers who have since cultivated cocoa, bananas, and the usual West Indian fruits and food-stuffs and kept livestock. Tobacco, another small farmers' crop, is grown in the south-west and sent for sale in Trinidad.

Although about 40% of the island is cultivated, agriculture is not as prosperous as it could be. In some peasant areas, notably the central belt shown on Map 6r, soil erosion has become serious and yields are poor. This may be the reason why in recent years the sale of food crops to Port of Spain has virtually ceased, and at times Tobago has to buy them from Trinidad. In other areas, particularly the moun-

6s. *Fishing from a beach in Tobago. Describe the method shown in the picture. What other methods are used in the Caribbean?*

tainous north-east and the north coast between Parlatuvier and Charlotteville, communications are so poor that the exploitation of forests and the culti-vation of cocoa and bananas is difficult or altogether impossible. In addition to these problems, hurricane Flora in 1963 destroyed about half the coconuts in the island, and plant diseases are affecting cocoa and coconut trees. They have almost wiped out the old lime industry.

THE PEOPLE

Unlike Trinidad, Tobago has few Indians (just over 400 in 1960), and over 90% of the population is Negro. Numbers are rising more slowly than in neighbouring islands because many young men are leaving to go to live in Trinidad where there are more varied opportunities for employment.

Most of the people live in the south-west, in the central belt, and along the coast. There are many small agricultural villages but the only two towns of importance are Scarborough and Plymouth. Scarborough (2,000) is the chief market, as it has the best access to the most productive cocoa and coconut districts. Its harbour is poor, however, being reached with some difficulty through a narrow channel in a reef. Partly for this reason, and partly because Tobago is dependent on Trinidad and has little direct contact with overseas markets, the town is still a small one. It does not dominate the settlement pattern as do the chief towns in the other West Indian islands.

COMMUNICATIONS AND TRADE

Except in the south-west, road communications in Tobago are poor. As we have seen, this has retarded development. Some parts of the north coast are cut off to such an extent that they have to rely on an intermittent shipping service. For communications overseas Tobago is dependent on sea and air transport to Trinidad. The airstrip has been built at Crown Point in the extreme south-west.

TOURISTS

Tobago has been called "Robinson Crusoe Island" from the belief that Daniel Defoe's story of that name had its setting there. This is in itself a tourist attraction and a number of small hotels have been built to accommodate visitors, most of whom come from North America and Trinidad. There is good bathing on the sheltered, white-sand beaches, fishing at Buccoo Reef, and most tourists make at least one trip to Little Tobago Island—two miles off-shore—where there is a sanctuary for Birds of Paradise, which were introduced there many years ago from the Dutch East Indies.

THINGS TO DO

1. Using the following table, draw a diagram to show the relative value of each of the major classes of goods imported and exported by Trinidad.

		$'000
Imports, 1964	Total	731,400
Food, beverages and tobacco		90,900
Mineral fuels, lubricants, etc.		371,700
Chemicals		29,000
Manufactured goods		126,000
Machinery and transport equipment		95,700
Exports, 1964	Total	686,300
Petroleum and petroleum products		573,900
Natural asphalt and tar		11,200
Ammonium compounds		10,500
Cement		3,000
Sugar, rum, molasses, bitters		51,000
Cocoa and coffee		9,700
Citrus and citrus products		4,700

2. Compare these figures with those of Jamaica.

3. Find out how oil is discovered, raised to the surface, and refined.

QUESTIONS

1. Name two important agricultural exports which are grown in either Trinidad or Jamaica mainly for export. State clearly the part or parts of the island from which each is obtained and describe the conditions affecting production. C.S.C. 1951.

2. Compare the importance of agricultural and mineral production in Trinidad.

3. What goods does Trinidad supply to (*a*) the other West Indian islands, (*b*) other parts of the world? Describe how one of these products is prepared for export. J.C.E. 1958.

4. Compare the physical geography and economic production of Jamaica and Trinidad. C.H.S.C. 1954.

5. "Tobago bears a closer resemblance to its northern neighbours than it does to Trinidad." Discuss this statement.

6. (i) Explain why the western part of Trinidad is more densely populated than the eastern part.
   (ii) Write a geographical description of the island of Tobago. C.S.C. 1960.

CHAPTER SEVEN

Barbados

Area: 166 square miles; population (1965): about 245,000; density of population: 1,415 per square mile

DEVELOPMENT

Barbados, the most easterly of the West Indian islands, is not really a part of the chain of the Lesser Antilles, as it lies in the Atlantic Ocean about a hundred miles east of its nearest neighbour, St Vincent. Map 8a shows this clearly. It was known to Europeans at least as early as 1536, when a Portuguese navigator left some hogs there so that shipwrecked mariners would not be without food. At that time the island was covered with light forest and scrub, only a few acres of which remain today. Having no deposits of precious minerals it was not considered a valuable possession by the Spaniards, and it was left unoccupied until a party of British settlers landed there in 1627. They established small farms along the fertile lowlands of the west coast on which they grew a variety of food crops for subsistence, and tobacco, cotton, ginger and indigo for export. Population increased rapidly as more and more immigrants arrived and spread throughout the country. By 1643 there were over 37,000 white settlers in Barbados, a population density of 220 per square mile.

Owing mainly to the rise of the North American colonies the prices of the two chief crops—tobacco and cotton—fell, and sugar cane, introduced in 1639, proved to be three times as profitable. Its cultivation spread rapidly but because it was not a good crop for small holders their properties were bought up and incorporated into estates. In 1645 there were 11,200 land-owners in Barbados, but by 1677 there were only 745. Over 30,000 dispossessed colonists left the island and went to other West Indian territories or to America. Today the number of white people in Barbados is less than a third of what it was in 1643. Even so the proportion remains the highest in the Commonwealth Caribbean territories.

Though some white servants remained on the sugar estates, the bulk of the labour force in the eighteenth century consisted of African slaves. They were brought to the island in such numbers that nearly 83,000 were living there in 1834. Their emancipation made little difference to the economy of the island. Because nearly all of the land already belonged to the estates, there was little opportunity for freed slaves to obtain land of their own and they had to continue to work for the planters. Because of the dry climatic conditions the planters were unable to find an alternative crop to cane. They were therefore faced with the double problem of providing work for large numbers of people and of overcoming the recurrent crises that struck at the sugar industry throughout the nineteenth century. They did so by keeping operations on a relatively small scale, by limiting the use of labour-saving devices and by raising yields per acre rather than per man.

With a population density of about 700 per square mile at the time of the emancipation of the slaves, and a rising population ever since, Barbados has not been able to provide adequate opportunities for employment and there have been several waves of emigrants. At different times, migrants have gone to Trinidad, Guyana and Surinam, Central America and the Panama Canal Zone, the Netherlands Antilles, the United States and the United Kingdom.

In spite of this migration and in spite of the fact that the birth-rate is one of the lowest in the region, Barbados has become by far the most densely peopled Caribbean territory. Today there are almost four people per cultivated acre. Though it is true that the agricultural resources of a tropical country can support more people than those of a temperate one, this is more than any agricultural country can properly sustain. The fact that the density is increasing year by year is the greatest single problem in the island.

THE LAND

The rocks forming the basement of Barbados are called the Scotland Series. They consist of great thicknesses of sedimentary deposits, mainly shales,

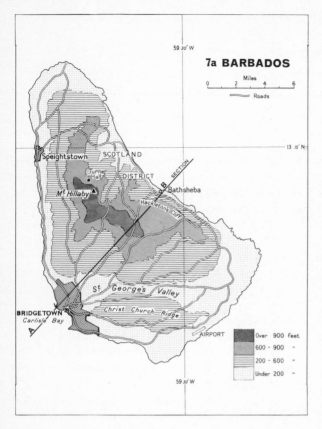

7a BARBADOS

Miles

0   2   4   6

—— Roads

59 30' W

13 15' N

Speightstown

SCOTLAND

Turner
Hall

DISTRICT

Mt Hillaby

SECTION

B

Bathsheba

Hackleton's Cliff

St George's Valley

Christ Church Ridge

BRIDGETOWN
Carlisle Bay

AIRPORT

59 30' W

	Over 900 feet
	600 - 900 "
	200 - 600 "
	Under 200 "

where they were covered by deposits of a chalk-like rock known as the Oceanic Series. In geologically recent times these rocks were covered by a cap of coral formed in very shallow water. This coral is the most important rock today. It reaches a maximum thickness of 300 feet and extends over the surface of the whole island except the Scotland district of the north-east where erosion has stripped it away to expose the older underlying rocks.

The highest point in Barbados is Mount Hillaby (1,115 feet) in the north centre of the island. From here the land falls on the northern, western and southern sides by a series of coral terraces. These were formed when the island was uplifted in stages from beneath the sea, the sides of the terraces being the old sea cliffs. They run generally parallel to the present shoreline and may be as much as 100 feet or as little as 5 feet in height. Some are vertical and rocky, others more gentle and grass-covered. From the air only the biggest and steepest cliffs are easy to see, and the island appears to be a gently rolling country.

Eastwards from the highest terrace there is a great contrast. The land falls steeply for hundreds of feet and in some places by a sheer cliff to the Scotland district. Southwards the main highland mass also descends steeply, in this case to the broad St George's Valley. Farther south still the land rises again to nearly 400 feet in the gently folded Christ Church Ridge before dropping finally to the sea.

Surrounding the island except along the coast of the Scotland district there are coral reefs, best developed along the south-eastern shore. If these

sands, clays and conglomerates laid down about seventy million years ago in a shallow, muddy sea. Later these rocks were folded, faulted and uplifted by a great earth movement. After a considerable period they were submerged deep beneath the sea,

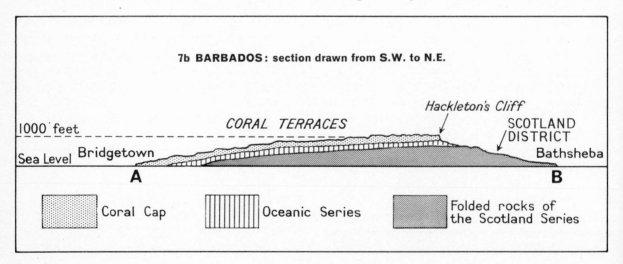

7b BARBADOS: section drawn from S.W. to N.E.

1000 feet

Sea Level

CORAL TERRACES

Hackleton's Cliff

SCOTLAND
DISTRICT

Bridgetown

Bathsheba

A

B

| | Coral Cap | | Oceanic Series | | Folded rocks of the Scotland Series |

were uplifted by a small earth movement they would form a new terrace just like the others in the island.

Coral has the power to absorb a lot of water, with the result that most of the rain falling on it soaks into it. In addition, the acids contained in rain and ground water have dissolved many caves and sink-holes in the rock. The water flowing down through these adds to the supply which collects underground. As it can be easily reached by wells it forms the most important source of water for domestic purposes. A little is also used for irrigation.

Surface drainage on the coral is consequently non-existent, except for brief periods after heavy rains. Temporary streams have nevertheless been able to carve steep-sided gullies which in places are 100 feet deep and 100 feet across. Bridges have had to be built in some places to enable roads to cross them.

The Scotland district, which takes up about a seventh of the island, is very different in character. It is a vast eastward-facing amphitheatre created where erosion has removed the coral cap and worn the underlying weak materials of the Scotland Series into a landscape of knife-edged ridges and ravines. Overgrazing and overcropping have hastened the processes of erosion, and in some parts the land is completely spoiled. Though care is now being taken to conserve the soils, some will never reach even a moderate standard of fertility.

RAINFALL

As far as rainfall is concerned, the year falls into two parts, the period between June and November being fairly wet, and that from the beginning of December to the end of May being relatively dry. The annual average is about 60 inches, the central and eastern parishes having the heaviest and most dependable rainfall.

However, as can be seen from Table 7d there are considerable variations from year to year. Shortage of rainfall is always a cause for anxiety, as a drought or a delay in the arrival of the rainy season can seriously affect the cane yield. The sugar output, and therefore the island's income, can drop by over a quarter in a dry year.

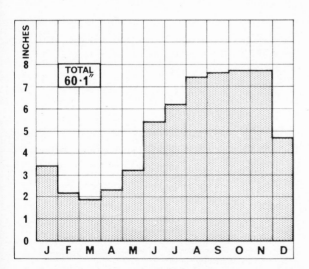

7c. *Average monthly rainfall of Barbados.*

7d. *In this table the average rainfall for the wettest and the driest districts are shown in heavy type.*
In addition, a wet year and a dry year have been chosen to show the great variations which can occur in the island's rainfall.

	WETTEST DISTRICTS			DRIEST DISTRICTS		
	Average over many years	*A wet year*	*A dry year*	*Average over many years*	*A wet year*	*A dry year*
JAN.	**4·4**	4·5	4·9	**2·6**	2·3	2·1
FEB.	**2·7**	3·6	1·3	**1·5**	2·5	0·6
MAR.	**2·9**	3·5	0·8	**1·7**	1·1	0·5
APRIL	**3·0**	2·5	1·8	**1·9**	1·2	1·9
MAY	**3·7**	4·1	1·2	**2·3**	4·7	0·5
JUNE	**6·5**	5·2	8·9	**4·4**	3·4	4·4
JULY	**7·9**	8·5	9·2	**5·3**	5·4	4·2
AUG.	**8·9**	12·1	3·4	**6·1**	5·8	2·8
SEP.	**9·5**	12·2	3·7	**6·5**	7·4	2·7
OCT.	**8·8**	11·8	5·8	**6·4**	12·1	2·7
NOV.	**9·3**	30·9	4·8	**6·8**	25·7	2·4
DEC.	**6·2**	10·0	3·2	**3·9**	5·7	2·7
	73·8	108·9	49·0	49·5	77·3	27·5

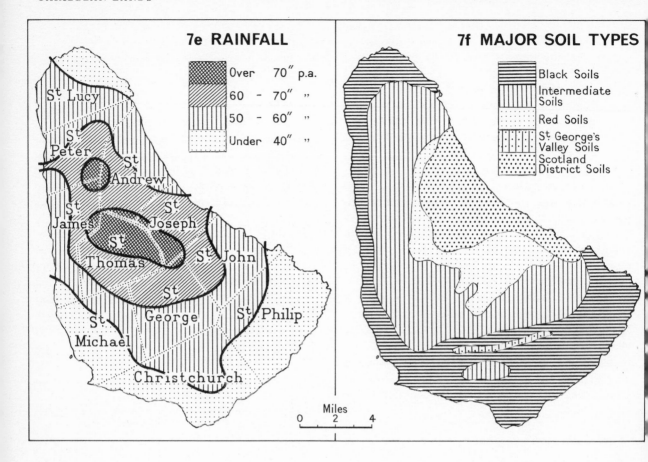

SOILS

The most important factors determining the character of a soil are the underlying rock and the climate. Barbados shows both these relationships very clearly.

In the Scotland district the great variety of rocks has given rise to a diversity of soils, some of which are fertile, though most are so badly eroded that they will never support good crops. Indeed in some places the soil has been stripped away altogether so that the underlying rock is exposed.

Elsewhere, as we have seen, the island is covered with a coral cap and we might expect the soil above this to be everywhere the same. But because of differences in rainfall this is not so. On the highest lands —that is, over 700 feet—where rainfall is heaviest, the soil is red or chocolate brown in colour and supports the best cane. On the drier lowlands—that is, under 200 feet—it is black, less easy to work and usually not so fertile. In the St George's Valley this black soil is much thicker than elsewhere and needs deep ploughing and draining, after which it becomes very fertile.

Between these two extremes are the intermediate soils, with a gradation in character marked by a gradual change of colour from red to black.

Though the soils overlying the coral are usually thin, they tend to get waterlogged after heavy rains.

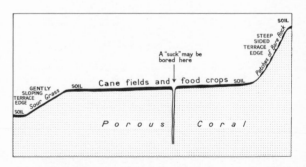

7g. *Section across terrace to show the way the land is commonly used and drained.*

Farmers have discovered an easy way to drain them by boring holes known as "sucks" down into the coral. Most fields have one or more of these sucks.

Mixed with the soil is a certain amount of volcanic dust, which, it seems, must have been blown to Barbados after eruptions of the volcanoes in the nearby Windward Islands. It is said that the island was covered with 1½ inches of grey volcanic dust after the eruption of the St Vincent Soufrière in 1812.

A knowledge of his soil is of value to the farmer, as each different type needs different treatment and special manuring if it is to give its best yield. This is especially true in Barbados where the soils would have lost their fertility were it not for careful fertilization over the centuries.

LAND USE

Though most of the land in Barbados has been put to the best possible use, by no means all of it—as can be seen from Table 7h—is fit for agriculture. In all, about 63% of the total area is cultivated—made up of 56% under sugar cane and the remainder mostly under food crops. The fact that 56% of all land (seven-eighths of the cultivated land) is devoted to cane shows how dominant this crop is. Not all of this land is reaped in any one year, however.

Total area	106,000 acres
Cultivated land	67,000 acres
Sour grass pastures, rab land and gullies	27,000 acres
Built-up areas, roads and waste land	12,000 acres

7h. Land use in Barbados.

"Sour grass" pasture, found mainly on the sides of terraces, is used for feeding cattle and other livestock, and for mulching the cane fields. "Rab" land is unfit for cultivation or for pasture but in places it is being planted with trees, chiefly casuarinas.

About 80% of the farmland is owned by estates, of which there were 244 in 1960. They range in size from 10 to 1,000 acres, though the majority are between 150 and 200 acres. The rest of the farmland is taken up with small holdings under ten acres in size. Some small farmers spend all of their time on their own land, growing cane and food crops and keeping livestock. If they are well-off, they may even employ casual labour during the cane harvest. Most, however, have such small plots of land that they must find their primary source of employment at other tasks.

AGRICULTURE

For three centuries sugar has dominated the island's exports. It will continue to do so in the foreseeable future because no other crop is so suited to the climate or brings such returns per acre or employs so many skilled and unskilled workers. If the land were turned over to food crops, for instance, Barbados would be able to supply only a fraction of its needs, and there would be nothing to sell overseas to enable the island to buy manufactured and other goods. However, even cane has its limitations. In contrast to many other things, the price of sugar has not risen much for over 100 years and the standard of living of those who depend on it remains low.

Cane is grown more intensively in Barbados than in any other Caribbean territory. The old method of planting it in separate, hand-dug holes is still commonly used as it gives the best results. About 15% of the output comes from 10,000 acres worked by small holders whose yields, on an average, are about two-thirds of those of the estates. The best cane lands are in the central and eastern parishes. The drier areas not only produce less in good years but also suffer most in times of drought.

Cane is planted in November and takes fifteen to eighteen months to mature. From then on ratoons can be reaped each year, so at any one time canes are at two stages of growth, and not all can be cut in any one year. About one-fifth of the land is young cane at harvest time and is not reaped. Harvesting lasts from mid January to June, the dry Christ Church lowlands being reaped first.

Before the war less than half of the total cane acreage was under ratoons, but since then new varieties of cane have been introduced which enable farmers to ratoon successfully for four or five years without appreciable loss of yield. These varieties also produce more sugar and are more resistant to droughts, pests, and disease. In consequence costs have been lowered and output has risen. The annual sugar production for the period 1920–4 was just over 50,000 tons. In recent years, with only a small increase in acreage, it has been about 170,000 tons. The output of 196,000 tons in 1965 was a record. At the same time, however, with improved mechanization and the closing of the least efficient factories—including all those worked by windmills—the number of people employed in the industry has decreased by several thousand.

7i. Cane fields in Barbados. What can you tell about the landscape and about the climate?

The crop is handled by twenty-one factories, rather more than the number operating in Jamaica, where the output is nearly three times greater. Rum, considered not only by Barbadians to be the best in the West Indies, is produced on one estate and in two refineries. In addition several factories prepare "fancy molasses"—a special type of molasses made from cane juice—which is canned and sold in Canada and the United States, where it is used to make confectionery.

No other country in the world depends to a greater extent on one crop than Barbados does on cane. Sugar and its by-products always account for over 90% of the domestic exports. In 1957 the figure was 96%; in 1958, an unusually poor year, it was 93%.

Practically all the sugar exports go to the United Kingdom and Canada, the island's export quota under the Commonwealth Sugar Agreement being 163,000 tons a year. In addition, about 12,000 tons are consumed locally.

Food crops such as yams, sweet potatoes, maize and pigeon peas are grown in all parts of the island. Bananas and fruit trees are grown in the moister districts and sometimes on the banks of gullies. Groundnuts are grown in drier areas. When these crops are harvested, there is sometimes enough to allow a small export, mainly to Trinidad. However, other foodstuffs, including large quantities of meat, dairy products, fish, flour and rice have to be imported. Altogether these amount to almost a third of the total imports.

In order to limit food imports as much as possible all estate-owners are required by law to devote at least 12% of their arable land to provisions. So, when the cane cycle of a field is complete—the last possible ratoons having been cut—the field may be "thrown

	1957		*1958*	
Sugar (tons)	180,733	($36,649,270)	130,237	($26,532,165)
Molasses (gals.)	9,103,049	($4,832,348)	12,639,527	($4,856,766)
Sugar Confectionery		($373,945)		($238,049)
Rum		($2,084,059)		($2,249,048)
Margarine (lbs.)	1,140,809	($476,295)	1,082,785	($458,741)
Other items		($1,153,407)		($776,975)
Re-exports		($4,100,370)		($4,611,669)

7j. Barbados exports for 1957 and 1958.

7k. How does this Barbadian sugar factory compare with those shown in plates 6l and 17l?

out"; that is, may be ploughed and, in May and June, planted with food crops. Sometimes a second planting is made and the next canes may have to be planted through the unreaped food crops in the following November. This system of intensive farming is unique in the West Indies.

Until recently cotton, grown on poorer soils in drier parts of the island, formed a minor export, but prices have become so poor that this has virtually ceased.

LIVESTOCK AND FISHING

In contrast to the sugar industry, which does not provide work all through the year for all of its employees, livestock rearing does provide a regular income. In spite of this and a law which requires estates to keep some animals, livestock rearing is not a major occupation in Barbados, chiefly because of the shortage of fodder. Good pasturage is scarce, and

imported animal foodstuffs are expensive. Of the 11,000 cattle in the island, most are reared for their milk.

As every source of food is valuable to this crowded island, it is fortunate that the waters around Barbados provide a fairly plentiful supply of fish. Flying fish, caught mainly between November and June, form the bulk of the catch. With the introduction of more modern methods of fishing and the increased use of powered boats, fishermen are getting better returns than before, but at the same time fewer are finding employment. Some flying fish are frozen for export.

Though this fishing industry is the most important in the West Indies, it is insignificant in comparison with the fisheries of Britain and Newfoundland. The main reason for this is that the Caribbean Sea is not rich in fish. It contains no continental shelf like those off the west coast of Europe and the east coast of Canada on which trawlers can operate, and no

79

7l. A street in Bridgetown. How many different modes of transport are shown in this picture?

up-welling currents of cold ocean water, or large rivers to provide a plentiful supply of fish food.

Sea eggs, considered a delicacy in Barbados, are plentiful on the reefs surrounding the island. As the sea-egg season starts at the beginning of September, there is work for some of the fishermen at a time when flying fish are scarce. Farther afield a Barbadian company operates a fleet of trawlers to catch shrimp off the South American coast. Some are processed for export to America.

7m. The deep-water harbour at Bridgetown. Compare the landscape with that shown in plate 8g.

OTHER OCCUPATIONS

In order to reduce the island's dependence on sugar, special encouragement has been given to light industries, and Barbados produces more manufactured goods than any of the other small islands. The most important of these industries is the conversion of copra into soap, edible oils, lard and margarine. Other light industries include the making of soft drinks and beer, bay rum, ice, biscuits, glass bottles, bricks and tiles, cigarettes (from imported tobacco), shirts and other clothes, boots, shoes, plastics and furniture. At Chalky Mount in the Scotland district there is a small pottery industry based on local supplies of clay. The articles made there are taken to Bridgetown where they are sold mainly to tourists. Other handicrafts include basket-making, needlework and turtle-shell ornaments.

Barbados is not rich in minerals. Though

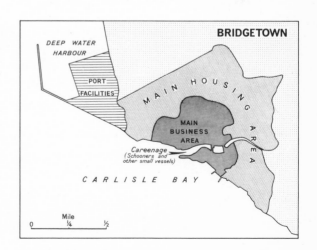

7n. Compare this harbour with that of St George's (Diagram 8f).

81

prospecting has gone on for many years and though trial borings have reached 15,000 feet, petroleum has not been produced in commercial quantities, though it is reported to exist at Fisherpond in St Thomas and perhaps elsewhere. A small amount of natural gas, obtained from a well at Turner Hall, is used in Bridgetown and its suburbs. Small quantities of pitch, or *manjak*, found in the Scotland district, are exported for use in electrical industries.

With its fine climate and excellent bathing-beaches Barbados has developed the largest tourist industry in the Lesser Antilles. Tourist earnings exceeded $27,000,000 in 1965. The main hotel area is the coastal strip between Bridgetown and Speightstown.

POPULATION, COMMUNICATIONS AND TRADE

The population of Barbados is less diverse, racially, than in most of the other West Indian territories. Over three-quarters of the people are of direct African descent, 5% are European and the remainder are mostly coloured.

Apart from the windswept eastern coast the whole island is densely peopled. Bridgetown and its suburbs contain about 85,000 people. Elsewhere, villages cluster in corners of estates and along roadsides.

Bridgetown, the capital, is the chief business and banking centre in the island. Lying 500 miles nearer to England than does Jamaica it is the first port of call for many ships coming to the Caribbean. In consequence it has become the chief commercial centre in the Lesser Antilles. Its port can berth large ships and has facilities for storing and loading sugar in bulk and molasses by pipeline.

Bridgetown handles virtually all the trade. Of the exports in 1964, 44% went to the United Kingdom, 10% to Canada and 8% to the United States. Their value was greater than the combined exports of the other Commonwealth Eastern Caribbean territories. Of the imports, 30% came from the United Kingdom, 11% from Canada and 16% from the United States.

Roads radiate from Bridgetown to all parts of the island, none of which is much more than half an hour's drive away. With four miles of road to every square mile of land, Barbados has one of the densest road networks in the world.

THINGS TO DO

1. Draw diagrams to show (*a*) land use in Barbados (*b*) the direction of trade.
2. Compare and contrast Barbados and St Kitts.
3. Find out the conditions which support big fishing industries in Britain and in Newfoundland, and the methods used to catch, preserve and market fish there. Compare these things with conditions in the country in which you live.

QUESTIONS

1. What attempts have been made in Barbados to escape from a one-crop economy? How far have they been successful?
2. Draw a map to show the position of Barbados in relation to (*a*) England; (*b*) the other West Indian islands; and (*c*) North, Central and South America. In what ways has its position influenced the island's development?
3. Among the problems faced by farmers in the West Indies are insect pests, unreliable rainfall, soil erosion and hurricanes. Select *two* of them, and discuss the problems involved, showing how the farmer attempts to deal with them. L.G.C.E. (O) 1966.

CHAPTER EIGHT

The Commonwealth Eastern Caribbean Territories

The main Commonwealth Eastern Caribbean islands are Grenada, St Vincent, St Lucia and Dominica (formerly grouped together to form a colony—the Windward Islands), and Montserrat, Antigua, and St Kitts and Nevis (formerly known as the Leeward Islands). Geographically they may be compared and contrasted in at least two ways. From the point of view of physical geography there are the volcanic islands of Grenada, St Vincent, St Lucia, Dominica, Montserrat, St Kitts, and Nevis which are mountainous, and the islands of Antigua, Barbuda, and Anguilla which are largely or wholly made of limestone and are low-lying. From the point of view of economic geography there are Antigua and St Kitts which (like Barbados) have long relied on sugar as a primary source of income, and the other islands where sugar cane has almost or entirely disappeared. Some of these now rely heavily on banana exports, but others (for instance, Montserrat and Nevis) have never established a major alternative to cane.

All the islands have some features in common. (Poverty has been suggested as the chief of them.) All possess some individuality. Isolating these things will be a useful exercise when reading this chapter.

They will be described in the order given at the beginning of the first paragraph, that is from south to north.

Grenada

Area: 120 square miles; population (1965): about 92,000; density of population: 767 per square mile

THE LAND

Grenada lies at the southern end of the arc of volcanic islands, and apart from a little limestone in the north it is wholly volcanic. It differs from its northern neighbours in that its mountains are older and considerably more eroded than those of St Vincent but rather younger and higher than those in the northern part of St Lucia. The only remaining traces of former volcanic activity in Grenada are a few cold mineral springs.

The main mountain mass, which lies in the south-centre of the island, consists of a number of ridges surmounted by several peaks which rise to over 2,000 feet. Several of these contain old crater basins and one is occupied by a large crater lake—Grand Etang, 1,740 feet above sea-level. It is shown in Plate 1a.

Lying to the north of these mountains and separated from them by a narrow col is a younger, higher and narrower ridge which rises to 2,756 feet in Mt St Catherine. It is flanked by numerous spurs. Close to the north-east coast there are two further crater lakes, Lake Antoine and Levera Pond.

The mountains rise steeply from the west coast and descend somewhat more gently to the east. The only lowlands are those in the north-eastern and south-western tips of the island. The south coast is very rugged and deeply embayed.

SETTLEMENT AND DEVELOPMENT

The first successful attempt to colonize Grenada was made by the French in 1650. They quickly overcame Carib resistance, which it was easier to do in Grenada than in the more mountainous islands of Dominica and St Vincent. Their first crops, tobacco and indigo, were supplemented by sugar, cocoa, cotton and coffee before the island was captured by the British in 1762. Under the British the population increased rapidly as many settlers migrated there from the Leeward Islands and elsewhere and many slaves were brought in to work on the estates. Sugar became by far the most important crop, the output trebling in twelve years. Cane took up most of the lowlands, while cocoa, provisions and small quantities of other crops were grown in some parts of the highlands.

After Emancipation many of the freed slaves left the estates. Some emigrated, mainly to Trinidad. Others settled in the highlands where there was plenty of unoccupied reasonably fertile land not too steep for cultivation. Attempts to replace them with indentured labourers from Malta, Madeira, Africa and

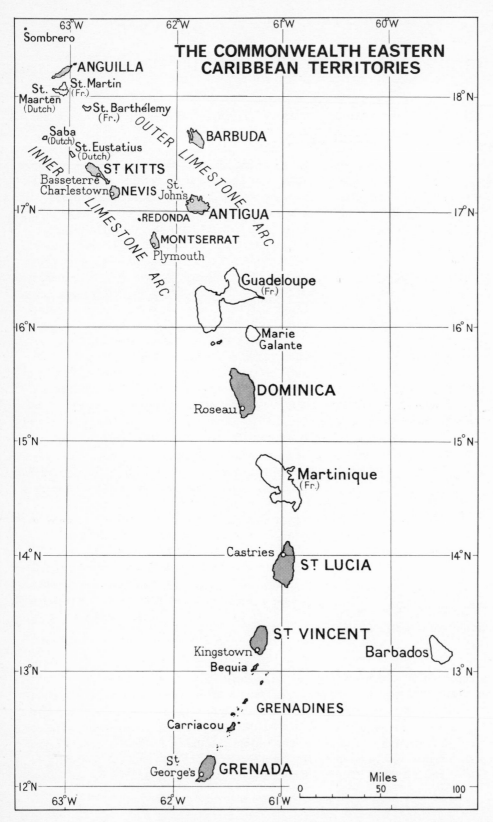

THE COMMONWEALTH EASTERN
CARIBBEAN TERRITORIES

8a. *This map includes some of the neighbouring islands including the French territories and the Netherlands Windward Islands.*

Sombrero

ANGUILLA

St. Martin (Fr.)

St. Maarten (Dutch)

St. Barthélemy (Fr.)

Saba (Dutch)

St. Eustatius (Dutch)

ST KITTS

Basseterre

Charlestown NEVIS

St. John's

REDONDA

OUTER LIMESTONE ARC

INNER LIMESTONE ARC

BARBUDA

ANTIGUA

MONTSERRAT

Plymouth

Guadeloupe (Fr.)

Marie Galante

DOMINICA

Roseau

Martinique (Fr.)

Castries

ST LUCIA

ST VINCENT

Kingstown

Bequia

Barbados

GRENADINES

Carriacou

St. George's GRENADA

Miles
0   50   100

18°N
17°N
16°N
15°N
14°N
13°N
12°N

63°W   62°W   61°W   60°W

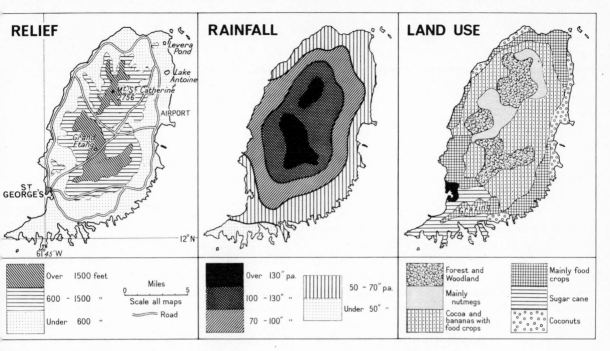

RELIEF

Levera Pond
Lake Antoine
Mt St Catherine 756
AIRPORT
Grand Etang
ST GEORGE'S
12° N
61° 45'W

Over 1500 feet
600 - 1500 "
Under 600 "

Miles
0 — 5
Scale all maps
Road

RAINFALL

Over 130" p.a.
100 - 130" "
70 - 100" "
50 - 70" p.a.
Under 50" "

LAND USE

Grazing

Forest and Woodland
Mainly nutmegs
Cocoa and bananas with food crops
Mainly food crops
Sugar cane
Coconuts

GRENADA *8b. Relief.*   *8c. Rainfall.*   *8d. Land use.*

India were not very successful (the Indian population in Grenada in 1965 was 3,800), and the output of sugar fell from over 4,000 tons in 1846 to under 1,000 tons in 1881. By this time cocoa had become the chief crop on the estates. The change was brought about by the estate-owners, who encouraged labourers to plant cocoa on small plots of land by allowing them to grow their own food crops there, and by buying the cocoa trees when they began to bear. With the money they earned in this way the labourers often bought land of their own and planted cocoa for themselves. One result of this system was that the island's cocoa exports rose from 170 tons in 1846 to 2,600 tons in 1881. Another was that Grenada became a land of small holdings. By 1890 over 80% of the farms were under 5 acres in area. Today the figure is 87%, and one of the island's problems is that so many holdings are of uneconomic size.

In the early part of this century the output of cocoa rose to over 6,000 tons a year and formed almost 90% of the exports. But in the 1920s a combination of poor prices and witch's broom disease caused a decline, and the exports of nutmeg and mace, which had been a subsidiary crop since 1843, grew to about equal importance. Sugar cane became confined to a small area a few miles south of St George's where a central sugar factory was built in 1935.

The population density, which was over 200 per square mile at the time of the emancipation of the slaves, had more than doubled by the beginning of this century. In spite of the fact that a higher proportion was cultivated than in any other island except Barbados and St Kitts, there was considerable pressure on the land. Many people took the opportunity to emigrate to Panama, Curaçao, Aruba, Trinidad and elsewhere and for many years the population remained stable at about 60,000. Since then, however, most outlets have been closed to migrants and numbers have increased. The population density of 739 per square mile in 1960 was the second highest in the West Indies. It has increased since then.

CLIMATE

The main features of the climate of the Eastern Caribbean have been explained in Chapter Two. As for Grenada, the coastal areas, especially the south-western lowlands, receive least rainfall, the average being 60 inches a year. In contrast, the mountain summits, which are often cloud-capped, receive over 150 inches. The dry season lasts from January to May, the wet season from June to December, with November as the wettest month.

With so much of its income derived from tree crops Grenada suffers severely whenever a hurricane strikes. It takes years for the island to regain former levels of production.

LAND USE

Only the highest and most inaccessible areas have been left in the forest that once covered most of Grenada, and in 1960 only 24% of the island was forested. At the heads of valleys and on steep slopes just below the forests grow most of the island's nutmeg trees. They merge at lower levels with cocoa. Food crops are grown in the drier coastal areas, bananas, together with cocoa, in the humid valleys and on hillsides, and coconuts in sandy places near the sea. There are patches of thorny scrub in the dry, flat lands of the south-west, but most of this area is devoted to stock rearing. Bordering on this zone are the cane fields supplying the sugar factory at Woodlands. In all about half the island is cultivated.

AGRICULTURE

Cocoa

Though some cocoa is planted above the 1,000-foot contour, it grows best below that level. After the war the areas worst stricken by witch's broom disease were cleared and planted with high-yielding plants. Mainly because the soil was so suitable they were very successful, and output was rising until the hurricane of 1955 set back production. Since then, however, there has been a recovery, and cocoa is again the leading export.

Except that cocoa is seldom grown under shade, cultivation and processing methods are similar to those in Trinidad. Windbreaks are common, however, and for these, rows of mango trees are often used. In addition, cocoa is often grown along with nutmegs. The reason for this is that it is only after nutmeg trees have been growing for about seven years that a grower can tell which are the males and which are the females. As only the female trees bear, most of the males have to be cut down. Instead of replanting with more nutmegs farmers often put cocoa in its place.

Nutmegs and Mace

Nutmeg trees flourish best at relatively high altitudes where the annual rainfall is over 80 inches and the mean temperature is below 75°F. They are slow to grow, and reach their peak production about twenty years after planting. When the fruit is ripe it splits and exposes a shiny, dark brown nut covered with a delicate scarlet latticework of mace. Both nutmeg and mace are in demand as spices and the latter is also used to some extent in the manufacture of toothpaste and perfumes.

The nuts are allowed to fall to the ground, where women collect them in large baskets. They are carried to sheds where the mace is stripped off carefully because it fetches a higher price if it is unbroken. It is sun-dried and stored for several months in the dark, after which time it has turned yellow and is ready to be packed in plywood chests for export. The nuts are spread in a thin layer on wooden trays where they are dried until their kernels are fully cured. Just before shipment women break open the shells with wooden hammers, extract the kernels, sort them according to size and pack them in sacks for export. Defective nutmegs are converted into oil, which is also exported.

Though nutmegs are exported from Indonesia and also to a small extent from St Lucia, St Vincent, and Trinidad and Tobago, Grenada is the world's largest producer. The price of nutmegs on the world's markets therefore depends largely on the amount available from Grenada. Thus when the hurricane of 1955 reduced the volume of nutmegs and mace to 5% of what it had been previously, the price rose so much that the value of exports was only halved.

In most years the United States buys most of the nutmegs while the United Kingdom takes most of the mace.

Bananas

Bananas, which had been only a minor export before the 1955 hurricane, became a major export afterwards, as the following figures show:

Year	1955	1960	1965
Stems	92,000	1,009,800	1,622,600

Grenada does not rely as much on banana exports as do certain other islands, especially St Lucia and Dominica. Usually they form about a quarter of the total export value.

. "Dancing cocoa" in Grenada. What is the purpose of this? Why do you think the process has not been mechanized?

It is very common to see the bananas interplanted with cocoa or nutmeg trees. About 40% of the production comes from small holders.

Other Crops

The cane grown in the south-west of the island is made into sugar in a single factory. The output of about 1,300 tons in 1965 was not sufficient for local consumption let alone for sale overseas. Rum is made at several distilleries.

Some coconuts are grown in the island and there is a factory to make edible oil and soap. Some lime oil is made in Grenada and exported.

Because the island concentrates so much on the three major export crops—cocoa, bananas and nutmegs—foodstuffs form a higher proportion of the imports than is usual for an agricultural country.

TOWNS AND COMMUNICATIONS

The capital, St George's, is situated on a deep, sheltered inlet, part of which is an old, submerged volcanic crater. The inner part of the harbour, known as the Carenage, has long been used by schooners and other sailing-ships. More recently a wharf has been built to accommodate ocean-going vessels, as, for example, those loading bananas.

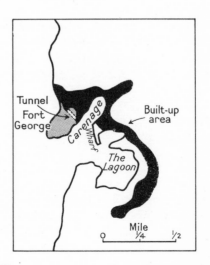

8f. St George's Harbour.

8g. Part of St George's harbour. In what direction was the camera pointing? Describe the site of the town.

St George's is connected by road to all the coastal districts of Grenada, including the airport on the east coast. The west coast road enters the town through a short tunnel which has been built through the promontory on which Fort George stands.

The Grenadines

The Grenadines are a group of over a hundred small islands and many more rocks and reefs standing on a shallow submarine volcanic ridge which extends northwards from Grenada almost as far as St Vincent. Their total area is about 35 square miles and their total population about 12,000, the same as Montserrat. Those lying south of Carriacou (13 square miles, population 7,000) belong to Grenada. The remainder, including Bequia (7 square miles, population 2,600) belong to St Vincent.

Sugar and cotton were once exported from the main islands but the former industry has died out and the latter has declined. On the ten islands which support population today the chief occupations are the growing of provisions—chiefly corn, groundnuts, cassava, peas, yams and sweet potatoes—and rearing of livestock. Settlement is dense on cultivated land, but agriculture has suffered because slopes are steep and the volcanic soils have been severely eroded. In consequence people have left the islands to become seamen and to migrate to other countries.

The chief exports are coconuts, groundnuts, limes, lime juice and lime oil from Carriacou, coconuts from Bequia, and cotton. Fish are caught off coasts and sometimes whales are caught and processed on Bequia. Schooners and other small wooden ships are built for inter-island trade and for fishing. Bequia has a small tourist industry—the visitors arriving mostly in yachts.

THE COMMONWEALTH EASTERN CARIBBEAN TERRITORIES

St Vincent

*rea: 133 square miles; population (1965):
7,000; density of population: 654 per square mile*

HE LAND

Vith its jumbled array of peaks, ridges and ravines,
t Vincent almost rivals Dominica as the most
nountainous island in the Lesser Antilles. Indeed
ne interior range is so high and so steep that the
land is the only one that is still not crossed by a
oad.

St Vincent is entirely volcanic in origin, being
nostly composed of ash and other fragmented
naterial, though there are some lava flows in places.
'he northern end of the island is dominated by
oufrière. Part of the irregular rim of its main crater
–which dates from an eruption in 1718—reaches a
eight of 4,048 feet only two miles from the sea.
oufrière is one of the two active volcanoes remain-
ng in the Caribbean and, as with its partner Mt
elée in Martinique, its sporadic outbursts are of an
xplosive type. The eruption of 1902–3 killed 2,000
eople and devastated nearly a third of the island.
'he previous explosion of 1812 was even more
estructive. At present, however, Soufrière is quiet.
n places the inner walls of its mile-wide crater fall
lmost sheer for 1,000 feet to the surface of a large
rater lake which was formed after the 1812 eruption.
'hough the mountain is so young, some deep narrow
ullies have already been cut in it by the streams
vhich flow off its slopes after heavy rains. They
adiate like the spokes of a wheel.

South of Soufrière there is a broad trough and then
he land rises again to another volcano—Morne Garu,
,523 feet. From here a sharp-crested ridge runs to
he southern end of the island. Many spurs breaking
way from this central ridge run down to the wind-
vard and leeward coasts and terminate in high cliffs.
Erosion has proceeded further in this older area than
n the north. Each stream has carved a ravine in its
pper course and deposited an alluvial fan where it
eaves the hills.

The mountains drop more steeply towards the lee-
vard than towards the windward coast, where a
eries of well-defined natural terraces indicates that
he land has been uplifted in stages. These terraces,
noulded by erosion into a rolling landscape, support
some of the best agricultural land in the island. Flat
land is very limited in extent. Indeed only 5% of the
island has slopes of five degrees or less.

SETTLEMENT AND DEVELOPMENT

Because St Vincent was one of the chief Carib strong-
holds, it was one of the last of the Lesser Antilles to
be colonized by Europeans. In fact, in order to gain
a foothold there at all the early French and British
settlers had to make treaties with the Carib inhabitants. In 1773, ten years after the island became
British, the last of these treaties allotted special
reserves to the Caribs, the largest of which was in the
north-east of the island.

Many pure-blooded Caribs were killed in the 1812
and 1902 eruptions of Soufrière and most of the 1200
Caribs listed in the 1960 census are descendants of
the Black Caribs, a race which sprang from a mixture
of Carib and Negro stock. Their numbers are small
because most were deported to the Bay Islands in
1796 after an unsuccessful uprising. Their later story
is told in the chapter on Belize.

During the eighteenth century cotton was extensively grown in St Vincent, but after the island became British sugar cane became the foremost crop.
Thus the sugar output of 3,200 tons in 1787 rose to
over 14,000 tons by 1828. Many slaves were brought
in to work on the estates and there was a slave population of 23,000 by the time of emancipation. After
emancipation Portuguese and Indian indentured
labourers were brought to St Vincent and the
descendants of those who remained there form a
small proportion of the population today.

When sugar exports declined in the later nineteenth
century, a third crop, arrowroot—which had been
brought to the island by the Caribs and exported
in small quantities since 1830—rose to prominence.
Today some cotton and coconuts and a large quantity
of arrowroot are grown, but bananas are the most
valuable export.

About two-thirds of the farmland is operated by
small holders. St Vincent was one of the first islands
in the Caribbean to start land-settlement projects and
today there are many people living on and cultivating
lands which have been acquired by the Government
from estate-owners. Partly in consequence farming
practices in St Vincent are better than those in many
other parts of the West Indies.

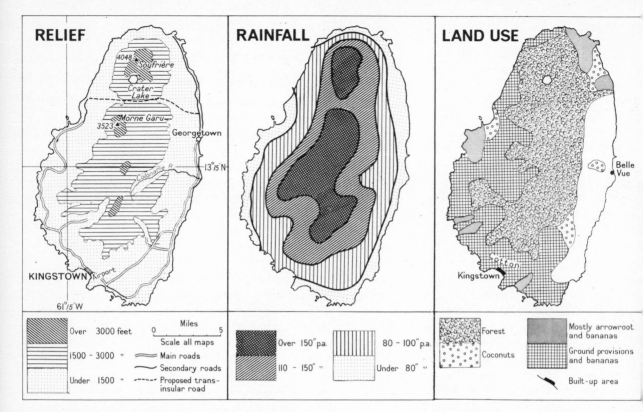

ST VINCENT *8h. Relief.*   *8i. Rainfall.*   *8j. Land use.*

RAINFALL

The rainfall of St Vincent is heavy, very little of the island having less than 80 inches a year. The mountainous interior, which receives over 150 inches, is the source of many streams. One of them—the Colonarie River—provides hydro-electricity. Several others are put to use by the arrowroot factories, where plentiful supplies of pure water are required. It is in the drier months from January to April that sugar, cotton and the bulk of the arrowroot are harvested.

LAND USE

The steep slopes of Soufrière and the central ridge have been left in forest, which though of little economic value, does help to reduce the danger of landslides. Out of a total area of 85,120 acres, about 30,000 are forested, half of which is forest reserve. Below the forest there is a zone of shifting cultivation where food crops are grown on peasant small holdings. The bulk of the export crops are grown in the coastal areas and on slopes up to 1,000 feet. Many of these slopes have been terraced to prevent soil erosion. Altogether about 30,000 acres are under permanent cultivation.

THE CROPS

Arrowroot

Arrowroot, a plant which grows to a height of 4 to 5 feet, is cultivated for the sake of the starch in its root, which reaches a length of 6 to 8 inches. It is planted on sloping ground and when it is ready for harvesting in October the labourers begin at the bottom of the fields and work their way uphill, the last of the crop being reaped by May. Immediately the plant is dug up, a section of the root is cut off and re-planted. It grows into a new plant which is itself ready for harvesting about a year later. Normally the stem, the shiny green leaves and any weeds in the field are dug into the soil to provide plant food, but every five years or so the field is cleared and forked before replanting. Arrowroot cultivation requires a large

8k. Digging arrowroot. Notice the way the soil is being conserved. Draw a sketch-map to show land use in this area.

81. Carrying arrowroot into a factory.

labour force for at least half the year, which is fortunate as St Vincent is the third most densely populated of the Commonwealth Caribbean territories.

The roots are carried by truck to one of the island's factories. There they are washed, shredded and pulped by a machine and carried in a plentiful supply of pure water through a series of sieves which extract the coarser fragments. The remaining suspension of starch particles in water is allowed to stand in vats until the starch settles to the bottom. Then the water is drained off and the starch is dried, graded and packed for export.

Eighty to ninety per cent of the arrowroot is grown on estates which, partly because they have the best land, have far higher yields than the peasants who grow the remainder. There are over twenty factories on these estates, but some of the estates and many of the peasants send their crop to a Government-owned

factory at Belle Vue on the windward coast. This factory, which has modern equipment to dry and prepare the finest quality starch, processes about a fifth of the total crop. There are plans to build several more factories of this type. The whole crop is marketed by a co-operative association.

St Vincent, with an annual export of 9 to 10 million pounds, supplies about 98% of the world's arrowroot requirements. Most of it is sent to the United States but the United Kingdom, Canada and Trinidad are also important buyers. Because arrowroot is so easily digested it is used in the preparation of baby foods and invalid diets. It is also used in the manufacture of biscuits.

Sugar
The eruptions of Soufrière at the beginning of the present century almost obliterated the already declining sugar industry. Though it struggled on, it never

recovered. Throughout the 1950s sugar production seldom surpassed 4,000 tons a year, and exports never came near the quota of 1,500 tons. In 1962, the island's only sugar factory was closed, and St Vincent is now a sugar importer. The failure of the St Vincent industry provides a good example of the way that only large-scale sugar enterprises based on large areas of easily accessible cane are profitable and successful.

Cotton

The variety of sea-island cotton grown in St Vincent is one of the finest in the world. It has a specially long staple which produces a strong, smooth cloth. But because of competition from nylon and other synthetic fibres and from the vast cotton crop in America, prices for St Vincent cotton are poor and uncertain and output is limited. Thus cotton formed only 5% of the island's exports in 1959.

The chief growing area is the relatively dry south-western part of the island. A Government-owned factory at Kingstown gins the whole crop as well as a smaller amount sent from some of the Grenadines.

Bananas

Bananas are grown by peasants and on estates in almost every area connected to the capital by road. Pure stands are few, the fruit being generally grown together with other crops. Exports, which go entirely to the United Kingdom, rose from 26,626 stems in 1954 to 2,474,000 in 1965. In 1962 they brought in 42% of the income compared with 30% from arrowroot.

Other Crops

Coconuts are grown mainly on estates, the chief producing area being in the north-east. The output of copra is usually over 2,000 tons a year. Most of this is exported, but some is processed at the cotton ginnery into edible oil, soap and stock feed.

Cassava, on the other hand, is grown mainly by small farmers. The starch is extracted at the arrowroot factories and some of it is exported. Sweet potatoes —which because of their short growing season are good money earners—are exported in considerable quantities to Trinidad. There are also smaller exports of groundnuts, yams and vegetables. Food imports are of less importance to St Vincent than to any other of the West Indies Associated States.

LIVESTOCK AND FISHING

Animals are kept to provide meat, milk and eggs. Some cattle, sheep and goats are exported and there is a ham and bacon factory that exports some of its products.

In addition to a small fishing industry, whales, porpoises, and blackfish (which look like a cross between the two) are harpooned off the coasts of St Vincent and the Grenadines for their blubber.

POPULATION

The rapid increase of population (or population explosion as it has been called) is particularly noticeable in St Vincent. It has resulted in a population density of nearly three people to every cultivable acre, and in virtually half the total population being under fifteen years old (that is below the age at which they can be expected to contribute to the economy).

TOWNS AND COMMUNICATIONS

Kingstown, the capital, has grown up on a large sheltered bay. Though it is the chief port, it has no deep-water pier (though one is planned) and even such small ships as schooners have to anchor in the bay. The town is connected by road to all the coastal districts except the north-west. Motor-boats and canoes ply between this isolated region and the capital. Unlike two other very mountainous islands —Dominica and Montserrat—it has been possible to locate the airport near the capital.

St Lucia

Area: 233 square miles; population (1965): about 94,000; density of population: 404 per square mile

THE LAND

The volcanic island of St Lucia may be divided into two physical regions:

1. The south and centre of the island is young and mountainous. A number of peaks rise to over 2,000 feet and the highest of all, Morne Gimie, reaches to 3,145 feet. Extremely steep slopes are common in the region. This is especially true of the pitons, which are the resistant lava plugs left standing like pinnacles when the rest of the volcanoes have been weathered

away. Two of these, Grand Piton and Petit Piton, which rise from the sea to 2,619 feet and 2,461 feet respectively, are among the most remarkable and best known scenic features in the West Indies. One of them is shown on the front cover of this book.

Many ridges radiate outwards from the region, those running westwards terminating very close to the sea. The southern flanks of the mountains lie buried beneath a recent outflow of volcanic mud, ash and boulders which slopes down to the sea like a giant fan. It has given rise to fertile soils on which most of the island's cocoa is grown.

Hot sulphurous streams, and the large active fumarole near Soufrière from which sulphur was once dug for export, show that vulcanicity in the southern part of St Lucia has not entirely died down. At present this fumarole—like the others in the Lesser Antilles—emits mainly hydrogen sulphide gas. If this were to be replaced by sulphur dioxide, it would be an indication of potential danger.

2. The older northern half of the island has been so worn down by erosion that the outlines of the old volcanoes are no longer traceable. The backbone of this region is a central ridge about 1,000 feet in height which with its offshoots is surmounted by numerous pitons, the highest of which is La Sorcière, 2,221 feet. There are also many lower individual hills. In contrast to the gorges of the south, the rivers in this region flow in wide, flat-bottomed valleys.

DEVELOPMENT

The first European attempt at settling St Lucia was made by the British in 1638, but the Caribs living there were too powerful, and they were forced to withdraw. A few years later the French were more successful. From then until 1803, St Lucia was one of the most disputed islands in the Caribbean and it changed hands no less than fourteen times. French influence there is still very marked. It shows in the place-names, the patois, and in some of the laws, especially those relating to the ownership of property.

The contests and uncertainties of the eighteenth century retarded the development of St Lucia. Thus sugar cane did not supersede the early crops—tobacco, cotton and ginger—until a century after it had become the mainstay of Barbados, Antigua, and St Kitts. However, sugar did in time become the most important export, production rising to a maximum of 5,000 tons in 1830, by which time over eighty factories were in operation and over 13,000 slaves were at work. Then in the difficult years that followed, the output dwindled again, falling to only 2,260 tons in 1843. Shortage of labour was one of the chief problems, the freed slaves preferring to find their own employment or to emigrate to the gold fields of French Guiana and elsewhere. Over 2,000 Indians were brought to St Lucia to take their place as field labourers but they soon found other employment and most of the estates were broken up into small holdings. Towards the end of the nineteenth century several central factories were erected, but none has survived. Limes were introduced and exported for many years, but disease caused a decline in the 1930s. Cocoa exports also increased, but most of the land was given over to subsistence crops. Shifting cultivation became common and soil erosion inevitably followed.

The lack of interest in commercial farming was due to better paid employment being constantly available for hundreds of workers in Castries. The large, deep, sheltered harbour there was selected as the chief coaling station in the West Indies. Coal imported from the United States and from Britain was stored on a wharf and loaded on to ships which tied up there for refuelling on their voyages from Europe and North America to South America and the Pacific. As the loading operation was never mechanized, the coal had to be headed aboard a hundredweight at a time.

From the 1880s to the 1920s this coal brought in over a half of the island's income and it was common for a thousand ships to call at Castries in a year. In 1911, for instance, 139,000 tons of coal were sold, amounting to three-quarters of the total exports. But in the 1930s, as fuel oil replaced coal, the trade declined. Fewer and fewer ships called at Castries and in 1938 only 22,000 tons of coal were loaded.

The unemployment and depression which would otherwise have followed were averted because labour was needed to build the United States Army and Navy bases at Vieux Fort and Gros Islet. In 1948, soon after they were closed, Castries was destroyed by fire and workers were needed to rebuild the capital. Thus only in recent years has St Lucia had to rely on agriculture as the sole source of income.

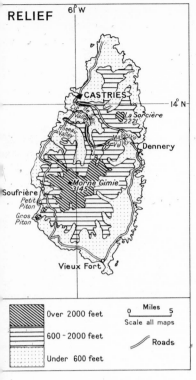

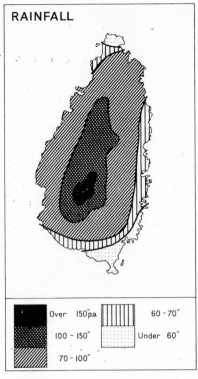

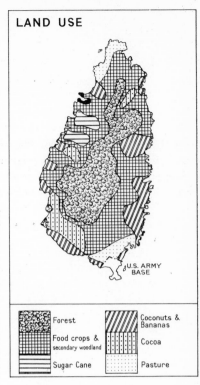

ST LUCIA *8m. Relief.*   *8n. Rainfall.*   *8o. Land use.*

RAINFALL

Over most of St Lucia the rainfall is heavy and there is no really dry season. This can be seen by referring to diagram 2h on page 11 which shows the average monthly rainfall for Castries, by no means one of the wettest places. The low-lying northern and southern tips of the island have the least rain and in these areas each of the first four months of the year usually has less than 4 inches.

In contrast to its easterly neighbour, Barbados, drought is seldom a problem in St Lucia. Instead, especially on the older and more eroded soils in the northern half of the island, the combination of steep slopes, heavy showers of rain and recklessly cleared land create a situation where landslides can easily occur. A serious landslide in 1938 did much damage and killed a number of people.

LAND USE

About a third of the land may be classified as forest and woodland, but of this only the rain-forest in the inaccessible mountainous districts is in good condi-

tion today. The remainder is secondary woodland which has grown up on land that was cleared for agriculture until soil erosion caused its abandonment. The northern tip of the island is very badly eroded and supports only scattered patches of thorny scrub.

Prosperous agriculture in the northern half of the island is limited to the alluvial flats, most of which are in banana estates. The southern part of the island is more fertile. There is no landslide problem and peasant farming is more successful. However, for the island as a whole, only about 30% is permanently cultivated. About 30% is waste land or in shifting cultivation.

AGRICULTURE

Banana exports began in the 1920s, declined in the 1930s because of Panama disease and ceased during the war when there were no ships to carry the fruit. After the war a new start was made with disease-resistant bananas. The pre-war record output was surpassed in 1954, and over 3,500,000 stems were exported in 1961. When the sugar industry ceased

8p. *Castries and its harbour. Note the old, eroded, volcanic landscape in the background. In what direction wa the camera pointing? Compare and contrast Castries with St George's (Plate 8g).*

shortly afterwards, large areas of land were released for banana cultivation in the large and fertile Roseau and Cul de Sac Valleys, and there was a second wave of expansion. In 1965, over 6,330,000 stems were exported, the ships being loaded at Castries and Vieux Fort. They formed 90% of the total exports, thus adding another one-crop economy to the Caribbean, though it is the only one to depend on bananas.

Coconuts are a relatively minor crop. Nearly two-thirds of them are produced on farms over 100 acres in size. Coconut oil is made in a factory at Soufrière, and St Lucia is the leading producer of this oil in the Lesser Antilles. It is exported to neighbouring islands and to Guyana. Fresh nuts and copra produced in areas not accessible to Soufrière are exported to Barbados for processing.

Cocoa is grown in most parts of the island and especially in the south-west. Small quantities of beans are shipped from Castries to Port of Spain, where they are exported to the United Kingdom and the Netherlands. High-yielding trees are being planted in order to increase output.

Citrus is not important and the output of limes is

decreasing, though some lime juice is still made in number of small factories.

Fruit and vegetables are grown everywhere, mostl for local consumption, but some are sent on sma boats to Barbados. Some rice is grown in the sout of the island. However, St Lucia produces only fraction of the food it needs, and the cost of importe food amounts to about half of the value of all th exports.

Lumber is cut for local use such as the making o furniture and shingles. Some charcoal is exporte to neighbouring islands, principally Barbados.

In order to increase the catch of fish a fishin school has been established at Vieux Fort. There is small export of lobsters, cured turtle flesh and turtl eggs.

TRADE, POPULATION AND COMMUNICATIONS

With no valuable mineral deposits, little estate agri culture and limited opportunities for employment St Lucia is a relatively poor country. Thus the export per head of population are about one-eighth of thos of Trinidad. Many St Lucians have emigrated i

:cent times, mainly to Curaçao, Aruba, Trinidad nd the United Kingdom.

Castries (15,000) and Soufrière (5,000) are the chief >wns. The centre of Castries, which is built on a nall alluvial flat, was largely destroyed by fire in 948 but was later rebuilt on modern lines. The town es beside one of the best and most sheltered har->urs in the West Indies and handles nearly all of the land's overseas trade. It is connected by road to all le major producing districts of the island.

Dominica

rea: 305 square miles; population (1965): about 7,000; density of population: 220 per square mile

HE LAND

hough many of the islands of the Lesser Antilles are iountainous, Dominica is undoubtedly the wildest nd most complex of them all. Indeed it is such a

mass of peaks, ridges and ravines that in proportion to area it is more rugged than Switzerland.

In the north the isolated massif of Morne au Diable (2,826 feet), a volcanic pile of intermediate age, forms a blunt peninsula ending in high northward-facing cliffs. There is little flat land in this region apart from that behind the town of Portsmouth, and this tends to be swampy.

In the centre of the island, separated from Morne au Diable by a low col, is a maturely eroded highland. Probably the remnants of an old plateau, its summits rise mostly to about 1,500 feet, though some ridges and isolated peaks rise to 2,000 feet. It is dissected by the gorges of many streams and by the relatively wide basin of the Layou River. On top of the plateau stand two young, inactive volcanoes. That in the south is the well-preserved cone of Morne Trois Pitons (4,672 feet), a mountain surmounted by three huge pitons similar in shape to the one shown on the front cover of this book. That in the north is Morne Diablotin (4,661 feet), from which high ridges radiate to the

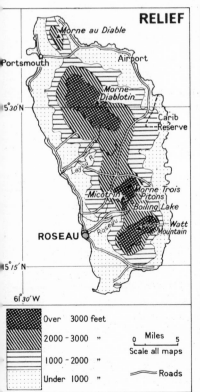

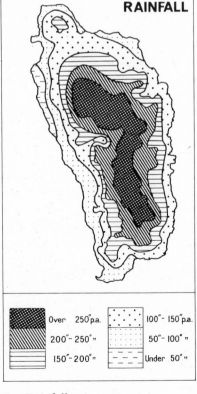

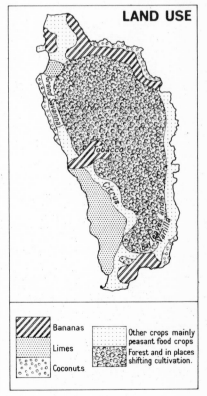

DOMINICA *8q. Relief.* *8r. Rainfall.* *8s. Land use.*

north, south and west—those in the west reaching almost to the coast. To the east, however, the descent is more gradual.

South of Morne Trois Pitons and Micotrin (4,006 feet) is the basin of the Roseau River which falls by a series of cataracts to the capital. Farther south still there is another complex volcanic mass of inter-mediate age, the highest peak of which, Watt Mountain, rises to 4,017 feet.

By world standards these mountains are not high, and in fact half the island lies below 1,000 feet. It is steepness of slope rather than altitude which gives Dominica its particular character and makes trans-port and agriculture so difficult. Remoteness in such a country is not a matter of distance but of difficulty of access. For instance, Roseau is only 20 miles in a direct line from the airport, but the journey by car on the narrow, winding road takes two to three hours.

Hardly any non-volcanic rocks have been found in Dominica, and the numerous fumaroles and hot streams indicate that there is still some subdued vol-canic activity there. So does the boiling lake in the Valley of Desolation, the turbulent surface of which is constantly being broken by jets of boiling water which may spurt up 10 feet and more. The steaming, sulphurous fumes emitted from the lake have killed much of the surrounding vegetation. Dead trees stand between occasional clumps of ferns, and coarse grass and dead logs cover much of the ground.

One of the volcanic rocks in the island—pumice— is extracted for export.

RAINFALL AND VEGETATION

Rainfall varies considerably from place to place, but in no district is it scanty. Over 80 % of the island has at least 100 inches a year, and even the sheltered lee-ward side of the island can expect rain on two days out of three. The mountainous interior gets 250 inches and more a year. June to October are the wettest months and February to May are the driest. The average monthly rainfall at Roseau, one of the driest places, is shown in diagram 8t.

About three-quarters of the island is forested, the highest proportion of forest in the West Indies. The high mountains are covered with elfin woodland, but below 3,000 feet this changes to tropical rain-forest which in Dominica is particularly luxuriant. On the leeward side below 1,000 feet there is a deciduous

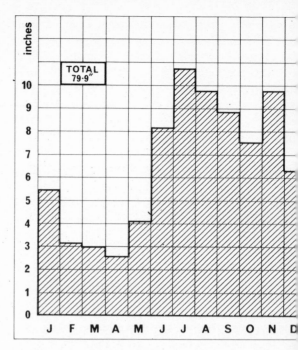

8t. Average monthly rainfall of Roseau. Describe it i the terms given below diagram 2h.

forest where trees shed their leaves towards the en of the least rainy months, and lower down beside th coast there is a narrow belt of thorn bush and scrub In one area close to the coast a recent lava flow ha given rise to such poor soil that it supports only grass

Though there is no organized lumber industry several varieties of timber, including white and re cedar, balata and mahogany are exported in smal quantities.

SETTLEMENT AND DEVELOPMENT

Because the rugged and forested interior of Dominic provided a natural refuge for the Caribs, European were unable to settle in Dominica for two centurie after its discovery. Then French settlers gained precarious foothold and began the cultivation o several crops, of which coffee became the most im portant. Though Dominica later came under Britis control, French influence is still to be seen in th place-names and heard in the patois.

While, as a result of disease, the output of coffe declined in the nineteenth century, that of suga

creased. However, the island never became a large
sugar producer, and in recent times the output has
almost ceased as there is not enough flat land to
grow the cane required to support a modern factory.
Cocoa became important for a time, the output
reaching its maximum about the beginning of this
century before West African competition caused a
decline. Limes were introduced about 1870 and,
because they could grow at elevations up to 1,500 feet
in higher more exposed areas than sugar or cocoa,
they soon became the mainstay of the economy. By
1920 lime products accounted for 80% of the total
exports, and for a time Dominica was the world's
leading producer. However, set-backs occurred in the
1930s, when a process was discovered in Europe for
manufacturing citric acid synthetically and when
diseases and hurricanes destroyed many trees. Most
of the lime plantations on the windward side of the
island were abandoned. By 1934 production had
fallen to 5% of that of 1922, but since then there has
been a slow and intermittent recovery.

It was at this time that several attempts were made
to establish a banana industry in Dominica, but they
were only temporarily successful. Now that ships call
regularly and roads have been built into some of the
more remote areas, cultivation is widespread and
bananas form the bulk of the exports. Thus Dominica
has had several periods of relative prosperity, each
based on a different crop.

Dominica is the only West Indian island to have
an area set aside for the Carib population. Several
hundred people, few of whom are of pure Carib
descent, live in a reserve some 3,000 acres in size
which stretches along 8 miles of the windward coast
and up into the ridges behind. They cultivate food
crops and catch fish. They have lost their old
language, but they have retained their traditional
craft of basket-making.

Because the development of the island was retarded
for so long and because so little of it was suited to
plantation agriculture, relatively few slaves were employed there. In consequence the population was never
large and the island is still considered by some to be
under-populated. It is true that Dominica is the only
Commonwealth Eastern Caribbean territory in which
a large proportion of the resources are still undisturbed, but it is hard to see how an increase of population could create any overall economic benefits.

*8u. Part of the Layou Valley. In what ways does a
landscape like this hinder development?*

AGRICULTURE

Only about 15% of the total area is under permanent
cultivation and most crops are confined to the river
valleys and alluvial flats.

The pre-war banana industry, brought to an end by
Panama disease and by the shipping shortage during
the war, has been revived and enlarged. The rise in
the exports of disease-resistant Lacatan bananas to
the United Kingdom can be seen from the following
table:

Year	1948	1952	1959
Stems	15,000	856,000	2,235,000
Percentage of total exports	1	26	68

In 1965 just over 4 million stems were exported and
their value was over 70% of the total.

Cultivation, which is mostly in the hands of
peasants, is widespread wherever there is lowland.
The biggest single banana-producing area is in the

north-east of the island where some of the fruit is grown on estates.

Dominica is the only one of the Eastern Caribbean territories where citrus fruits are of importance. Oranges and grapefruit are grown on estates, packed in a Government factory and exported to the United Kingdom in the same ships that carry the bananas. Some canned grapefruit segments are also exported.

Most of the limes are grown on estates in the south-west of the island below a height of 1,000 feet. A few are exported as fresh fruit to other West Indian islands, particularly those such as Antigua and Barbados with tourist industries, but the bulk of the crop is converted into lime products. The best fruit is selected and made into marmalade and preserves. The rest is crushed, and the resulting liquid is allowed to stand in large vats for two weeks or more, in which time it separates into two layers. Lime oil, which forms the surface layer, is separated from the underlying juice, steam-distilled and packed in four-gallon cans for export. It is used to flavour such things as soft drinks, confectionery and jellies.

The juice is strained, preserved by adding sulphur dioxide, and sent abroad in wooden casks. It is a very popular drink in countries with temperate climates where limes cannot be grown.

The demand is limited, however, and the output of limes in Dominica is much smaller than it was in the peak years before the war. In addition Dominica suffers competition from Mexico, the world's largest lime producer. Altogether, limes and their derivatives brought in 12% of foreign earnings in 1960.

Vanilla, long associated with Dominica, and made from the dried pods of a plant belonging to the orchid family, has almost gone out of production.

Cocoa is widely grown on small holdings in sheltered valleys. The output is small and most of it is consumed locally. In recent years new cuttings have been planted to replace some of the old trees. Coconuts are another subsidiary crop. They are sometimes interplanted with bananas. The bulk of the crop is made into soap and cooking oil. Bay oil is extracted from the leaves of bay trees (few of which have been deliberately planted) and exported, mainly to the United States. A small amount of sugar cane is grown to supply an old mill and rum distillery near Roseau. The supply is supplemented by small shipments of molasses from Montserrat.

Shifting cultivation is common among the peasant and extends into parts of the forest. Some fruit an vegetables have at times found a market oversea especially in the Bahamas.

OTHER COMMODITIES

The manufacture of straw goods, especially of floo mats, is the largest and most profitable local industry They are exported to a variety of countries, includin Barbados, Bermuda and the United States Virgi Islands. Other small industries include the making o cigarettes, pipe tobacco and cigars—from tobacc grown mostly in the Layou Valley—and the makin of soft drinks.

TOWNS AND COMMUNICATIONS

Roseau (11,000), the capital, is situated on a smal alluvial fan created by the Roseau River on th western coast. Only small ships can tie up at the jetty Larger ones stand off-shore where they are loade and unloaded by lighters. Portsmouth (2,000) has much better harbour but it has never been used ver much. Most of the other settlements have been buil on small, isolated alluvial flats and in all about 90 % of the population lives within a mile of the sea.

Set as it is between the French islands of Martiniqu and Guadeloupe, Dominica is isolated from the othe Commonwealth Eastern Caribbean territories. How ever, the ruggedness of the terrain has been a bigge handicap to development than has isolation, and th construction of roads has been the most difficul problem. Long stretches of the coastline are so rugge that there is no continuous coastal road. Until 195 Roseau and Portsmouth were connected only by track, and products had to be carried from one tow to the other by motor-launches and sailing-boats Even now that they are connected by the trans-insula road it is a fifty-mile journey, though the towns ar only 20 miles apart.

Because of the lack of communications and th high proportion of mountainous land, only small isolated parts of Dominica have been opened up fo commercial cultivation. Thus, in spite of the relativel low population density, there have been few opportu nities for employment and Dominicans took par in the recent emigration to Britain. They have als found employment at times on sugar and banan plantations in the neighbouring island of Guadeloupe

Montserrat

area: 39 square miles;[1] population (1965): about 13,000; density of population: 332 per square mile

THE LAND

Montserrat, which lies about midway between Guadeloupe and Nevis, is part of the inner volcanic arc of the Lesser Antilles. It consists of three main volcanic masses. That in the north is the oldest. It has been reduced by erosion to rounded hills, the highest of which—Silver Hill—rises to 1,285 feet. In contrast, in the south, the Soufrière Hills, which rise at their highest point to 3,002 feet, and South Soufrière, which reaches 2,505 feet, are recent steep-sided cones deeply incised by ravines. They contain fumaroles which emit sulphurous fumes that have killed off all but the most resistant vegetation in their vicinity. In general, however, their upper slopes are wooded and their lower, more gently sloping shoulders are in pasture and vegetable cultivation.

[1] The correct area was first discovered by a group of teachers who were attending a course organized in Montserrat by the University of the West Indies. Previously the figure was said to be 32½ square miles.

Between the Soufrière Hills and the Central Hills, which rise to 2,450 feet, there is a belt of lower land. This provides a route between the eastern and western coasts and contains some of the best cultivable land. In places, however, the volcanic material contains many boulders which add to the difficulties of cultivation.

DEVELOPMENT

During the period of slavery sugar estates occupied the best agricultural land, and in 1789 there were 6,000 acres under cane, a figure very similar to the total area under crops today. Then, in the recurrent financial crises of the second half of the nineteenth century, the land-owners resorted to share-cropping rather than sell their land. Whenever conditions improved they employed labourers again. Even so, the area under cane declined, sea-island cotton taking its place.

Unfortunately, if cotton is to grow well, the fields have to be kept free from weeds with the result that they are very susceptible to erosion. This is particularly evident in the north of the island.

MONTSERRAT *8v. Relief.*   *8w. Rainfall.*

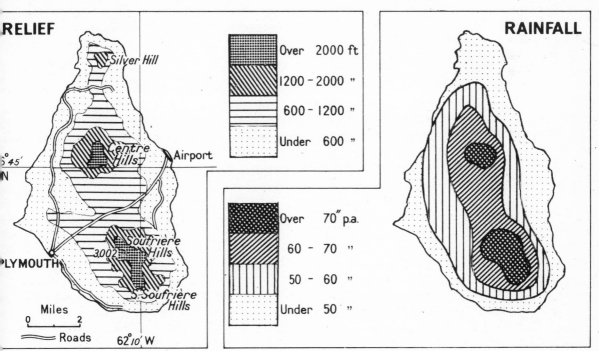

RAINFALL

The Central and Soufrière Hills rise high enough for their summits to be cool and wet. The east coast, exposed to the drying influence of the Trade winds, is somewhat drier than the west coast. The northern and to a lesser extent the southern parts of the island are drier still.

ECONOMY

Only some 6,000 acres—that is, a quarter of the island—are under cultivation. The chief crop, sea-island cotton, is grown on the lowlands and on slopes up to 500 feet. Now that share-cropping is dying out, about two-thirds of it is produced by small farmers on their own lands. It is processed in a large ginnery at Plymouth and two smaller ginneries elsewhere, and the lint is shipped to Britain. Cotton-seed cake and meal are also made, some being used locally as animal fodder and some being sold abroad.

Though the economy of the island is based on its cotton exports, these are supplemented by a variety of fruits and vegetables. Of the small quantities exported, tomatoes are the most important. Tomatoes have been sold at different times in Canada, Bermuda, Puerto Rico, Barbuda, St Thomas, Trinidad, Guyana and Florida, depending on the transport available. Transport is, in fact, the chief problem hindering further development. Like all small islands Montserrat does not buy or produce enough to attract much shipping, but until ships do call regularly there is no incentive to produce more. The same is true of bananas. At present those that are grown have to be sent to Dominica for re-export. Carrots, onions, pumpkins, tamarinds and mangoes have also been sold in various countries, but because of the lack of transport the chief market for these and other fruits and vegetables is the neighbouring island of Antigua and, to a lesser extent, St Kitts.

About 200 acres are under cane. Most of the crop is made into rum, a little of which is exported. Some is made into muscovado sugar for local consumption, but most of the sugar needed has to be imported. Though the cane area is expanding slowly the island is unlikely to export sugar again as there is not enough flat land to support a large factory and make a rebirth of the industry worth while.

Limes, introduced about the middle of the nineteenth century, were once an important export. Some are still grown, mostly by a few estates on the leeward side of the island, but because climatic conditions proved to be not particularly suitable and because trees have been damaged by hurricanes, diseases and insect pests, the output is declining and only a little lime oil is exported today.

The forests provide another resource. Some timber —chiefly cedar—and some shingles and charcoal are exported and there is a small boat-building industry. With over 5,000 cattle in the island there is usually no shortage of locally produced meat and milk. Some animals are occasionally exported to the French West Indies and Antigua.

Because exports are limited and because the prices of cotton, fruit and vegetables are never high, Montserrat is a poor island, even by Caribbean standards. Nearly half of the imports are paid for by remittances sent home by people who have emigrated to other countries. Emigration has been going on for years and Montserrat is the only West Indian island where it has caused a decline of population. Numbers fell by 2,000 between 1944 and 1960.

Plymouth (2,500) is the island's chief port. It lies on an open roadstead, but the water is deep enough to allow ships to come close to the shore. Roads extend some distance to the north and south of the town but none encircle the island.

Antigua

Area: 108 square miles; population (1965). about 60,000; density of population: 555 per square mile; area of dependencies (Barbuda and Redonda): 62½ square miles

THE LAND

Antigua is divided into three distinct structural regions:

(i) The area south-west of a line joining Five Island Harbour and Willoughby Bay consists of the eroded remnants of old volcanic mountains. These steep-sided hills rise to over 1,000 feet, the highest point Boggy Peak, reaching 1,319 feet.

(ii) Stretching from north-west to south-east across the centre of the island is a narrow clay lowland about 10 miles in length and 3 miles in width. It is flat or gently undulating country, rarely rising more than 50 feet above sea-level.

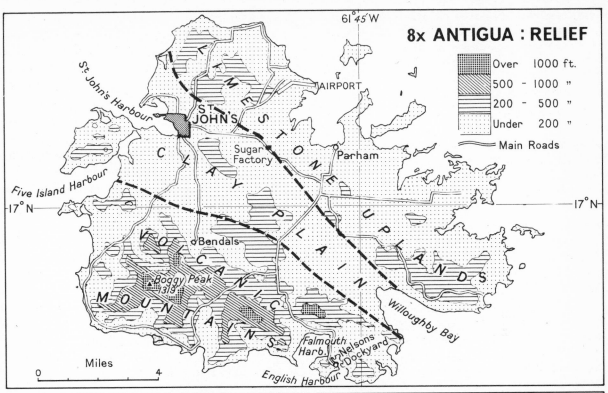

8x ANTIGUA : RELIEF

Over 1000 ft.
500 - 1000 "
200 - 500 "
Under 200 "
Main Roads

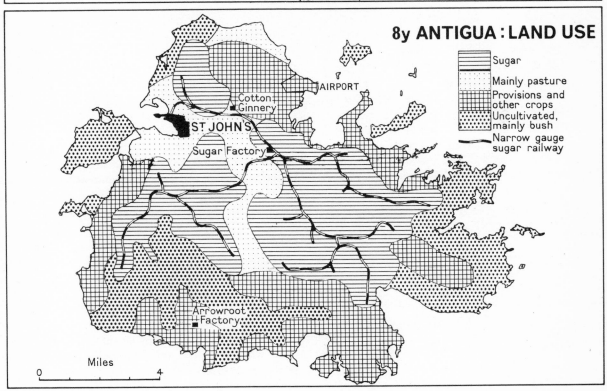

8y ANTIGUA : LAND USE

Sugar
Mainly pasture
Provisions and other crops
Uncultivated, mainly bush
Narrow gauge sugar railway

(iii) The northern part of Antigua is composed of a rolling limestone upland which rises fairly steeply from the central plain to heights of over 300 feet.

The coast is rugged and contains many bays, some of which have fine white sand beaches. Elsewhere, especially on the west coast, are small areas of mangrove swamp. The island is surrounded by coral reefs.

There is little mineral wealth in Antigua. Some barytes is worked and some clay is used to make pottery.

RAINFALL

Antigua is something like Barbados in being a low island with a low and uncertain rainfall, the average annual total being only 45 inches. The amount received, which varies considerably from year to year, largely determines the island's prosperity. For example, when in 1953 only 29 inches fell the output of cotton was reduced by half, and as the drought lasted well into 1954 the succeeding sugar crop suffered also. The cotton crop was only slightly larger and the island's exports in 1954 were worth less than half of those of the previous year. Going to the other extreme, Antigua can also experience floods, especially after hurricanes. Two hurricanes struck Antigua within three weeks in 1950 and did much damage.

As there are no streams of any size, a great deal of work has had to be done to provide water by drilling wells and by making ponds, reservoirs and catchments in the hills. Even so, in the dry months from December to April, and also during long droughts at other times, water shortage often becomes a severe problem.

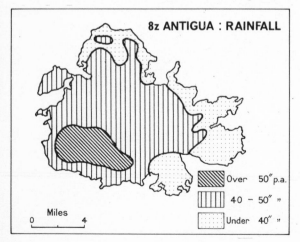

8z ANTIGUA : RAINFALL

Over 50″ p.a.

40 – 50″ ″

Under 40″ ″

Miles
0   4

DEVELOPMENT

The history of Antigua resembles that of Barbados and St Kitts in that there was a brief period when small holders cultivated tobacco, cotton and indigo, followed by nearly two centuries of slave-worked sugar estates. By the middle of the eighteenth century there were 35,000 slaves but only 2,500 white people in the island. The original forest cover had been largely removed to make way for cane, which was grown everywhere, even on top of the volcanic hills. Throughout this period there was so much specialization in this one industry that the inhabitants had to rely on imports for practically everything they needed, even for the bulk of the food supply. Thus the depressions which struck the British West Indian sugar industry in the nineteenth century were felt particularly severely in Antigua. The better-situated lowland estates struggled on in spite of greatly reduced profits, but marginal land went out of use altogether and in many places it has never been cultivated since. The remains of many old stone windmills that once crushed the cane are still to be seen in the hills standing amidst brush and thicket now cropped only by goats.

After their emancipation in 1838 many of the freed slaves wanted to obtain land of their own, but proprietors were reluctant to sell their estates despite their declining value. With no great development of peasant farming in the nineteenth century, with insufficient demand for wage labour, with the failure to find an alternative to cane, a shortage of locally produced foodstuffs, and a population density of 400 per square mile, the island inevitably entered a period of depression. This was made worse when the naval station at English Harbour was abandoned. Throughout the sailing-ship era it had been the chief British naval base in the Caribbean, but with the coming of steamships its strategic importance ended and it fell into decay. The recently restored ruins of the massive fortifications, shops and harbour works of Nelson's Dockyard are still to be seen. They are one of the island's tourist attractions.

In the present century the dependence on one export crop has been reduced by the introduction of sea-island cotton. In addition, though estates still own about half the total area of the island including much of the best land, the land shortage has been partly overcome by a successful land-settlement scheme.

8aa. English Harbour. In what direction was the camera pointing? What can you tell about past and present land use?

Abandoned properties have been purchased by the Government and split into small holdings which have been sold or rented to peasants. By 1957 more than 21,000 acres, or over a quarter of the total area of the island, had been disposed of in this way, though only about half of this was fit for cultivation. Other peasants rent small holdings from the estates. This system has not proved to be as satisfactory because many of the leases are drawn up on a year to year basis and the peasants have no security and therefore no incentive to improve their land.

The natural increase of population was offset for a long time by workers emigrating to Cuba, Panama, the United States, the banana plantations of Central America and the oil refineries of Aruba and Curaçao.

Thus the 1938 population of 34,000 was rather smaller than that 150 years earlier. Now, however, most of these outlets are closed and the population is increasing rapidly.

AGRICULTURE

The following approximate figures show the use to which land was put in Antigua in 1961.

Cultivated land	20,000 acres
Pasture land	5,100 acres
Land fit for cultivation but uncultivated	8,900 acres
Forest, scrub, built-up areas and other uncultivated land	31,000 acres

8bb. Antigua: Land use statistics.

105

Sugar cane is grown on most of the central plain where, except for the light rainfall, conditions are very suitable. A little is also grown in valleys in the volcanic hills and on the limestone uplands. About 60% of the cane is produced by estates, the highest yields being obtained by a group of estates which have amalgamated in order to improve their efficiency. This syndicate owns about half of the total cane acreage in the island.

The annual sugar export quota is 32,000 tons and a further 1,600 tons are needed for local consumption. As can be seen from Table 8cc this quantity has almost been reached in good years, though in bad ones the amount has fallen by more than half.

Year	1959	1960	1961	1962	1963	1964	1965
Tons	31,800	20,200	21,000	19,000	27,700	21,000	14,000

8cc. Antigua: Sugar production (tons).

8dd. Picking sea-island cotton in Antigua.

Antigua is one of several examples in the Caribbean where, in spite of a high population density, labour is in short supply in the cane fields. This has led to the mechanization of certain operations, and in 1965 70% of the estate canes and 20% of the small holders' canes were mechanically loaded. Cane cutting itself has not been mechanized and workers from St Lucia and St Vincent are helping to reap the crop. One large central factory in which the Government has a financial interest produces all the sugar and molasses. A light railway is used to transport cane to this factory and to take the products to St John's for export.

Though both the area and the output of sea-island cotton fluctuate considerably from year to year, depending on price and on rainfall, in general they are declining. The cotton is grown mainly on the limestone uplands in the north-east of the island and around English Harbour in the south. About 80% of the crop is grown on small farms. Planting begins in August, and harvesting takes place about five or six months later. To reduce the ravages of insect pests the bushes are then destroyed and those seeds that are retained for replanting are fumigated. The Government purchases the whole crop, which is then ginned in a large factory which also processes the crop from Carriacou in the Grenadines. The output of anything from a quarter of a million to one and a third million pounds of cotton is sold mainly to the United Kingdom. Because the price paid for sea-island cotton is so variable, Antigua has reduced its dependence on the cotton itself by making cotton-seed oil, meal, and cake for local consumption and export.

In 1957 the Government, after investigating the supply of water available in the volcanic hills, set up an arrowroot factory there and is encouraging peasants in the neighbourhood to grow the crop.

Antigua is not self-sufficient in foodstuffs and has to import corn, butter, salt fish, flour and rice from various sources and even some fruit and vegetables from Montserrat and Dominica.

Though the pasture land is not rich, cattle, pigs, sheep and goats are reared, mainly by peasants, in enough numbers to supply the island with about half of its requirements of animal products.

OTHER OCCUPATIONS

The forest found in Antigua today is not the original vegetation but a secondary growth of low trees and thickets growing on once-cleared land. Certain areas, especially steep hillsides, are maintained in this forest in order to conserve soil and water. Some trees are cut when they reach sufficient size to make lumber. Others are used to make charcoal, a little of which is exported.

Antigua has few industries other than those concerned with the processing of sugar and cotton. Locally made pottery is exported to Bermuda and the United States. Cornmeal, soap, light hardware articles, cigarettes, and salt are also made and leather tanning is carried on. There is a growing fishing industry, and frozen fish and lobsters are sent to Puerto Rico and St Kitts. The most recent development has been the building of a small oil refinery at St John's to supply petroleum products to ships as well as to the local market.

Antigua has taken advantage of the tourist attractions of its dry, sunny climate, its history, its white sand beaches and its easy accessibility from America. By 1967 over thirty hotels had been built to accommodate tourists, and there is, in addition, the Mill Reef Club, which is owned by a group of rich Americans who have bought several square miles of land in the east of the island and built their homes there. Tourism has been the big development of the 1960s and tourist earnings more than account for the gap between exports and imports. In consequence Antigua is better off than the rest of the Commonwealth Eastern Caribbean territories.

TOWN, COMMUNICATIONS AND TRADE

St John's (13,000), the capital and only town, lies at the western extremity of the central plain and has good road communications with the rest of the island. The airport is a few miles away to the north-east. In spite of the fact that its harbour is so shallow that ocean-going ships have to anchor up to 3 miles offshore and be loaded and unloaded by lighters, St John's handles all the trade.

In 1964 sugar and molasses made up 92% and cotton $5\frac{1}{2}$% of the exports (not including re-exports) which were worth $3,677,000. Seventy-four per cent of the exports went to the United Kingdom and 16% to other West Indian territories. In return $23,000,000 worth of goods were imported, an amount which had more than doubled in eight years largely to satisfy the needs of tourism. Twenty-six per cent of these came from the United Kingdom, 28% from the U.S.A. and 14% from other territories in the West Indies. Re-exports were worth nearly a million dollars, bringing the total export figure to $4,662,000.

Barbuda

Area: (including the lagoon): 62 square miles; population: about 1,200

Extending northwards from Antigua is a shallow, submarine bank on which—some 24 miles away—stands the island of Barbuda. Two-thirds of the island is a flat, monotonous plain only a few feet above sea-level, but in the east, a series of steep-sided, flat-topped coral terraces rise to just over 200 feet. There is a narrow belt of sand dunes round most of the coast. Everywhere the soil is shallow and much bare rock is exposed.

The rainfall is low, averaging 36 inches a year, and severe droughts are common. When rain does come, it often falls in heavy showers and the heavy, impermeable clay pan which lies beneath the thin layer of topsoil causes the plain to become waterlogged. In these conditions no large trees can grow, and the vegetation consists of low woodland and bush with patches of savanna in the south-east.

The island has never supported a large population, and today only about 1,200 people live there. Agriculture has never been developed on a large scale, and exports are small. Some sea-island cotton and coconuts are grown, and a variety of food crops, including peas, beans and groundnuts, is sent to Antigua for sale. The people also rear livestock, and make and sell charcoal. Lobsters are caught and sent to Antigua for sale. Some tourists visit the island to catch fish and shoot game.

Codrington, the only village, stands on the large, shallow lagoon on the western side of the island.

Redonda

About 25 miles south-west of Antigua is Redonda, a small volcanic island one mile long, a third of a mile wide and 1,000 feet high. It is of no economic significance.

St Kitts, Nevis and Anguilla

Total area: 139 square miles; population (1960): 56,500

St Kitts (St Christopher's)

Area: 68 square miles; population (1960): 38,300; density of population: 563 per square mile

SETTLEMENT AND DEVELOPMENT

The small party of colonists who landed in St Kitts in 1624 were the first British settlers in the West Indies. They gained a precarious foothold and a year later welcomed French help to drive the Caribs out of the island and defend it from Spanish attacks. St Kitts was then divided up between them, the British occupying the middle and the French the two ends of the island. With so much rivalry between the two nations this arrangement was not successful for long, and the island changed hands several times.

In the early days the settlers came as small holders to grow food crops for themselves, and tobacco, cotton, ginger and indigo for export. Population increased rapidly, the total for St Kitts and Nevis reaching 20,000 by 1640. This growth came to a halt around 1650 when sugar cane was introduced. Indeed, as the sugar estates grew in size so the population fell, many of the small holders preferring to emigrate rather than work for other people on land that had once been their own. Their place was taken by African slaves who increased in numbers from 3,000 in 1707 to 24,000 in 1774.

Things went well for the sugar planters until the slaves were emancipated in 1838 and labour was no longer free. In addition many of the liberated slaves left the estates altogether. Some settled on the foothills of the mountains as peasant farmers, but because most of the land was already owned by the estates and was not available to them, others emigrated to places such as Trinidad and Guyana where land was plentiful. In their place the planters brought in some indentured labourers from Madeira and India, but few of these people chose to remain in the island when their contracts expired. Nevertheless despite these and other problems the sugar industry struggled on and in 1911 a central sugar factory was built to improve the efficiency of production. Since then the industry has taken a new lease of life. Cultivation and manufacturing methods have improved to such an extent that the sugar export has risen from about 11,000 tons reaped from 7,500 acres in 1908, to about 50,000 tons reaped from a little over 13,000 acres in recent years.

THE LAND

St Kitts may be divided into two parts, the high main body of the island and the relatively low south-eastward-pointing peninsula.

The backbone of the main body of the island consists of three groups of young, rugged volcanic peaks, all of which rise to at least 2,800 feet. The youngest and highest group in the north-west is dominated by Mt Misery, 4,314 feet, a dormant volcano with some fumarole activity in its crater. Like Verchild's Mountain a little farther south, it contains a crater lake. The mountains, which rise steeply above 1,100 feet, are composed of volcanic ash, cinders and some boulders. Around their base is a more gently sloping apron of volcanic ash dissected by deep ravines called "ghauts" or "guts". There is a basalt lava flow ending at Black Rocks on the north-east coast. There is also some limestone in the island. It is quarried for local use at Brimstone Hill.

The older and lower southern peninsula ends in a triangular knot of volcanic peaks, the highest of which rises to 1,188 feet. This part of the island is undeveloped and is not served by a road.

RAINFALL AND VEGETATION

The land above 1,200 feet receives a heavy rainfall, probably over 90 inches a year. In heavy rains the streams running down the flanks of Mt Misery are liable to flood. The mountains are largely covered with palm brake and rain-forest which extends down to about 700 feet in places, though most of the land between 700 and 1,000 feet has been cleared for peasant cultivation.

The driest area is the southern peninsula, parts of which have as little as 40 inches a year and a dry season of 4 to 6 months. Most of it is covered with low shrubs and cacti, though in the flatter and less rocky places it has been cleared for pasture.

Most of the cane fields lie between the 50-inch and 70-inch isohyets, though some exist where the rainfall is over 70 inches.

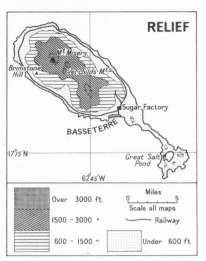

RELIEF

Mt Misery
Brimstone Hill
Verchilds Mts.
Sugar Factory
BASSETERRE
17°15'N
62°45'W
Great Salt Pond

Over 3000 ft
1500 - 3000 "
600 - 1500 "
Under 600 ft

Miles
0   5
Scale all maps
Railway

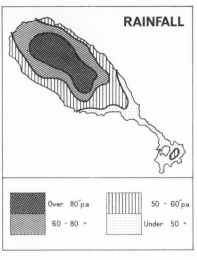

RAINFALL

Over 80" p.a
60 - 80 "
50 - 60" p.a.
Under 50 "

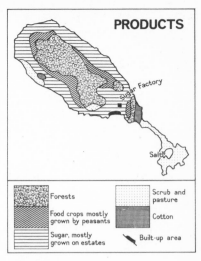

PRODUCTS

Sugar Factory
Salt

Forests
Food crops mostly grown by peasants
Sugar, mostly grown on estates
Scrub and pasture
Cotton
Built-up area

ST KITTS *8ee. Relief.*   *8ff. Rainfall.*   *8gg. Products.*

8hh. The town is Basseterre. Compare the landscape of this part of St Kitts with that of Nevis (Plate 8ll). Draw a sketch-map to show land use.

AGRICULTURE

From the time cane was first introduced St Kitts has been known as an island particularly suited to its growth. With careful manuring the fine volcanic ash has remained very productive. Today the sugar industry dominates the economy of the island, just as it does in Barbados. About 16,000 acres—that is, over a third of the total area—is under cane. Apart from about 500 acres all of this land is owned by forty-nine estates. No other island has maintained an estate economy to anything like this degree. All the canes are ground in a single central factory which maintains a narrow-gauge railway about 36 miles long to collect the cane and deliver the sugar to the wharf. The cane is grown in a belt round the main body of the island. It extends from the sea up the hillsides to a point where increasing gradients, absence of roads and distance from the railway make its cultivation uneconomic.

The sugar export quota of St Kitts is 40,900 tons, of which 29,500 is the negotiated price quota. About 5,000 tons are consumed locally each year. The average annual output from 1960 to 1965 was 44,000 tons and production has exceeded 50,000 tons in very good years. In addition between 1 and 2 million gallons of molasses are exported each year. Together sugar and molasses bring in over 90% of the foreign earnings, and St Kitts is more dependent on its sugar industry than any other island. Barbados and Antigua both have tourist industries that help to offset their dependence on sugar.

To escape from this dependence on one source of income, efforts have been made at various times at growing other crops. Experiments with cocoa, citrus, tobacco and rubber have all failed. Only sea-island cotton has been a partial success, but because of the uncertain market only 285 acres were planted in cotton in 1964. There is a privately owned ginnery in the island, which extracts a small quantity of cotton-seed oil and makes cotton-seed cake for animal feed.

Food crops are grown mainly by peasants between the upper limits of the cane fields and the lower edge of the forest. In addition cane fields which have yielded three or four ratoons are ploughed and planted in vegetables. However, the production of fruit and vegetables is less than the requirements and there is a considerable import, especially from Nevis.

TOWNS

Basseterre (16,000), the capital of the colony and the only town of any size, is situated on a bay on the south-east coast of St Kitts. Though it has no real harbour, the roadstead is sheltered and Basseterre is a busy port. In addition to handling the imports and exports of St Kitts it acts as a distributing centre for merchandise to neighbouring islands, including such non-Commonwealth ones as Saba, St Martin and St Eustatius. There is a regular motor-boat service to Charlestown, the chief town of Nevis.

Most of the other settlements in St Kitts are situated in the lower courses of the guts where they widen out a mile or so from the sea.

Nevis

Area: 36 square miles; population (1960): 12,700; density of population: 355 per square mile

DEVELOPMENT

For a long time the development of Nevis was very similar to that of St Kitts. There was an initial period of settlement by British small holders followed by a much longer period of slave-run sugar estates. The slave population rose from 4,000 to 10,000 between 1707 and 1774.

The divergence between the two islands came about when many of the Nevis sugar estates were unable to continue operating during the years of depression in the later nineteenth century. The rest followed during the drop in sugar prices after the First World War. The ruins of many of the old Great Houses, wind-mills and boiler works are still to be seen, but only a handful of properties, mostly in coconuts, are run on plantation lines today. Much of the land has reverted to scrub and at present only about 7,000 acres are cultivated out of a potential cultivable area of 23,000 acres. Estate-owners have been able to hold on to their land only by resorting to the share-cropping of cotton. Under this system the land-owner provides peasants with the cotton seed and takes a certain amount of the crop—usually a third—in place of rent. Share-cropping is still common in Nevis, though in recent years land has been made available to peasants by the Government, which has purchased some estates, subdivided them, and leased or given away the small holdings. On these lands attempts are being made to control soil erosion, which has become serious in some areas.

THE LAND

Nevis is an almost circular island with a diameter varying between 6½ and 8 miles. The centre is dominated by one symmetrical volcanic cone, Nevis Peak, which is 3,232 feet high. There are also some subsidiary peaks, including the Cone Mountains which rise to over 2,000 feet in height. Because the volcanic activity was more explosive than in St Kitts, the material contains many more stones and boulders. The fields, even those on the lowlands, have had to be cleared of great quantities of rocks before they could be cultivated.

RAINFALL

The rainfall varies from just under 40 inches a year on the sheltered south-western lowlands to over 90 inches at heights above 1,200 feet. Nevis Peak is commonly enveloped in cloud, especially during the afternoons.

AGRICULTURE

The chief export from Nevis is sea-island cotton. Mainly because of price fluctuations the area under cotton varies considerably from year to year, but in good years about 3,000 acres are planted, much more than in St Kitts. It is grown by peasants below the 700-foot contour, mainly on the drier, leeward side of the island. Their tiny holdings are usually rented for only a year at a time or are held on a share-cropping agreement, so there is little incentive for them to improve the land, and yields are low. The crop is sent to one large Government-owned ginnery for processing.

Sugar production, once greater than that of St Kitts, is very small today. About 1,000 acres of cane are cultivated by peasants—only a sixteenth of the area in St Kitts. Most of the cane is sent in lighters to the central factory in St Kitts for manufacture and export, but some is made locally into muscovado sugar and syrup for home consumption. Standards of cultivation are not high, the yield being only about a third of that of St Kitts. A large-scale revival of the sugar industry in Nevis, though desired by the people,

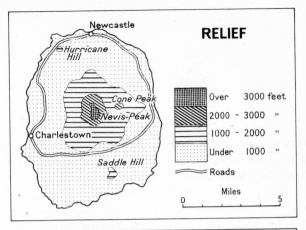

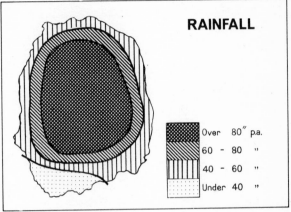

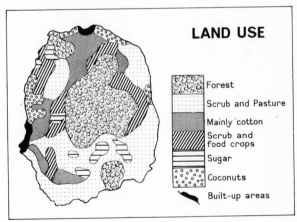

NEVIS 8ii. Relief. 8jj. Rainfall. 8kk. Land use.

8ll. Nevis. What can you tell about the geological history of the island from this picture?

is unlikely to take place because there is not enough flat land to support a large sugar factory.

Many different fruits and vegetables are grown, partly for local consumption but also for sale in the Basseterre market. Indeed Nevis has become the chief supplier of foodstuffs to the sugar-specializing island of St Kitts. There is a brisk daily trade across the 2-miles-wide channel that separates the two islands. An increase of this traffic would seem to be the most suitable development for the island.

There are about 4,000 acres of pasture in Nevis, much of which is of poor quality. On this land some 3,000 cattle are reared as well as other livestock and poultry. Some meat and live animals are sold in St Kitts.

OTHER OCCUPATIONS

Clay is dug at Newcastle and women make it into pots which are sent to Charlestown and Basseterre for sale. Some charcoal is made and sent there as well. There is a small boat-building industry, lighters being made for local use and for use in St Kitts and Anguilla.

Anguilla
Area: 35 square miles; population (1960): 5,500

Anguilla, which lies about 60 miles north of St Kitts, is some 16 miles long by 1½ to 4 miles wide. Like Barbuda it is a low-lying coral island, rising at its highest to just over 200 feet. Over about a third of the area the edges of the coral terraces are exposed as bare rock ribs. Over a larger area the soil is too thin for cultivation but supports scrub suitable for low-grade grazing. The remainder of the island has patches of quite fertile soil.

The rainfall of about 40 inches a year is too low to support forest and the island is largely covered with low bushes.

Just over a tenth of the island is under cultivation. Cotton, the chief export crop, is grown on 50 to 60 acres. There is one small ginnery where it is processed. Food crops, especially maize, sweet potatoes, pigeon peas and beans, are grown and some are exported to the neighbouring island of St Martin. Some cattle are kept and there is a small export of live animals and of hides and skins. Other exports are fish, lobsters and charcoal. The major commercial product is salt obtained from the evaporation of sea water in salt ponds.

However, the island has never been prosperous and today its livelihood rests largely on the money sent home by emigrants now living in Curaçao, Aruba, St Thomas, St Croix, the Greater Antilles and the United Kingdom, and from the earnings of its schooners and sloops.

QUESTIONS

1. What are the chief similarities and the chief differences between St Kitts and Nevis? How can they be explained?
2. Under the headings (a) relief, (b) climate, (c) occupations compare the islands of *either* Antigua and Dominica *or* Trinidad and Barbados. O.C.S.E.B. (O). 1966.

3. What are the chief factors making crop production difficult in the West Indian islands? To what extent can they be controlled by mankind? J.T.C. 1953.
4. The following table shows the number of stems of bananas exported from the West Indies to the United Kingdom in 1961 and 1965.

	1961	1965
Jamaica	10,244,000	15,143,000
St Lucia	3,466,000	6,336,000
Dominica	2,323,000	4,006,000
St Vincent	1,822,000	2,474,000
Grenada	932,000	1,623,000

(a) What percentage of the total came from St Lucia in each year?
(b) Draw a comparative diagram to show the exports from each territory in each year.

CHAPTER NINE

The French West Indies

Area: 1,113 square miles; population (1965): about 637,000; density of population: 572 per square mile

Martinique and Guadeloupe and its dependencies are all that remain of the former extensive French possessions in the West Indies, though they still retain a colony—French Guiana—in South America. The two islands were first occupied by the French in 1635. After an initial period when tobacco, cotton, and indigo were the chief crops, the islands became very prosperous with slave-grown sugar. There followed a decline in the late nineteenth century, but following the allocation of a sugar export quota and with the rise of banana exports, there has been considerable recovery. Most of the trade is with France.

Martinique, with an area of 425 square miles and a population of 290,000, lies midway between Dominica and St Lucia. Like those two islands Martinique is mountainous, its volcanic interior rising to over 3,000 feet in several places. Unlike them it contains an active volcano—Montagne Pelée, 4,700 feet high.

The last major eruption of Mt Pelée took place in 1902. Early in the year it began to emit smoke and there were occasional falls of ash. The eruptions increased in intensity, breaking through the sides of the mountain because the main vent was blocked by a solid plug of lava. In April an outburst of lava, mud and ash destroyed several sugar estates and killed a number of people. The climax came on the morning of May 8, 1902, when there was an explosion and a blazing mass of ash, lava and gas burst out of the southern face of the mountain. Burning, melting and smashing everything in its path it swept down at hurricane speed to overwhelm the town of St Pierre. When the cloud cleared a few minutes later, it revealed only the shattered relic of the town. Of the seventeen ships in the harbour only one escaped to tell the tale. "We have come from the gates of Hell," said the captain when he reached St Lucia. "You can inform the world that not a soul remains alive at St Pierre." Of the 30,000 or 40,000 inhabitants, one did survive —a prisoner protected by the thick walls of his cell.

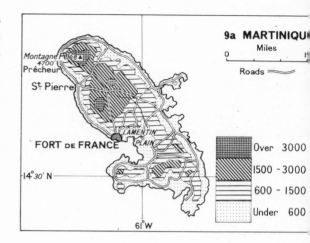

After this catastrophe activity continued on a more moderate scale for several months. In addition the lava plug blocking the main vent of the volcano was pushed slowly upwards until it projected several hundred feet above the rim of the crater. Exposed as it was to heavy rains and severe weathering, it was soon worn away.

Between 1929 and 1932 minor eruptions occurred again. St Pierre, which by this time had been rebuilt on a smaller scale, was untouched and no lives were lost, but for a time the road from St Pierre to Prêcheur was blocked by a lava flow and a layer of ash.

Mt Pelée is a young and slightly eroded cone. Elsewhere the mountains of Martinique are broken by deep valleys which allow roads to penetrate into the interior and to cross from coast to coast. There is not much flat land in the country, the largest expanse —the Lamentin Plain—being the chief cane-growing area in the island. There are twelve sugar factories and several more rum distilleries. In 1964 over 53,000 tons of sugar and nearly 2 million gallons of rum were exported, bringing in about a quarter and a sixth of the income respectively. The major export, bananas, made up about a half of the total. Other exports are coffee, cocoa, pineapples and pineapple slices. In addition food crops are grown for local consumption and in 1963 there were 45,000 cattle, 30,000 pigs and 27,000 sheep in the island, which provided most of the requirements of animal products.

Fort de France (95,000), the capital and chief commercial centre, lies on one of the biggest and best sheltered harbours in the Caribbean. It has a dry dock where ships can be repaired.

Guadeloupe (583 square miles, population 316,000) really consists of two islands divided by a narrow channel, the Rivière Salée, which is 4 miles long and up to 17 feet deep. The two parts are very different in character.

The western part, Basse-Terre, belongs to the volcanic arc of the Lesser Antilles and it is traversed by a forested mountain range which is almost inaccessible from the western side. Its highest peak, La Soufrière, 4,870 feet, last erupted in 1797 and 1836, when heavy showers of ash fell over the surrounding area. Today sulphurous smoke and steam rise from small vents in the crater and flames can be seen at times. Hot streams on the flanks of La Soufrière are another indication of its dormant vulcanicity.

In contrast, the eastern part of Guadeloupe is composed of the remains of a low limestone plateau, most of which has been worn down to a lowland from which steep-sided, wooded hills rise for 200 to 300 feet.

The higher, wetter part of Basse-Terre is particularly suited to tree crops such as coffee, cocoa and vanilla, whereas the lowlands to the east and south are in sugar cane and bananas. The farmland of Grande-Terre is mainly under cane with a small area in pineapples. In 1963 twelve factories produced 168,000 tons of sugar. In addition the island exported nearly 2 million gallons of rum and 108,000 tons of bananas. Together these brought in about 90% of the income.

Each part of the island has its own large town. Basse-Terre (25,000) is the capital, but because it lies on the less productive side of the island and because it has only an open roadstead to accommodate ships, it is smaller than Pointe-à-Pitre (80,000). Pointe-à-Pitre is the chief commercial centre and nearly all the imports and a large proportion of the exports are

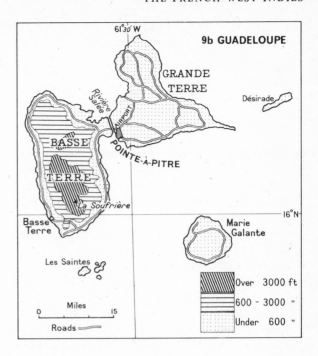

9b GUADELOUPE

loaded and unloaded there. Its harbour can dock ships of up to 20,000 tons.

The dependencies of Guadeloupe are Marie Galante, Désirade, Les Saintes, St Barthélemy, and St Martin—the northern part of a small island of which the rest belongs to the Netherlands. Together the dependencies have an area of about 105 square miles and a population of 26,000. Marie Galante is very similar in form to Grande-Terre. The chief products are sugar and cotton. Désirade is a long limestone block on which some cotton and maize are grown and some animals are raised. Les Saintes produce a small amount of sugar and coffee. A variety of crops, including bananas, tamarinds, cotton, corn and pineapples, are grown in small quantities on St Barthélemy. The chief occupation in St Martin is the growing of cotton. Fishing is a minor occupation on all the islands.

QUESTIONS
1. To what extent are Guadeloupe and Martinique similar to the Commonwealth Eastern Caribbean territories?
2. How far is it true to say of Guadeloupe that "all the typical aspects of Caribbean geography are represented there"?

115

CHAPTER TEN

The Netherlands Antilles

Area: 366 square miles; population (1963): 202,000; density of population: 552 per square mile

In addition to the mainland territory of Surinam in South America, the Netherlands owns six islands in the Caribbean. Three of them—Aruba, Bonaire and Curaçao—lie close to the shores of Venezuela (Map 17a). The other three—St Eustatius (Statia), Saba and St Maarten which together form the Netherlands Windward Islands—lie hundreds of miles away between St Kitts and the Virgin Islands (Map 11a).

The Dutch who occupied these islands in the seventeenth century were not seeking rich agricultural lands. One of the things they wanted was salt for their North Sea herring fisheries, and this they found in St Maarten and Bonaire. They also wanted bases from which they could trade with other Caribbean territories. These they established on Curaçao and Statia, which became two of the richest *entrepôts* in the region, handling large numbers of slaves and vast quantities of European goods. When Statia was captured by the British in 1781 and everything stored there was auctioned, the goods fetched about £4,000,000, even though prices in such circumstances were not at their best. Though the island was restored to the Dutch, it never recovered, and the population density has dwindled from about 2,500 per square mile to under 180 per square mile.

Curaçao, with an area of 173 square miles and a population of 131,000, is the largest and most important of the Netherlands Antilles. Its early prosperity waned in the nineteenth century when slavery was abolished and Caribbean trade declined. Its recovery came with the development of the Venezuelan oilfields. A shallow and shifting sand-bar across the mouth of the Gulf of Maracaibo allowed only vessels of shallow draught to gain access to the second largest oilfield in the world. It was therefore necessary to find a near-by port where the petroleum could be transhipped to ocean-going tankers, and this was the obvious place to build a refinery. Curaçao was chosen

because of the large, deep-water harbour at Willemstad. In 1917, the first year of its operation, 8,500 tons of refined products were exported. Since then, even though a channel has been dredged to allow tankers to enter the Gulf of Maracaibo, the refinery has grown in importance. In 1957 it employed 11,000 workers and exported nearly 18 million tons of refined products. Willemstad is now one of the busiest ports in the world; 85% of its exports are crude petroleum, 13% are refined products. The remaining 2% are varied. They include phosphates, sent mainly to the United States.

Aruba has had a similar history, the first of two oil refineries there dating from 1925. In that year the population was 9,500. By 1963 it had reached 59,000, a density of over 800 per square mile.

In the early days of the refineries many contract workers from the British West Indies found employment there. Today the employees are mostly Dutch West Indians. The remittances sent home by those who have gone to Curaçao and Aruba from Bonaire, St Maarten, Statia and Saba make a significant contribution to the income of those four islands.

Because Curaçao and Aruba offer passengers a wide variety of nearly duty-free goods, they are visited by many of the ships taking tourists on Caribbean cruises. Some hotels have been built for those who wish to stay on the islands for longer periods.

As both islands have little more than 20 inches of rain a year, a drought that usually lasts from February to September, and no streams or rivers, agriculture is of little importance. Even most of the drinking water has to be distilled from sea water in large factories.

Bonaire has not shared in this prosperity and its population has remained small—6,000 on 95 square miles. Agriculture is restricted by the lack of rain, and salt is no longer of value, but there is a small tourist trade and a local clothing industry.

116

10a. Looking from Willemstad over the oil refinery—the largest single industry in the West Indies. What factors account for the location of refineries in the world?

The three northern islands are much smaller and less populated. Indeed, *St Maarten* (16 square miles, population 2,000) is only the smaller southern portion of an island, the rest of which belongs to France. *Saba* (5 square miles) is a single, extinct volcanic cone, rising sharply from the sea to a height of nearly 3,000 feet. Most of the population of 1,200 live in the village of Bottom which lies in the old crater, 700 feet above sea-level, where the only flat land is to be found.

The chief occupations in the Netherlands Windward Islands are the growing of food crops, livestock rearing and fishing. There are plans to develop the small tourist industry there. In the days when Statia (8 square miles) was a commercial centre and sugar producer it had a population of over 20,000. Now the population is 1,400 and the chief export is pumice.

QUESTIONS

1. To what extent is it true to say that in the Netherlands Antilles the best use has been made of a naturally adverse environment?

2. The development of a new industry (such as petroleum refining in Aruba and Curaçao) is one example of a circumstance which results in an exceptionally rapid rise of population. What other examples can you think of in the West Indies? What social problems have arisen as a result of the population increase in these places?

117

CHAPTER ELEVEN

The Virgin Islands

The Virgin Islands are a group of seven main islands and a large number of islets and cays that lie to the east of Puerto Rico. Indeed, apart from St Croix, they are the summits of a submarine continuation of the range that forms the backbone of Puerto Rico. Some islands are owned by the United States, the rest by Britain.

The United States Virgin Islands

These were purchased by the United States from Denmark in 1917 mainly in order to control the Anegada Passage into the northern Caribbean. Their total area is 132 square miles and their population in 1964 was about 33,000—that is, 250 per square mile.

The largest islands are St Croix (82 square miles), St Thomas (28 square miles) and St John (20 square miles). The last two are of rugged build and rise to 1,700 feet and 1,300 feet respectively. St Croix is lower and there is a considerable area of flat land in the south.

Cane was once their chief crop, but the sugar industry dwindled in the later nineteenth century and had collapsed entirely by 1930. Since then, aided by the Virgin Islands Corporation—an American venture to develop the islands' resources—there has been a partial recovery in St Croix. In 1957 sugar production amounted to 14,700 tons. Other occupations are the cultivation of food crops, livestock rearing and the manufacture of rum and bay rum. Alumina is manufactured in St Croix from bauxite imported from Surinam and West Africa.

The exports are small and total only about a third of the imports. The trade deficit is more than paid for by the large number of American tourists who, attracted by the climate, the beaches, the free port shopping in Charlotte Amalie and the National Park in St John, visit the islands each year. There is a direct jet service to New York and Miami.

St Thomas, the chief tourist centre, supports about half the total population. St Croix has most of the remainder. The capital and chief town is Charlotte Amalie (13,000) on the south coast of St Thomas.

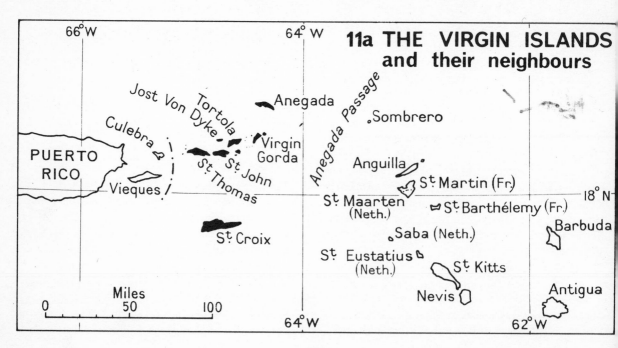

11a THE VIRGIN ISLANDS and their neighbours

The British Virgin Islands

The colony of the British Virgin Islands consists of Tortola (24 square miles; 6,200 people), Virgin Gorda (9 square miles), Anegada (13 square miles), Jost Van Dyke (4 square miles) and a number of small islets which bring the total area to about 60 square miles. Apart from Anegada, a limestone block nowhere over 30 feet in height, the largest islands are mountainous and rugged, Tortola rising to a maximum height of 1,780 feet and Virgin Gorda to 1,370 feet.

In the days of slavery the British Virgin Islands had prosperous sugar and cotton industries, but since then all the estates have been broken up. The land has been taken over for small-scale shifting cultivation and grazing, and soil erosion is widespread. No cotton and very little cane is grown there today and no sugar is manufactured, though there is a small export of rum, mainly to St Thomas.

The small patches of fertile soil that still remain on the hill-crests and in the valley-bottoms support a variety of food crops and fruits. Some of these, especially bananas and sweet potatoes, are sold to the United States Virgin Islands. Parts of the steeper hill-slopes and valley-sides are covered with scrub and secondary woodland which are of little use except for making charcoal and small boats. Most of the rest of the land is used for grazing, and livestock rearing has become the chief occupation. Most of the exports go to the United States Virgin Islands, though some cattle are also sent to Guadeloupe and Martinique. Fish caught off the coasts provide a small extra source of income. A little salt is made from evaporated sea water and some is exported. Tourism has so far not been developed to any great extent.

Life and living conditions in the colony today are dominated by the United States Virgin Islands. Not only do they purchase most of the exports, but the higher wages paid there, especially by the hotels, have attracted many workers from the British islands. It was estimated that in 1960 at least one-tenth of the colony's population of 8,000 had taken contract employment in the American islands, mainly in St Thomas. The result has been a decline of agriculture and of exports. This is shown by the fact that one of the chief sources of income is the sale of postage stamps to collectors.

QUESTION

In what ways would you expect the British and American Virgin Islands to develop in future?

CHAPTER TWELVE

The Bahamas

Area: about 4,375 square miles; population (1963): 131,000; density of population: 30 per square mile

(This chapter ends with a brief description of the Turks and Caicos Islands)

THE LAND

The Bahamas are an archipelago of about 700 islands and many more small cays and rocks which lie east of Florida and extend southwards almost as far as Hispaniola. Together they are almost as large as Jamaica. Nowhere more than 400 feet, and rarely more than 200 feet high, they stand, together with many coral reefs, on two shallow submarine banks in which passages deep enough for shipping are hard to find. The only deep water between the islands lies outside the barrier reef off the east coast of Andros. Americans based on Andros are using it as a test area to track atomic submarines. The islands themselves are composed mainly of calcareous sand, originally derived from marine shells, which was piled up into low ridges and rounded hills by wind action at a time when the whole shelf stood above the sea. Some rocks are still loose and sandy, but others have been consolidated by age and weathered in upland areas into typical karst scenery. The lowlands often contain brackish swamps, and in four islands— Grand Bahama, Abaco, Andros, and New Providence—there are "pine barrens", that is large stretches of pine forest.

The only mineral of commercial value is salt— extracted by solar evaporation of sea water in Great Inagua and Long Island. It is exported to the United States and Canada. Bat phosphate, taken from some of the innumerable caves in the islands, is used locally as a fertilizer.

RAINFALL

The rainfall of the Bahamas is not heavy, the annual total being between 40 and 60 inches in most places. Most falls in heavy showers between May and October. Because rain soaks quickly into the ground, the people are dependent on wells for most of their water supply. Water shortage is often a handicap to agriculture. For instance, farmers have to wait for the rains to set in before they can plant their crops, and so they can reap only one harvest a year. Much of the water supply in Nassau is obtained by de-salting sea water.

Differences in climate between the islands have not yet been recorded but as they stretch through 7° of latitude and vary in size from mere rocks to ten times the size of Barbados, it must be supposed that they exist. For instance, it is thought that the average annual rainfall for Inagua may be as low as 25 inches. Again, Andros is known to be a major source of thunderstorms which sometimes spread eastwards to affect New Providence.

POSITION

Though they lack valuable natural resources of their own, the Bahamas have been able, by virtue of their position, to share at times in the prosperity of other countries. In the seventeenth century, because they controlled the sailing-ship routes leading out of the Caribbean, they became the lair of many buccaneers and pirates. Since then their proximity to America has been more important. They prospered from the slave trade, from the contraband traffic to the continent during the American Civil War, and during the years of Prohibition in the 1920s from smuggling liquor into the United States. Today American tourists provide the largest source of income. In 1960 tourists outnumbered the population of the Bahamas by six times.

OCCUPATIONS

Forestry

Some of the islands, notably Andros (1,600 square miles), Grand Bahama (430 square miles) and Great Abaco (776 square miles), are extensively forested with pine trees. The sale of pulpwood is the major

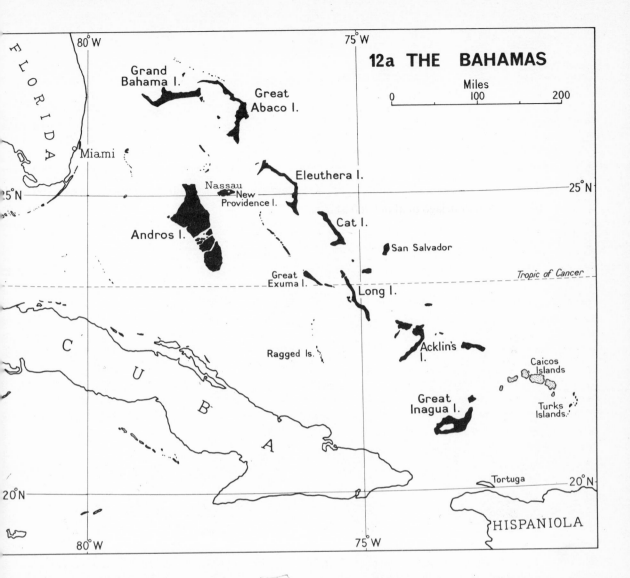

Miles

0   100   200

source of income on the first two of them. Pine lumber is also exported and, in all, forest products amount to 60% of the exports of the Bahamas (not including re-exports). Mahogany, lignum vitae and other broad-leaved trees are used locally, especially for boat-building for which Abaco, Andros, the Ragged Islands (45 square miles), and Harbour Island (1½ square miles), are especially well known.

Agriculture
Only for one short period of their history was plantation agriculture important in the Bahamas. This came about when some of the American colonists who had remained loyal to Britain during the American Revolution left the mainland with their slaves after the war in 1783 to settle in the Bahamas, notably on Harbour Island, Long Island and the Abaco Islands. There they established cotton plantations which flourished at first but quickly declined as the soil became exhausted and insect pests appeared. Production ceased altogether after the emancipation of the slaves in 1834.

Those Bahamian soils best suited to cultivation take up little more than 1% of the total area. They exist in pockets between low ridges where they are sheltered from the salt-laden sea air. Even here they are often thin and are therefore easily exhausted. Moreover, they drain very quickly. Unfortunately the

12b. Local and foreign enterprise in Nassau. The house is covered with plaques of firms which have been attracted to the Bahamas by the tax concessions granted there.

small farmers who carry on most of the agriculture today have not taken measures to maintain the fertility of the soil or conserve the moisture in it. Bush burning—the commonest way of clearing the land—dries up the soil, leaves it exposed to strong, drying winds, and reduces its humus content, thus lessening its power to retain moisture. Yields, naturally, are often low. Nevertheless small farmers grow food crops for their own needs and supply hotels with a great variety of tropical fruits and tropical and temperate vegetables. In recent years large farms have been established on several islands for the same purpose. Pineapples, tomatoes, okras and onions are grown in sufficient quantities to permit export to the United States and Canada. Some of the pineapples and tomatoes are canned. Coconuts and cucumbers

e grown mainly on Andros. A little sisal is culti-
ated to supply the local straw goods industry. Straw
oods are sold to tourists and are exported in bulk to
merica.

Small farmers also keep most of the livestock,
iefly on Exuma (80 square miles), and Long Island
30 square miles). Recently large livestock farms
ave been established on Eleuthera (158 square
iles). This island now produces most of the eggs
nd fresh milk and some of the meat consumed in the
otels in the island and in Nassau. Other products
re tomatoes, pineapples, citrus fruits and bananas.

There is also an American missile-tracking station
n Eleuthera.

Another factor retarding agricultural development
is the distance of some of the islands from Nassau, the
chief market. Motor-boats provide a freight service
to and from the important places, but foodstuffs and
livestock carried to Nassau by sailing-boats from the
more remote islands may take over a week on the
voyage and consequently arrive in poor condition.
Again, farming in many islands is handicapped by
the lack of good roads and harbour facilities on the
islands themselves.

Fishing

The shallow waters of the Bahamas are rich fishing
grounds. Fishing is a major occupation in Abaco,

2c. Cruise ships in Nassau harbour.

Grand Bahama, Harbour Island and St George's Cay
($\frac{1}{2}$ square mile). Most of the catch is consumed in
Nassau, but large quantities of frozen crayfish are
sent to Florida. Conchs are eaten locally and the
shells are sold as souvenirs to tourists. Other small
shells are painted and made into jewellery.

Before the war the Bahamas, especially Andros, had
a prosperous trade in sponges, but during the 1940s
the beds were so severely affected by disease that they
had to be closed to fishing for some years. Since their
reopening the export has been smaller than it used
to be.

TOURISTS

American tourists spend so much money in the
Bahamas that each year the colony is able to import
goods worth nearly twenty times the value of the
exports. The Atlantic Ocean on one side and the
50-mile-wide Gulf Stream (at a temperature of over
70° F.) on the other ensure that the islands have a
winter warmth unknown anywhere on the continent.
The mean temperature of the coldest month, January,
is 68° F., which may be compared with 60° F. at
Miami and 31° F. at New York. As winter is also the
dry season it is naturally the most popular time for
visitors, though others are attracted there in summer
when hotel rates are cheaper. They travel by air, liner
and yacht, the flight from New York taking only two
and a half hours and that from Florida between 30
and 50 minutes. There were eighteen flights a day to
Florida in the height of the season in 1963.

The Bahamas have made much of their advantages.
No passports or visas are required by American
visitors. In New Providence luxury hotels have been
built and there are many other tourist attractions,
including sports clubs, horse-racing and motor-
racing. Other major resort areas have been established in Grand Bahama, Eleuthera and Abaco, and
new ones are being opened every year. Everywhere
there is excellent sea-bathing from white or pink
sand beaches. There is good fishing and on some of
the out-islands there is bird-shooting and hunting as
well. With the construction of over twenty airstrips
and the establishment of regular air services, the out-
islands have become better known and more
developed.

INDUSTRY

As the Bahamas lack raw materials, cheap power,
skilled labour, transport facilities and local capital
for investment, one would not expect large-scale
industrial development to take place there. Yet at
Freeport on the southern side of Grand Bahama
Island over 200 square miles have been leased for
that very purpose. The overriding attraction is that
for ninety-nine years after 1955 all industries at
Freeport will be exempt from almost all forms of
taxation, including income tax and customs duties.
Cement is manufactured and fuel is supplied to ships
using the busy sea lanes on the east coast of America.
But in general the scheme has developed slowly, the
problem being that big firms—the type benefiting
most from tax exemption—are very difficult to move
from one part of the world to another.

Instead, there has been a major growth of tourism
at Lucaya on the western side of Freeport, where
there are luxury hotels, apartments, duty-free shops,
a casino, a golf course, and an international airport.
This development resulted in the population of
Grand Bahama rising from 8,500 in 1963 to about
21,000 in 1965, a year in which the number of tourists
was 155,000.

POPULATION

Twenty-two of the islands are peopled. Even among
these there are great contrasts, some—such as Andros,
Eleuthera, Grand Bahama, Long Island, Abaco, Cat
Island and Exuma—having several thousand inhabitants, others a mere handful. New Providence (60
square miles), with over 60% of the total in 1963, had
a population density of 1,360 per square mile. This is
due to the fact that Nassau, the capital and only large
town in the Bahamas, is situated there. Nassau is the
hub of the whole colony, having direct air communications with London, New York, Florida, Canada,
Jamaica and Bermuda. It is becoming a business and
financial centre because English and American concerns are opening branch offices there with a view to
avoiding taxation. Its harbour, which is protected
from the prevailing North-East Trade winds by
Paradise Island, is deep enough to take all but the
largest ocean-going ships.

12d. Caicos Island—View of Cockburn Harbour.

The Turks and Caicos Islands

These two neighbouring groups of islands form a part of the southern Bahamas, to which they were once associated politically. Their total area is 166 square miles and their population was 6,300 in 1962.

The manufacture of salt by evaporating sea water in specially built ponds has long been the main occupation of the inhabitants of Salt Cay in the Turks Islands and of Cockburn Harbour (known locally as East Harbour) in the Caicos Islands. Some salt is also collected on the capital, Grand Turk, but in recent years the establishment of an American missile base there has provided more profitable employment.

The annual production of salt is declining, about 22,000 tons being exported in 1962. Other exports include conchs, several million of which are sent each year from the Caicos Islands to Haiti, and frozen crayfish, which are sent to Miami.

The small rainfall—20 inches a year—is a handicap to agriculture. Small farmers grow some food crops and produce a little sisal for export.

QUESTIONS
1. To what extent is the economy of the Bahamas a result of their position?
2. "The biggest problem of the Bahamas, as of Guyana, is the problem of communications." Discuss this statement.
3. Imagine that a syndicate is planning to build a hotel on one of the Bahamas. What information would be needed before work could begin? To what extent would this information provide a geographical account of the island on which the hotel was to be located?

CHAPTER THIRTEEN

Cuba

Area: 44,164 square miles; population (1963): 7,200,000; density of population: 164 per square mile

THE LAND

Cuba is by far the largest island in the Caribbean; in fact, it is almost as large as all the other West Indian islands put together. It is over 700 miles long and from 25 to 100 miles in width.

Almost three-quarters of the land surface is a rolling plain. The only really high mountains occur in Oriente. In the south-west of this province the narrow, precipitous ranges of the Sierra Maestra rise steeply from the sea, reaching a maximum height of about 6,500 feet in Pico de Turquino. To the east lie the Baracoa Mountains, separated from the Sierra Maestra by the Nipe plateau.

Two other parts of Cuba are mountainous. Near the south coast of Las Villas province lie the Trinidad and Sancti Spiritus Mountains which rise above 3,000 feet in places. In the westernmost province of Pinar del Rio there is the Cordillera de Guaniguanico which contains several separate ranges including the many isolated limestone peaks of the Organos Mountains and the long ridges and valleys of the Rosario Mountains.

Few other places rise above 1,000 feet and so, in contrast to the other West Indian islands, it has been possible to construct a railway and a main road along the watershed from one end of the country to the other. Altogether there are 3,000 miles of railway in Cuba, not including the considerable mileage maintained by the sugar centrals.

MINERALS

Most of the mineral wealth is concentrated in the mountains of Oriente. Nickel is usually the most valuable export, followed by copper, manganese, chromium and iron. The small deposits of alluvial gold which so interested the Spaniards have long ago been worked out. In recent years there has been considerable prospecting for oil, which has resulted in the working of small deposits in the central parts of the country.

CLIMATE

Cuba, despite its elongated shape, has nevertheless a greater latitudinal extent than any other West Indian island. It also lies closer to the tropic of Cancer than any other major island and is therefore most affected by the north–south apparent movements of the sun. The average minimum and maximum temperatures are 71°F. and 82°F. respectively. At Havana temperatures below 45°F. have been recorded during a severe norther, while on very hot days the temperature may reach as much as 100°F.

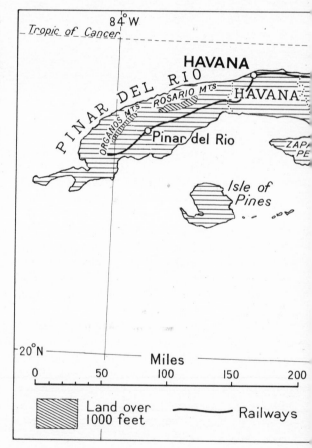

Rainfall is typical of the northern Caribbean in that about three-quarters of the total falls in the six months from May to October. Furthermore, in the province of Oriente there is the usual contrast between the rainy mountain summits and their northern slopes with 100 inches and more a year, and the dry rain-shadowed south with 30 inches and less. But in the central and western provinces the rainfall is much more evenly distributed than in the east, or for that matter than in Jamaica, Hispaniola and Puerto Rico. In part this is due to the lack of a mountain backbone to capture rain from the north or north-east winds which prevail for most of the year. However, it appears also that in summer the Trades, in being pulled towards the low-pressure system over the North American continent, blow at times across this part of Cuba from a south-easterly direction, as shown in Diagram 13b. In doing so they bring rain to the south coast—something which happens nowhere else in the Caribbean lands. The amount of rain that falls in west and central Cuba—about 50 inches a year—is rather too light to give the best results with sugar cane which is by far the most important crop. On the other hand it is not so light as to enforce the use of irrigation. Thus crop yields are satisfactory in good years, but when drought occurs, as it can at any time, the effect is serious. Western Cuba is also more subject to hurricanes than the east, which is protected by the Sierra Maestra and the near-by mountains of Hispaniola.

THE CROPS

Sugar

Though the output varies considerably from year to year, Cuba is usually the world's biggest producer and exporter of sugar. Certain special advantages account for this dominance.

(1) There are vast stretches of rich lowland where

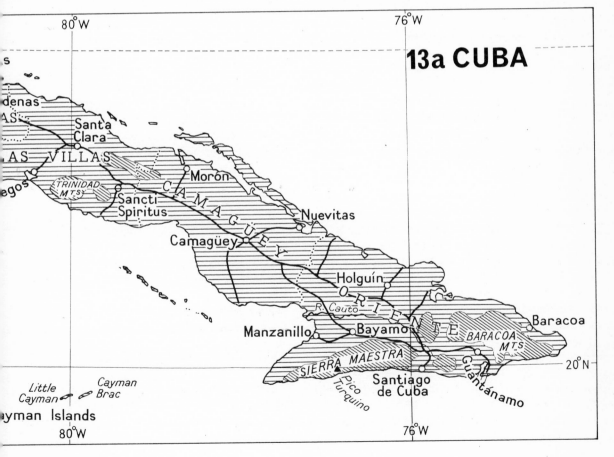

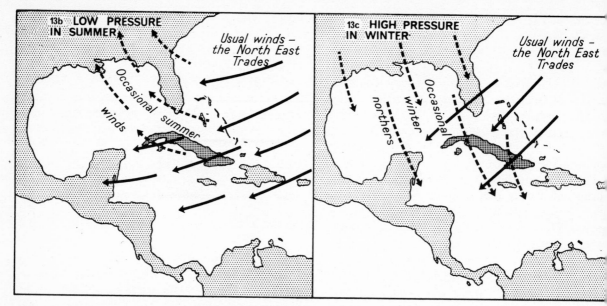

13b, 13c. Pressure systems over North America influence weather conditions in Cuba more than any other We. Indian island.

cane can be grown in sufficient quantities to supply many large central factories. Soils are so good in places that cane has been grown there for a hundred years without the application of any fertilizer.

(2) The long, narrow shape of Cuba and the numerous good harbours ensure short and inexpensive hauls to the ports. Thus, in spite of the island's size, sugar seldom has to be transported overland for more than 60 miles.

(3) As we have seen, rainfall is sufficient to enable farmers to do without expensive irrigation works, helping to keep down the cost of production.

(4) The great period of sugar expansion came at a later date in Cuba than in the rest of the Caribbean. Virgin lands were being opened up at a time when Jamaican soils, for example, were wellnigh exhausted. To this day cane can be ratooned in Cuba longer than anywhere else in the world. This late start also enabled Cuban planters to use techniques of cultivation and manufacture that had been developed over a long period and at considerable expense elsewhere. For example, most factories in Cuba were able to use steam power from the outset. Furthermore, before the end of the nineteenth century all new estates were laid out with narrow-gauge railways to carry the canes quickly and cheaply to the centrals. Thus

larger—and more efficient—factories could be buil in Cuba than in other Caribbean countries.

The expansion of the Cuban sugar industry too place in several distinct stages. The first began whe Haiti went out of production after the slave revol there in 1791 and Cuban farmers were encouraged to grow more cane to fill the gap in European supplie at a time when the price of sugar was very high Expansion continued throughout the nineteent century as Cuba benefited from the combined effect of the rise of sugar consumption in industria Europe and America, the relative cheapness of he slave-grown sugar[1] and the change in British economic policy from colonial protection to free trade. Production rose to over 1 million tons in 1894. Then it declined sharply for a few years during the civil war when Cuba—with American assistance—gained her independence from Spain.

The second period of expansion began after that war, when the American government granted Cuban sugar a preferential tariff so that it faced little competition even from the subsidized European beet sugar which flooded the other markets at that time. Encouraged by this, American investors poured money into developing Cuban sugar. Everything was

[1] Slavery was not abolished in Cuba until 1886.

done on the largest scale and in the most efficient way. Cheap labour was imported from Haiti and Jamaica to clear the land, construct the railways and buildings, and reap the harvests. More and more sugar was produced by factories ever decreasing in number and increasing in size. Peasant holdings were assimilated by the huge new estates, their former owners becoming employees. For them, and indeed for the country as a whole, economic dependence accompanied political independence.

The third and biggest phase of expansion came during and shortly after the First World War, when demand for sugar was greater than ever before. This brought another flood of investment, known as the "Dance of the Millions", and a new wave of immigration, including many refugees from Europe. But prosperity ended a few years later, when overproduction and the world economic slump combined to send sugar prices crashing. Many mills suspended operations, and many investors were ruined. The value of Cuban exports fell from $794 million in 1920 to under $83 million in 1933. The depression was widespread and very severe because the whole economy of Cuba had become geared to sugar and there was nothing else to take its place.

Production increased only when the United States entered the Second World War and agreed to buy all the sugar Cuba could supply. Following the pattern set thirty years before, output continued to rise even after the war was over. It reached a record of $7\frac{1}{4}$ million tons in 1952. This was more than could be sold, and again the country was threatened with

13d. *Loading cane in Cuba. Some of this machinery was made in Russia.*

13e. *In Cuba the problem of finding sugar workers is being met to some extent by townspeople who spend 15 days a year in the cane fields. Is there a similar labour problem in the territory where you live? How is it being met there?*

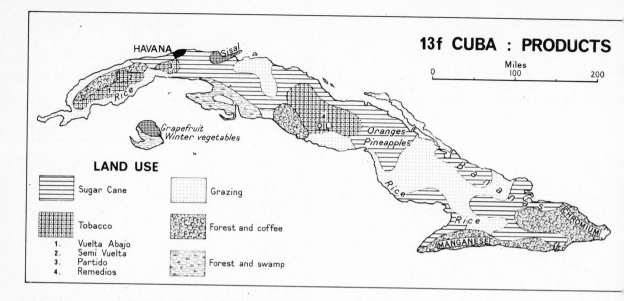

13f CUBA : PROGRAMS

LAND USE

Sugar Cane — Grazing

Tobacco — Forest and coffee
1. Vuelta Abajo
2. Semi Vuelta
3. Partido — Forest and swamp
4. Remedios

disaster. Measures were therefore taken by the Government to limit output from then on at about 5 million tons a year.

Though several hundred million gallons of molasses and large quantities of industrial alcohol and rum were also produced the resulting situation was equivalent to economic stagnation, and apart from the rise of tourism in the 1950s the Cuban economy was no better off than it had been between the wars. New crops were not planted because the sugar and cattle estates which held, but did not use, large areas of good agricultural land showed no desire to utilize their resources of capital and skill to diversify agriculture. Population was rising, and many people who could have been farmers were unemployed at a time when large quantities of American foodstuffs were being imported. New industries were not developed because trade agreements with the United States opened Cuba to American manufactures, against which Cuba could not compete. The resulting poverty and lack of prospects for the bulk of the population were the mainspring of the Revolution of 1959.

After the Revolution private farms were no longer allowed to exceed 3,000 acres and most were limited to 1,000 acres. A lot of the surplus land released was cut up into small holdings (each of which was over 66 acres in size—the "vital minimum" for a family of five) and distributed to the people. Other large properties were converted into State farms, and

it is on these that the bulk of the sugar is grown

Up to 1960 the chief market for Cuban sugar was the United States, which, after fulfilling its obligation to purchase specified amounts from Hawaii, the Philippines and Puerto Rico, gave Cuba priority over all other countries, buying about three million tons of raw sugar a year and imposing a specially low tariff on it. When the United States stopped buying Cuban sugar, new markets were quickly found in Russia and China, and Cuba is trading increasingly with these and other Communist countries. The crop is processed in 160 State-owned centrals scattered throughout the lowlands but with the greatest concentration in the two eastern provinces where over half the cane is grown.

Though attempts are being made to diversify agriculture, Cuba has been forced to continue to export sugar so as to obtain currency to pay for essential imports. The dominance of the sugar industry over all others in Cuba is illustrated by the following facts: that cane occupies over half of the cultivated land; that nearly a third of the island's workers are employed in the industry during the "zafra" (the harvest); and that sugar and its by-products make up 90% of the island's exports. So many people depend in one way or another on the industry that the out-of-crop period between June and December is known by the expressive name "tiempo muerto"—the dead season.

13g. Tobacco needs careful attention if it is to grow well.

Tobacco

If quantity makes Cuba famous for sugar, quality makes the country famous for tobacco. This crop occupies only 3% of the cultivated land but is the second most valuable export. Cuban leaf is so fine that it is exported to many countries, where it is used for blending. More famous than the leaf are Cuban "Havanas"—the best cigars in the world.

Cultivation is in the hands of small farmers because the crop needs much skill and attention throughout its growing season. The seedlings are planted in nurseries in August and September and transplanted to the carefully fertilized fields in October and November, after which the leaves require only 60 days to mature. Those plants to be used as the outer wrapping for cigars are shaded by cheese-cloth spread over a framework of poles. After the leaves are harvested they are hung to dry in large thatched curing sheds for 1 to 3 months. Then they are packed in small bundles and fermented for another month. After that they are sorted and graded and packed into large bales, by which time they are ready for the market.

Export tobacco is grown in the four regions shown on Map 13f, where the soil is specially suitable. The most famous district is the Vuelta Abajo in the province of Pinar del Rio, which produces a cigar of incomparable flavour. Blending tobacco is produced in the near-by Semi Vuelta district and around Remedios, while the Partido area south-west of Havana specializes in cigar wrappers. The bulk of the tobacco for the local cigarette industry is grown in Oriente.

Coffee

Coffee, like tobacco, is grown by small farmers. For most of the year the trees can be easily tended by the family, but from September to December, the busy harvesting season, help is obtained from gangs of migrant labourers who move from one farm to another. As coffee grows best above 1,000 feet, it is not found in the cane and tobacco areas. Ninety per cent comes from South and East Oriente, and most of the rest from the Trinidad Mountains. Cuba grows enough coffee to satisfy a large local market and in some years to send a little abroad.

Other Crops

Cocoa is grown in some of the hilly parts of Oriente, mostly by small farmers. Output is small and very little is exported. Citrus fruits for local consumption are grown in most parts of Cuba. Grapefruit is exported from the Isle of Pines. Bananas are produced on the northward-facing slopes and the narrow coastal plain of Oriente where rain is plentiful throughout the year. Small farmers are being encouraged to increase their output of food crops and to plant cotton, soya beans and groundnuts in order to reduce imports of textiles and edible oils. Until this is achieved, Cuba is having to ration certain foodstuffs.

LIVESTOCK

For many years after the discovery of the island Cuba was taken up by huge cattle ranches established on the savannas. The livestock industry declined as sugar became supreme and suffered especially in the revolutionary battles at the end of the nineteenth century, when many animals were slaughtered. Later it recovered and there are now over four million cattle in the island. The largest single area of grassland lies in the provinces of Camaguey and, to a lesser extent, Las Villas. Butter, cheese and canned milk are made in the towns of Havana, Sancti Spiritus and Bayamo. Cuba is almost self-sufficient in animal products.

FORESTS

The forests which originally covered about 60% of the island have been reduced, particularly in this century, to between 10% and 15% of the total area. Most of that which remains is in inaccessible mountain country, especially in the Sierra Maestra, which is the last remaining area of large stands of pine trees. The result of the reckless clearing of forest that has accompanied the spread of sugar cane is that Cuba can now supply only 20% of its timber requirements.

THE PEOPLE

While Cuba was a Spanish colony, its economic backwardness retarded settlement and until the end of the nineteenth century the population was relatively small. The rapid development that then took place attracted many immigrants. For instance, half a million people entered the island between 1907 and 1919. Of these more than 60% came from Spain. This immigration, together with the reduction of the death-rate brought about by improved health services, has resulted in an increase from about $1\frac{1}{2}$ million to over 7 million people in the past sixty years. Because so much immigration has taken place since the last slaves were brought from Africa, about 30% of the population is white, a much higher proportion than in Haiti and the Commonwealth Caribbean territories. Puerto Rico, which was also under-developed in the slave days, has an even higher proportion of white people than Cuba.

The settlement pattern is considerably influenced by the sugar industry, not only because it employs so many people, but also because it enforces a marked contrast between the busy villages and towns and the empty expanses of cane fields surrounding them. Some towns have grown very large in handling the trade and catering for the needs of so many agricultural wage-earners. At least a dozen contain over 100,000 people. On the other hand towns and villages are fewer and smaller in the subsistence-farming areas where population is spread more evenly throughout the countryside and where there is less money to be spent. Settlement is sparse in the grasslands and sparser still in the mountains.

THE TOWNS

The capital Havana, with over $1\frac{1}{4}$ million people, is by far the largest city in Cuba, and, for that matter, in the West Indies. Its importance dates back to the early colonial days when it was the pivot of the Spanish convoy system in the Caribbean. Massive fortresses—still to be seen—were constructed to protect the narrow entrance to the spacious harbour where treasure fleets from Cartagena, Panama and Vera Cruz gathered to refit and revictual before setting out on the final stage of their voyage home. Moreover, because of its proximity to the Spanish possessions of Florida and Mexico, Havana became, as a historian wrote in 1634, "the key to the New World, and the fortress of the Indies".

Since then each new development in Cuba has added to the size and importance of the city. Today the old Spanish centre is surrounded in turn by the busy commercial quarter where there are many tall, American-type buildings, and by the rapidly expanding residential suburbs. Havana has remained the biggest port, handling some 75% of the imports and 25% of the exports. There are railways and main roads connecting it to all parts of the island. It is also the chief banking, shopping, industrial and university centre. Among the many industries are oil refining, the manufacture of cigars and cigarettes, drinks, canned goods, textiles, clothing, shoes, soap, matches, paint and cement.

Most of the other ports of Cuba are engaged in the manufacture and export of sugar. Matanzas has many other industries as well, notably the manufacture of rayon, shoes, ammonia and metal goods. Cardenas, not far away, manufactures sugar and alcohol and processes rice and sisal. Baracoa exports bananas. Santiago de Cuba exports sugar, coffee and timber. Somewhat to the east is the United States naval base at Guantánamo Bay. On the south coast Cienfuegos and Manzanillo are the largest ports.

TRADE

As a result of the Revolution trade with the United States has ceased and Cuba has had to make a complete switch in the direction of its exports. This is shown by the following figures, given in millions of pesos.

	Russia	Communist China	Eastern Europe
1959	13	0	1
1962	301	92	65

Most of the imports come from these same countries, but some are bought elsewhere (for example, from Britain). They are paid for by sales of sugar on the world market.

The Isle of Pines

The Isle of Pines, with an area of about 830 square miles, lies some 30 to 40 miles south of the province of Pinar del Rio, from which it is separated by the shallow Gulf of Batabano. The low-lying southern part of the island is swampy. The somewhat higher northern section is made of limestone, metamorphosed in places to marble, which is quarried to some extent. The north was once well forested, but much timber has been cut and clearings have been made in order to cultivate grapefruit.

QUESTIONS

1. (a) Describe the cane-sugar industry of the Caribbean area using the following headings; (i) the general conditions favouring production; (ii) methods of cultivating; (iii) methods of treatment to produce sugar and its by-products for export. (b) Locate the chief areas of sugar-cane production in Cuba and name five other parts of the Caribbean which are important producers. C.S.C. 1956.

2. What advantages does Cuba possess over the other West Indian islands? How has she made use of them? J.C.E. 1956.

3. From Cuba and Trinidad select any *two* large towns. (a) Draw labelled sketch-maps to show their position. (b) Describe the growth and importance of *one* of them. L.G.C.E.(O). 1965.

4. With the aid of a sketch-map and by reference to specific commodities, explain why Cuba's foreign trade per head of population is much higher than that of any other West Indian island. O.C.S.E.B. (O). 1966.

CHAPTER FOURTEEN

Hispaniola

Area: 29,525 square miles; population (1963): 7,780,000

DEVELOPMENT

On his first voyage to the West Indies in 1492 Columbus, after discovering the Bahamas and Cuba, sailed across the Windward Passage and was following the north coast of Hispaniola when his biggest ship was wrecked on a reef. Some of the crew had to be left behind when Columbus returned to Spain. This, the first Spanish settlement in the West Indies, did not last long, being destroyed by the Arawaks before Columbus revisited Hispaniola two years later. The spot was abandoned and a new settlement was built near by. Soon afterwards the town of Santo Domingo was founded on the southern side of the island. It became for a time the base of Spanish operations in the Caribbean.

However, the island and its capital did not retain their prominence for long. Hispaniola lacked an abundance of precious metals, and Spanish interest shifted to the Central and South American mainland where they were plentiful. The island became depopulated as the Arawaks rapidly died out and few Spaniards went to settle there. Even so, the more favourable areas such as the Southern Plain and the Cibao Valley were developed into huge Spanish-owned, slave-run estates. Because of the sparse settlement, ranching rather than cultivation became the chief occupation. Beef and pork were provided for ships' crews, and live horses were exported to the mainland. The more remote parts of the country fell into foreign hands. Tortuga became the chief stronghold of French buccaneers, who also settled in unfrequented parts of Hispaniola itself, especially on the west coast. There they slaughtered wild cattle descended from those that had escaped from Spanish ranches, smoked the meat and sold it to buccaneer ships. Gradually French influence became so strong that in 1697 Spain was forced to cede the western part of Hispaniola to France. It became the colony of St Domingue.

During the era of French rule buccaneering ended and St Domingue became a rich agricultural country. Indigo and tobacco were among the first crops to be exported in quantity, but sugar soon took precedence. Sugar estates were established along the north coast where little irrigation was needed and in the Artibonite Valley and the Léogane, Cayes, and Cul de Sac Plains, where irrigation was essential. Coffee plantations thrived in the hills, and cotton was grown on the Arbre Plain and on those parts of the Cul de Sac Plain and Artibonite Valley which were too hot for coffee and too dry for cane.

HAITI AND THE DOMINICAN REPUBLIC

At the height of its prosperity St Domingue was the richest country in the tropics. But this ended in 1791 when the slaves, who made up 80% of the population, rebelled and killed the French colonists or drove them out of the country. A new republic was created. It was named *Haiti* after the original Arawak name for the country, meaning "land of mountains". An English attempt to conquer the country failed when thousands of soldiers died of yellow fever. A French expedition sent by Napoleon to recapture the country also failed.

During the thirteen years of fighting many of the estates and irrigation works were destroyed and exports virtually ceased. The country was left poverty-stricken and very backward. Some other reasons explaining this state of affairs were:

(i) Haiti had to pay a large sum of money to France in order to obtain recognition of its independence.

(ii) Much money was also spent in retaining a large army and in erecting fortifications against foreign attack. For instance, the Citadel, a colossal fortress built on a high hill near Cap Haïtien, was capable of housing 2,000 men. It still contains 300 cannons weighing over a ton each, none of which ever fired a shot. Today the Citadel is a big tourist

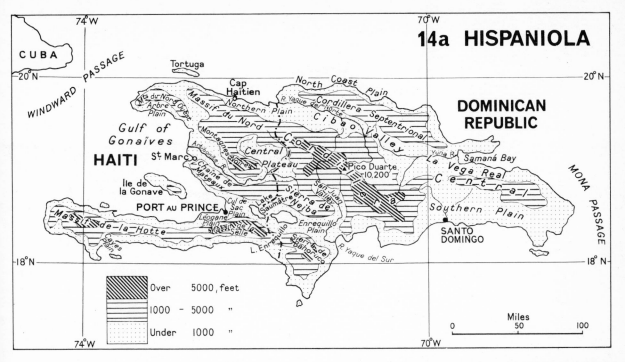

14a HISPANIOLA

CUBA

WINDWARD PASSAGE

Tortuga

Cap Haïtien

North Coast Plain

DOMINICAN REPUBLIC

Mts. du Nord Ouest

Acbre

Northern Plain

Massif du Nord

R. Yaque del Norte

Cordillera Septentrional

Gulf of Gonaïves

Cibao Valley

HAITI

St Marc

Montagnes Noires

Artibonite R.

Central Plateau

Chaîne de Matheux

Cordillera

Yuna R.

Samaná Bay

La Vega Real

Île de la Gonave

San Juan Valley

Pico Duarte 10,200

Central

PORT au PRINCE

Cul de Sac Plain

Lake Saumâtre

Sierra de Neiba

Léogane Plain

Massif de la Selle

Southern Plain

SANTO DOMINGO

Massif de la Hotte

Bates Plain

Enrequillo

L. Enrequillo

Enrequillo Plain

Sierra de Bahoruco

R. Yaque del Sur

MONA PASSAGE

Over 5000 feet
1000 - 5000 "
Under 1000 "

Miles
0   50   100

attraction, tourism in Haiti being second to coffee as a money earner.

(iii) The hostility of slave-owning countries to the newly freed nation expressed itself in an unwillingness to trade with Haiti.

(iv) To keep them going, estates needed skilled management backed with considerable capital reserves. The lack of a managerial class after the revolution, the backwardness of the Negroes, who had been held in subjection so long, and the discouragement of foreign investors prevented the estates from operating. Instead they were split up into small farms, each owner producing his own crops in his own way. Sugar suffered most. Thus in 1825 virtually none was exported. Coffee exports were about half of what they had been thirty years previously.

Since 1791 Haitian history has been one of temporary dictatorships interrupted by bloody revolutions. In 1957, for instance, there were six governments in as many months. This has handicapped agricultural and industrial enterprise.

The *Dominican Republic*, finally created in 1865, has also had a disturbed history. Both countries were occupied by American troops for a time, Haiti from 1915 to 1934 and the Dominican Republic from 1916 to 1924. This brought a few years of political stability

and honest administration, and there was a marked improvement in communications and health services. Since then the differences between the two countries have become more apparent. The Dominican Republic, with more favourable geographic conditions and with a single dictatorship between 1930 and 1961 made much more rapid economic progress than Haiti.

THE LAND

Hispaniola is the second largest Caribbean island and the most mountainous of all. It is here that the two great axes of folding which can be traced from Central America—one through Cuba and the other through Jamaica—merge in one island. They form a series of roughly parallel east–west chains. They give Haiti its peculiar two-pronged shape.

Though these mountains are complex and geologically varied, four main ranges can be traced, one in the north, one in the south and two in between. Because they run across the international frontier, they have different names in French-speaking Haiti and in the Spanish-speaking Dominican Republic.

In the north of the Dominican Republic, behind a narrow coastal plain, is the Cordillera Septentrional which rises to over 3,000 feet. Between this and the next range—the Cordillera Central—there is a large

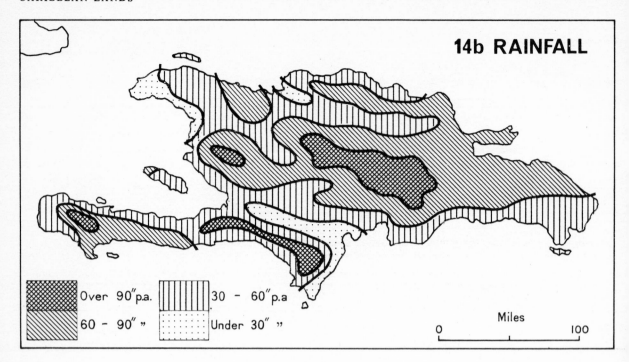

14b RAINFALL

Over 90" p.a.   30 - 60" p.a

60 - 90" "   Under 30" "

Miles

0   100

HISPANIOLA

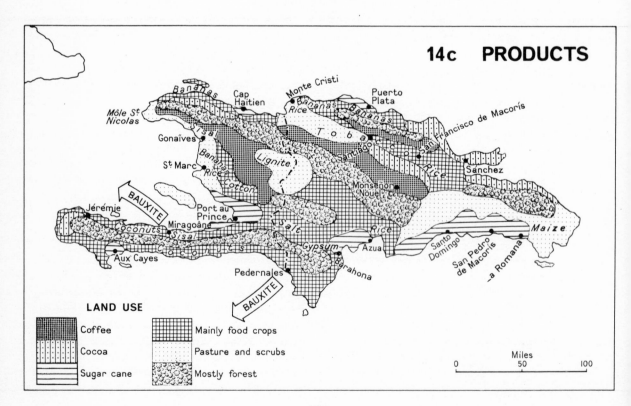

14c PRODUCTS

Môle St
Nicolas

Bananas   Cap   Monte Cristi   Puerto
          Haitien   Plata
                         Bananas   Bananas
                    Rice
Gonaïves   Tobacco   San Francisco de Macorís

St Marc   Lignite   Santiago   Rice   Sánchez

              Rice Cotton   Monsenor
                                      Noue
Jérémie   BAUXITE   Salt
          Coconuts   Rice   Maize
Miragoàne Sisal Port au
                  Prince   Santo San Pedro -a Romana
Aux Cayes   Coconuts   Gypsum   Azua   Domingo de Macorís
                        Pedernales   Barahona
                                BAUXITE

LAND USE

Coffee   Mainly food crops

Cocoa   Pasture and scrubs   Miles
                                          0   50   100
Sugar cane   Mostly forest

136

valley which stretches from the north coast of Haiti to Samaná Bay. It is nearly 30 miles wide in places. In Haiti it is known as the Northern Plain; in the centre it is the Cibao, and in the east the Vega Real. South of it lies the Cordillera Central of the Dominican Republic and its continuation the Massif du Nord of Haiti. This is the highest range in the West Indies, containing several peaks over 9,000 feet in height. The highest of all is Pico Duarte, about 10,200 feet above sea-level. The narrow San Juan Valley separates the Cordillera Central from the Sierra de Neiba, which continues westwards, south of the Central Plateau of Haiti and the Artibonite River, as the Chaîne de Mateaux. South of these mountains there is a rift valley, first thrown down to form a strait and then uplifted slightly in very recent times from beneath the sea. This lowland is known as the Enrequillo Plain in the Dominican Republic and as the Cul de Sac plain in Haiti. The two salt lakes, Saumâtre and Enrequillo, which occupy depressions in the trench, are below sea level.

The 140-mile-long southern peninsula of Haiti contains two ranges, the Massif de la Hotte in the west and the Massif de la Selle in the east. The latter rises to over 8,000 feet and continues a short way into the Dominican Republic.

The largest plains in the island are those in the south and south-eastern part of the Dominican Republic. Elsewhere lowlands are small and isolated from each other.

Rivers are too short and too steep to be of much use for navigation. In the dry season from December to April they dwindle and may dry up altogether, especially in limestone areas. In some places rivers have been harnessed to generate hydro-electricity. Two examples are the gorge of the Artibonite River which lies between the Central Plateau and the coastal lowland, and the Jimenoa Falls in the Cordillera Central. The lower courses of many streams, especially those in the Dominican Republic, provide water for irrigation.

CLIMATE AND VEGETATION

Because the landscape of Hispaniola is the most irregular in the West Indies, the climatic and vegetational contrasts are also the greatest. Thus the peaks of the Cordillera Central are as cool and wet as any in the West Indies, whereas the western lowlands are among the hottest and driest. Haiti, lying on the leeward side, is drier than the Dominican Republic. The Arbre and Cul de Sac Plains, for instance, get only 20 to 30 inches a year. The heaviest rains come between May and October.

Caribbean Pine forests cover the upper slopes of the Cordillera Central and certain other ranges such as the Massif de la Selle. Lower down, lush tropical forests occur in the wetter areas and thorn forests in the drier ones. Savannas are numerous and in such places as the Cibao and the north-western part of the Central Plateau they are extensive. Cactus and thorn shrubs occur in the driest areas. A belt of this type of vegetation extends all the way from the Môle St Nicholas to Port-au-Prince. It covers much of the Île de la Gonâve as well.

Haiti

Area: 10,714 square miles; population (1963): 4,450,000; density of population: 415 per square mile

Ever since the land of Haiti was divided into small holdings at the beginning of the nineteenth century, Haitian agriculture has been in the hands of peasants rather than estates. Today over 80% of the population are small holders. They have retained their traditional farming practices, burning and clearing the land and using the hoe and the machete as their only farming implements. Much of the land has been worn out by these primitive practices, and consequently crop yields have declined. Moreover, in searching for new lands the peasants have stripped the forests from many of the steeper and higher slopes, thus increasing soil erosion and reducing timber resources. Haiti is now the most eroded country in the West Indies. Forty per cent of the total arable area has either been ruined or severely affected.

The peasants produce crops primarily for family subsistence, so cash is in short supply and living standards are poor. The income per head of population is the lowest in the West Indies; a recent estimate put it at $14 a month.[1] Poverty is becoming increasingly acute because of the rapid increase of population, now over ten times what it was at the time of

[1] For currencies see page vi.

137

14d. Haitian peasants produce food primarily for family subsistence. What similarities and differences would a small farmer from your territory notice if he paid a visit to this family?

the revolution. It is difficult to improve things because of the isolation of many of the peasant communities and because the peasants speak patois and rarely master spoken or written French. About 80% of the population is illiterate. As a United Nations report, *Mission to Haiti*, put it: "The fundamental economic problem of Haiti derives from the relentless pressure of a steadily growing, insufficiently educated population upon limited, vulnerable and—as far as agriculture is concerned—alarmingly shrinking natural resources."

Being a republic, Haiti has never had the outlets for emigration open to Puerto Rico. Some people find employment for the few months of the cane harvest in the Dominican Republic, but they are not always welcome there.

THE EXPORT CROPS

The most important of these, coffee, brings in over 60% of the foreign earnings. It is grown by peasants along with their food crops on practically every suitable slope between 1,000 and 5,000 feet. There are no large plantations. Although the trees are usually grown with a minimum of care and much of the crop is poorly processed, the coffee itself has a good flavour and sells well in America and in several European countries. Output is about the same today as it was at the beginning of the century; that is, about 30,000 tons a year.

Sugar cane is grown on the Northern, Léogane, Cul de Sac, and Cayes Plains. By far the largest factory is that owned by an American company near Port-au-Prince. It obtains its cane from large,

14e. A Haitian market. Compare it with plates 4m and 4n and with the markets you know best.

irrigated estates near by and makes unrefined sugar and molasses for export and white sugar and rum for local consumption. About a third of the exports go to the United States, and another third to the United Kingdom. Other, smaller factories exist at Aux Cayes and at Jérémie.

Cocoa is grown at heights of 300 to 2,500 feet in some parts of the Northern Peninsula and at the extreme tip of the Southern Peninsula. Most of it is poorly processed, and prices are low. Output is rather less than it was a century ago.

A very successful recent development has been the establishment of large sisal plantations in Haiti. Exports bring in about 15% of the total income. In addition, hats, shoes, handbags, curtains and carpets are made from the fibre and are very popular with tourists.

Unstable political conditions in Haiti since the war have affected the banana industry. The output of 7 million stems in 1946 fell to about 300,000 in 1955. The chief areas of cultivation are the Artibonite and Northern Plains.

Cotton is grown in some semi-arid areas such as the Central Plateau and the Artibonite Plain. It is of good quality, but output has declined since the boll weevil made its appearance in the country in the 1930s.

Essential oils are extracted from vetiver, amyris, lemon grass and other plants. They are sent to America and to France, where they are used in the making of perfumes.

Rice, corn, cassava and many other vegetables and fruits are grown primarily for home consumption, but some are exported, especially to the Bahamas.

139

14f. Sisal being dried. What can you tell about the landscape and the climate of Haiti?

Livestock is kept in the grasslands. Some hides and skins are exported.

MINERALS

Bauxite is worked and exported by an American company with its headquarters at Miragoane. The output is not nearly as large as that of Jamaica, Guyana or Surinam. Small deposits of copper, manganese and silver ores are known to exist, but they are not worked at present. Nor are the deposits of lignite which occur in the north-west of the Central Plateau and near Aux Cayes.

TOWNS AND COMMUNICATIONS

Port-au-Prince (200,000), the capital, has grown to prominence because of its position on the largest and most productive lowland in Haiti. Its sheltered harbour has a pier that can take vessels up to 10,000 tons. It is the commercial centre of the country. It has a number of industries which include cotton ginning, and the manufacture of textiles, soap, lard, cement, plastics, handicrafts of sisal and wood, foodstuffs and drinks.

Port-au-Prince is the focus of communications. There are railways on the near-by sugar-cane lands and one line goes north to the Artibonite Valley.

Main roads of variable quality connect the capital to such towns as Aux Cayes (75,000), Gonaïves (65,000) and Cap Haïtien (25,000). Only about 250 miles of road have been asphalted.

TRADE

The trade of Haiti is small—only about a quarter of that of the Dominican Republic. Over a third of the exports go to the United States and the rest are distributed between many other countries, of which the most notable are Belgium, Italy, France, the Netherlands and the United Kingdom. About two-thirds of the imports are purchased from the United States.

The Dominican Republic

Area: 18,811 square miles; population (1963): 3,330,000; density of population: 177 per square mile

There are few similarities between Haiti and the Dominican Republic. The Dominican Republic, with nearly twice the area and a smaller population, has much less pressure on greater and more varied natural resources. The population density is nearly the lowest in the West Indies. Another contrast is that the stable political conditions that existed in the Dominican Republic during the dictatorship which lasted from the 1930s to the 1960s encouraged the investment of foreign capital for agricultural and industrial development.

About half of the country is forested, a fifth is cultivated and the remainder is largely pasture.

THE EXPORTS

Santo Domingo was the site of the first Spanish cane fields in the West Indies. But the development of a large-scale sugar industry dates from the 1870s, when civil war in Cuba curtailed the sugar output from that country and the Dominican Republic was able to capture her markets. Sugar has been the most valuable export since 1914. The country is now the second largest producer in the Caribbean.

The chief growing areas are those round Barahona, where the Rio Yaque del Sur provides irrigation water, on the Southern Plain, where irrigation is also essential, and on the North Coast Plain. The cane is grown on large estates round sixteen factories, one of which, with 70,000 acres under cane, is reputed to be the biggest in the world. Over half a million tons of unrefined sugar are exported every year, the bulk of which goes to Britain. Other purchasing countries include the Netherlands, Japan and the United States. Two factories manufacture refined sugar, some of which is exported, and one makes furfural from bagasse. This chemical is sold in the United States, where it is made into nylon. Sugar and its by-products make up over a third of the exports. They are shipped from Santo Domingo, from near-by Rio Haina, and from Barahona and La Romana.

The second most important crop is coffee, grown mostly in the higher slopes of the hills overlooking the Cibao. It is entirely a small holder's crop, but arrangements are made for it to be properly processed. The crop is about as large as that from Haiti. The United States takes over three-quarters of the exports.

The Dominican Republic is also a large producer of cocoa, most of which is grown in the north-east of the country and exported from Sánchez. The bulk of the crop is sold in the United States. Lesser amounts are sent to the Netherlands, Germany, Puerto Rico and elsewhere. Chocolate is manufactured both for local consumption and for export.

Tobacco, grown on the Cibao round Santiago, is exported to many countries including Spain, Germany, Algeria, the Netherlands and France. The rice output of some 80,000 tons a year permits a certain export. The chief growing areas are those round Monte Cristi and San Francisco de Macorís. Some of the maize produced in the country is sold to Puerto Rico. Bananas and groundnuts are also exported.

There are about a million cattle in the Dominican Republic; that is, about ten times as many as are in Haiti. Hides and skins are sold abroad, and some beef is sent to Puerto Rico.

Bauxite is mined and exported from Pedernales on the south coast near the Haitian frontier. Iron ore is mined in the Hatillo area and gypsum near Barahona. A small amount of gold is also produced. Nickel ore has been found near Monseñor Nouel, petroleum at Azua, and deposits of silver, copper and platinum are known to exist.

Fifty per cent of the Dominican Republic is still in forest, by far the highest proportion in the Greater

Antilles. A considerable amount of timber is exported and large reserves await future exploitation.

INDUSTRY

The Dominican Republic has a wider range of industries than Haiti. Besides those already mentioned they include metal goods, cigarettes, matches, cosmetics, pharmaceuticals, perfumes, cement, textiles, shoes and other leather articles, sacks and ropes, soap, foodstuffs and beverages.

THE PEOPLE

In contrast with Haiti, which is predominantly a Negro country with very few white or coloured inhabitants, just over 70% of the people of the Dominican Republic are coloured, 15% are white— chiefly of Spanish descent—and the remainder mostly Negro.

The population is concentrated in two areas, the South-Eastern Plain, and the Cibao and Vega Real. The former area is served by the capital and chief port, Santo Domingo (300,000), and the latter by Santiago. Santiago is connected by road and rail to Sánchez and through a pass in the Cordillera Septen-

trional with the port of Puerto Plata. Santo Domingo is connected by road with the other major Dominican cities and with Port-au-Prince, the capital of Haiti.

TRADE

Somewhat over half the exports from the Dominican Republic go to the United States. About a fifth are sent to the United Kingdom and the rest are distributed among many countries, including the Netherlands, Belgium, Puerto Rico, Japan, Germany and Ceylon. About two-thirds of the imports come from the United States. The rest come from many sources, which include the Netherlands West Indies, Canada, Germany, the United Kingdom and Belgium.

QUESTIONS

1. Account for the contrast in the development of the two independent republics on the island of Hispaniola. O.C.S.E.B. (O). 1965.
2. Compare the problems of developing Haiti with those of the territory in which you live.
3. "Political freedom retards economic development." Discuss this statement and its bearing on the West Indies.

14g. Santo Domingo at the mouth of the Ozama River. Using the picture, suggest reasons which explain the original choice of the site and the city's subsequent development.

CHAPTER FIFTEEN

Puerto Rico

Area: (with dependencies): 3,435 square miles; population (1963): 2,520,000; density of population: 734 per square mile

THE LAND

Puerto Rico, the smallest and most easterly of the Greater Antilles, is roughly rectangular in shape. As can be seen from Map 15a, there are two mountainous areas. The main backbone of the island is the Cordillera Central. It contains the highest mountain, Cerro de Punta (4,388 feet). Separated from the Cordillera Central by the valley of the Caguas River is the much smaller Sierra de Luquillo in the north-east. Here the second highest peak, El Yunque, is to be found. Together these mountainous areas take up about half the area of the island. Their core is mainly composed of volcanic and metamorphic rocks but they are flanked by limestone which, particularly on the northern side, has been severely eroded to produce a cockpit type of karst scenery with isolated conical buttresses separated by narrow pockets of fertile lowland. Surrounding the highlands is a coastal plain, mostly made of limestone but covered in places by alluvial deposits. It is about five miles wide in the north and rather less than that elsewhere.

CLIMATE

Lying in the same latitude and having much the same shape and topography as Jamaica, Puerto Rico has much the same climate. Mean temperatures on the plains range from 75° F. in January and February to just over 80° F. in July, August and September. The heaviest rain falls on the mountains, especially the upper north-eastern slopes of the Sierra de Luquillo which directly face the Trade winds. The coastal plains have much less, particularly in the rain-shadowed south-west where a small area has under 30 inches a year.

Puerto Rico has occasional summer hurricanes. About ninety have been recorded since the island was first settled in 1508.

DEVELOPMENT

Puerto Rico was ruled by Spain for four centuries. In 1898 it was ceded to the United States. Since then, though it has become economically closely linked to the mainland, it has become politically more and more independent. Today it is a "Free Associated State". Though not represented in Congress, Puerto Rico is self-governing in all local matters save defence and foreign relations. The people are spared American tax, and any customs duties collected on Puerto Rican goods entering America—for example that on rum—are handed back to the Puerto Rican treasury.

Under the Spaniards Puerto Rico was not a great sugar producer, even though cane was introduced as early as 1515. Some estates were established on the coastal plains and some sugar was exported, but the industry never developed as it did in Jamaica and Hispaniola. This was in part due to the fact that many of the early settlers left to seek their fortunes in Peru. Also for three centuries trade was curtailed by the Spanish decree that Puerto Rico could deal only with Spain. Of course this law was broken; in fact, it is believed that in some years the contraband trade was larger than the legal one. Even so, development was retarded and the population was little more than half that of Jamaica when the law was repealed in 1815. By this time, however, the slave trade had ended and Puerto Rico was unable to expand the sugar acreage quickly and share in the prosperity of the other Caribbean islands. The industry was further handicapped by plant diseases.

Cattle hides, tobacco and ginger were the chief exports of the seventeenth century. In the next century cotton was added and in the nineteenth century the exports of sugar increased, but coffee spread so rapidly throughout the highlands that by the time the country came under American control it was bringing in three times as much money as sugar.

143

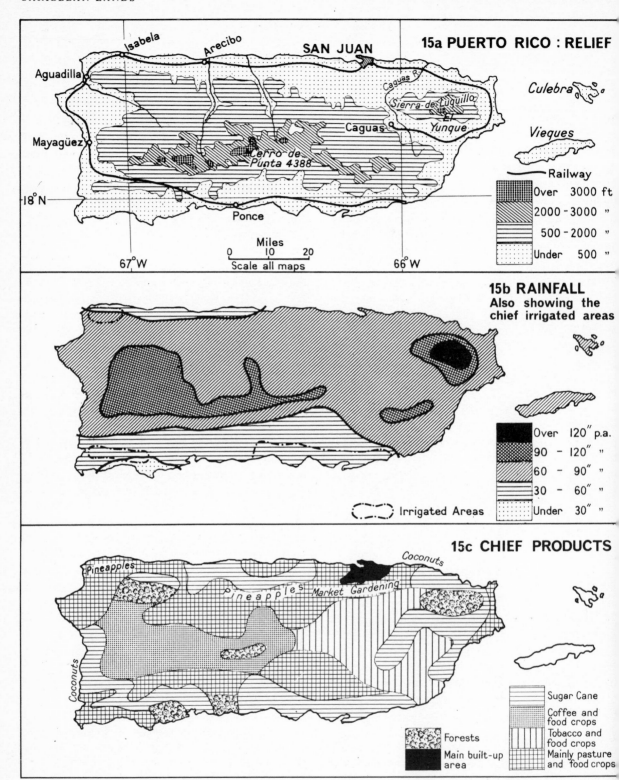

15a PUERTO RICO : RELIEF

Isabela
Arecibo
SAN JUAN
Aguadilla
Caguas R.
Sierra de Luquillo
El Yunque
Caguas
Mayagüez
Cerro de Punta 4388
18°N
Ponce
Culebra
Vieques

Railway
Over 3000 ft
2000 - 3000 "
500 - 2000 "
Under 500 "

Miles
0   10   20
Scale all maps
67°W   66°W

15b RAINFALL
Also showing the chief irrigated areas

Over 120" p.a.
90 - 120" "
60 - 90" "
30 - 60" "
Under 30" "

Irrigated Areas

15c CHIEF PRODUCTS

Pineapples
Coconuts
Pineapples   Market Gardening
Coconuts

Forests
Main built-up area

Sugar Cane
Coffee and food crops
Tobacco and food crops
Mainly pasture and food crops

Since 1900 great changes have taken place in the island's economy. Assured of a large and seemingly prosperous market at home, American businessmen bought huge estates in Puerto Rico and set up big modern centrals there. In thirty years the sugar output multiplied fifteen times. At the same time coffee declined, partly because of the better wages being paid to sugar workers and partly because Spain imposed tariffs on goods from her old colony, while, in America, Brazilian coffee was more popular than that from Puerto Rico. Then in 1928 began the world slump in which Puerto Rico suffered severely, the prices of her chief commodities falling to such low levels that it was rarely profitable to sell them. Coffee output in 1930 was only one-sixth of what it had been two years earlier. To add to her distress the island was struck by hurricanes in 1928 and 1932 and suffered a serious drought in 1931. For over ten years the mass of the workers faced starvation and were only kept alive by vast relief funds from the United States.

Since the war there has been another change. The Puerto Rican government has been carrying out a programme of land reform and industrialization that is rapidly improving the country. Land has been acquired from many American corporations, for by law no one is supposed to own over 500 acres. On some of this land, Government-owned "proportional profit farms" have been set up, where labourers, in addition to being paid standard wage rates, share in the profits and are allowed to have a few acres of land of their own on which to grow food crops. Others have been encouraged to borrow money from the government to buy farms for themselves.

THE CROPS

After the United States contracted to take over 1 million tons of Puerto Rican sugar every year, duty free, sugar became by far the greatest and most

15e. *Harvesting cane in Puerto Rico. Notice the contrast between the cane fields on the lowland and the wooded limestone hills in the background.*

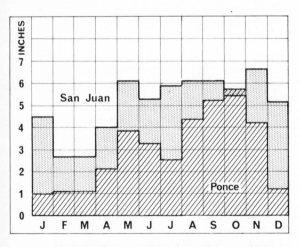

15d. *Average monthly rainfall of San Juan and Ponce. Compare the totals, and the length of the rainy season with those of Port Antonio and Kingston (Diagram 5g).*

15f. Pineapples on the north coast plain.

15g. Tobacco is grown and cured in some of the highland valleys.

profitable agricultural undertaking. However, in order to diversify the economy and reduce the problem of seasonal unemployment in the sugar industry the area under cane has diminished in recent years. It now occupies 40 % of the cropland, its place being taken by an increase of pastureland used mainly for dairying. In addition the number of sugar workers dropped from 85,000 in 1952 to 48,000 in 1962.

Puerto Rican sugar yields are higher than those in Cuba. They need to be, because only half of the country is cultivable and the land must be used in the best possible way. On the other hand Puerto Rican sugar is more expensive than that from Cuba, so it cannot compete on the world market. Output is therefore virtually limited to as much of the United States quota as can be produced and to home demand. Well-advertised rum is sold in America.

Pineapples, oranges, grapefruit and bananas are grown side by side with cane, especially along the north coast plain and also in the foothills. All these fruits are exported in quantity to America. Some are canned so as to reduce the risk of fetching low prices in a fluctuating market. Puerto Rico is also the largest exporter of fresh coconuts to the United States. Most are grown in a narrow belt close to the sea, mainly along the northern and western coasts.

About one-fifth of the cultivated land is under coffee, the main producing area being the rugged western mountains between 1,000 and 3,000 feet. Though, as we have seen, it was once the leading export, very little is now sent abroad.

Tobacco is grown on a large number of small hill farms in the east-central part of the country. Because of low prices output is lower than it was before 1930. Most of the crop is exported as leaf to the United States to be manufactured there, but there is also a small export of cigars made in Caguas. The season lasts from November to March, after which a harvest of food crops can be gathered before the next planting.

A large proportion of the arable land is under food crops, particularly in the hills. Maize, rice, sweet potatoes, bananas, plantains, avocado pears, yams and beans are the most widespread. In some places—as shown on Map 15c—they are more important than cash crops. Nevertheless, about half the foodstuffs required have to be imported. These imports no longer include large quantities of butter, milk and meat because Puerto Rico has developed its livestock industry considerably in recent years. Most of the animals are kept on the dry southern plain and the foothills of the Cordillera Central, though there is an important dairy industry on the northern plain.

Very little land has been left under the original forest cover, the chief remaining areas being the Sierra de Luquillo and the higher parts of the Cordillera Central.

PROGRESS IN INDUSTRY

Though agriculture has never been more prosperous, it can only employ about a tenth of the people living in Puerto Rico. Moreover, improvements in farming methods are tending to reduce this number. In order to create more employment the Government has, since the war, encouraged the establishment of manufacturing industries by offering to suitable firms factory sites and buildings, loans, and tax-exemption for periods of up to ten years. The plan, known as "Operation Bootstrap", has been very successful. Many American companies have taken advantage of these incentives—together with the relatively low wages paid to Puerto Rican workers and the fact that there are no tariffs on goods exported to the United States—to set up branch factories in the island. Over a thousand have already been built. They are to be found in all parts of the country, as special encouragement is given to firms operating in rural areas. Puerto Rican manufactures now earn twice as much as agriculture does, in spite of the lack of mineral resources. Some of the more important industries are oil refining, chemicals, cement, plastics, paper, rayon, textiles and clothing, hair-nets, fountain-pens, metal goods and the assembly of light machinery, particularly electrical components which are then air-freighted back to the United States. The largest pre-war industry—needlework—has been greatly expanded and is the chief employer of female labour. New generating stations, including hydro-electric plants, have been built to supply power to these factories.

The benefits are considerable. For instance, the *per capita* income rose from about $180 in 1940 to over $1,000 in 1962.[1] On the other hand it is doubtful whether many of these industries could carry on if

[1] For currencies see page vi.

Puerto Rican workers had to be paid the same wages as those in America.

Besides doing so much to promote the island's agriculture and industry, the Government has set about the tasks begun by the Americans of clearing slums and building new housing estates, roads, hospitals and schools, including one of the largest vocational schools in the world. All this has fostered a tremendous public urge for self-improvement. Illiteracy has already been reduced to less than 20% and will soon be 10%. Community self-help projects have been encouraged so that the people will develop their own initiative and not rely entirely on Government aid.

THE POPULATION PROBLEM

In spite of the progress that has taken place in recent years there are still many unemployed people in Puerto Rico. This is not surprising. In 1966 the density of population was over 750 per square mile, that is to say, well over one person per acre. This is about the same as the United States would have if all the people in the world were living there. Moreover, as a result of a high birth-rate and the improvement of medical services, the natural increase is now about 60,000 a year. The employment problem thus created is partly offset by the fact that the men have to serve for a period in the United States armed forces. More important is the annual migration of some 40,000 people to America, chiefly to New York, where over half a million Puerto Ricans are now living.

THE CHIEF TOWNS

A few years after the Spaniards colonized the island, which at that time was known as San Juan Bautista, they chose the best harbour on the north coast as the most suitable place to establish their chief port. This they called Puerto Rico—the "rich port". In later years the names were interchanged, so that the island became known as Puerto Rico and the capital, San Juan.

The older part of San Juan lies on an island which almost encloses the mouth of San Juan Bay, and several old forts—notably El Morro at the harbour entrance—remain to show how well it was protected. It is connected by a bridge to the newer part of the town and to the suburbs which stretch eastwards along the coast and southwards away from the sea. In recent years San Juan has grown rapidly and now contains half a million people. It is by far the most important port in the island, and has the busiest airport in the whole Caribbean. It is also the centre of the island's tourism, which expanded from 40,000 visitors in 1952 to over 400,000 in 1962.

Ponce, on the south coast, is the second largest port on the island. It exports sugar and rum, and has an oil refinery. The third port of importance is Mayaguez.

TRADE

Over 90% of Puerto Rican trade is with the United States. As we have already seen, much of the island's present prosperity is due to the availability of such a large and rich market for the exports. On the other hand it also means that Puerto Rico has to buy in return the world's dearest goods, so the cost of living is high. The chief imports are foodstuffs, including fish, grain and vegetables, textiles, minerals—including oil from Mexico and Venezuela for the island's refineries—timber and manufactured goods. The chief exports are sugar, rum, manufactures, fruit and tobacco. Canada takes some rum and fruit, Belgium some coffee. There is a small export of manufactures such as cement and glass bottles to near-by West Indian islands.

THE DEPENDENCIES

The outlying small islands of Vieques, Culebra and Mona are unimportant. Most of Vieques is controlled by the U.S. Navy. On the rest of it some crops are grown. The people in Culebra make a poor living by grazing and fishing. Mona is practically uninhabited.

QUESTIONS

1. What are the chief problems that Puerto Rico has attempted to overcome in recent years? What efforts have been made to overcome them and how far have they been successful?
2. Which Caribbean island do you think resembles Puerto Rico most closely? Give your reasons.
3. "For centuries the economy of Puerto Rico remained in a backward state but in the last 20 years, very spectacular progress has been made." Discuss. O.C.S.E.B.(O). 1965.

15h. Three Puerto Rican factories about ten miles inland from San Juan. They produce paper products, glass and cement.

CHAPTER SIXTEEN

Belize (British Honduras)

Area: 8,867 square miles (including cays); population (1965): about 106,000; density of population: 12 per square mile

THE CENTRAL AMERICAN SETTING

Stretching south-eastwards from Mexico for 1,000 miles is a long, tapering, twisted isthmus in which lie Belize and the six Central American Republics. The Republics are:

	Area (square miles)	Population
Guatemala	42,000	4,400,000
Honduras	43,000	2,300,000
El Salvador	8,000	2,900,000
Nicaragua	57,000	1,700,000
Costa Rica	20,000	1,400,000
Panama	28,500	1,300,000

The mountain chain which forms the backbone of the isthmus contains many volcanic peaks, some of which are active and rise to over 12,000 feet. The mountains are a source of minerals, especially silver and gold, and are high enough to have a marked effect on agriculture. Three climatic and crop belts are recognized. In the cool intermont plateaux and basins of the *tierra fria* live the majority of the people of Amerindian descent. Their subsistence economy is based on maize, potatoes, beans and livestock. Lower down, between 3,000 and 6,000 feet, is the *tierra templada* where the chief crop is coffee. Large quantities are grown in most of the Republics and coffee forms over three-quarters of the exports of El Salvador and Guatemala.

The hot, moist coastlands of the *tierra caliente* have a higher proportion of Negroes, many of whom emigrated to Central America from the West Indies to work on the banana plantations and on the construction of the Panama Canal. The Central American Republics supply most of the banana requirements of the United States. The plantations were originally developed on the Caribbean seaboard, but when the fruit was struck with Panama disease, the bulk of the production shifted to the Pacific coastlands where it has remained ever since. Other lowland crops are cocoa and sisal.

The Panama Canal has been built at the lowest and narrowest part of the isthmus. As it shortens some sea routes by thousands of miles it is of great economic and strategic importance, especially to the United States which owns the strip of land on either side of the canal.

DISCOVERY AND SETTLEMENT OF BELIZE

In 1506, four years after Columbus entered but did not explore the Gulf of Honduras, a small Spanish expedition penetrating farther west sailed up the coast to the Yucatán peninsula. These voyagers, the first Europeans to see the shores of what is now Belize, made no attempt to land or settle there. Lacking a good harbour and backed by impenetrable forests and swamps, the coast was too unattractive. When, a few years later, the Spaniards conquered Central America, they settled instead in the interior mountains and plateaux where transport was easier and where the precious minerals they sought were to be found. Thus throughout the sixteenth century the southern part of Yucatán was virtually uninhabited. The Mayan Indians who had once densely peopled it had moved northwards several hundred years before, leaving the forest to creep back and hide their cities and temples. The reason for this migration of perhaps three-quarters of a million people is still a mystery. War, sickness, a rebellion of the peasants against the priests, a climatic change and the ravages of soil erosion after centuries of intensive cultivation have all been suggested to explain it.

The Central American coast, so unsuited to the Spaniards, became instead the haunt of buccaneers who soon learned to take advantage of the protection offered by the hazardous and uncharted channels through the barrier reef fringing the shore. There,

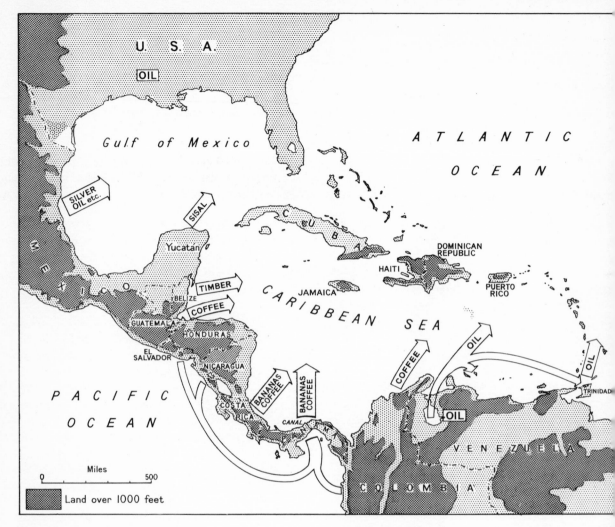

16a. The Central American setting.

hidden on the cays or in the river mouths, they could safely careen their vessels and prepare to attack the Spanish treasure ships leaving Mexico, Panama or Cartagena.

In the early seventeenth century, British settlements were established in Yucatán and along the "Mosquito" coast farther south to export logwood. This tree, from which dyes were obtained for the British woollen industry, was at that time fetching prices up to £100 a ton. Such a profitable trade attracted many ex-buccaneers and also settlers from Jamaica after its capture in 1655. For a short time the area became as valuable as any British colony then established in the Caribbean.

In the treaties between Spain and England the position of the British settlers in Central America was never clearly defined, and on a number of occasions Spaniards seized their ships and destroyed their homes. Gradually the logwood cutters became concentrated on the stretch of coast between the Belize and Hondo rivers, but even there they were far from safe. It was not until after they had beaten off an unusually powerful Spanish attack in 1798 that they were left in peace. During the revolutionary wars of the early nineteenth century, when the Central American countries succeeded in gaining their independence, Belize was the only country left untroubled

At the beginning of the nineteenth century, when

e population of Belize numbered some 200 whites, ,000 coloured people and free Negroes, and 3,000 laves, a unique immigration began. Several thousand *Black Caribs*, the offspring of Caribs and Negroes in t Vincent, were transported after an unsuccessful ebellion to the Mosquito coast and the Bay Islands f Ruatan and Bonacca. A few years later some were llowed to leave the Bay Islands for Belize, where, ontrary to expectations, they proved so hard-vorking and well behaved that more were encouraged o enter. Some were engaged to cut timber, but the najority chose to settle as a distinct agricultural and ishing community in the south. Their descendants, ome 4,000 strong, are still there to this day.

As there was a steady drift of escaped slaves away rom Belize to neighbouring countries, the population emained small until Emancipation, after which it ncreased fairly rapidly. A notable immigration took place about the middle of the nineteenth century vhen Spanish refugees from an Amerindian insurrec-ion in Yucatán settled in the Corozal District. They began a small sugar industry there, but as they uffered from frequent raids from across the border he success of the industry was limited and it remained mall until the 1960s.

An Anglo-American treaty, confirmed by Guate-nala in 1859, extended the southern frontier of Belize rom the Sibun to the Sarstoon River, thus doubling he former area of the country. Since then Guatemala las repudiated this agreement, partly on the grounds hat Britain has failed to fulfil a clause promising to .hare the cost of building a road from the capital of Guatemala to the Caribbean. Guatemala has epeatedly attempted to sell the whole territory to the British who maintain that, although it once belonged o Spain, this sovereignty was never transferred to Guatemala, so that the Republic has no right to offer it for sale. Public opinion in Belize itself is divided between those who want complete indepen-dence, those who favour the Guatemalan claim and those who wish to retain an association with the Commonwealth.

THE LAND

Belize, the only Commonwealth territory in Central America, is a long narrow country extending for 174 miles from north to south, whereas at its widest it is only about 70 miles from east to west. The frontier

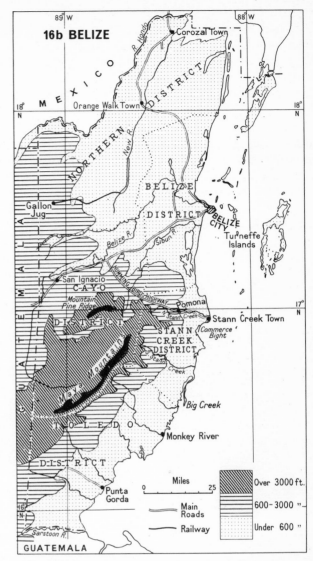

with Mexico follows the lower part of the Hondo River to its mouth. That with Guatemala runs for many miles along the mountains in the west and for a short distance along the Sarstoon River in the south. The area is about double that of Jamaica.

RELIEF

The Maya Mountains, an eastward extension of the much higher mountain backbone of Guatemala, take up over a third of Belize. They rise steeply from the surrounding lowlands to between 2,500 and 3,000 feet, at which elevation there are widespread rem-nants of an old peneplain dipping gently to the east.

151

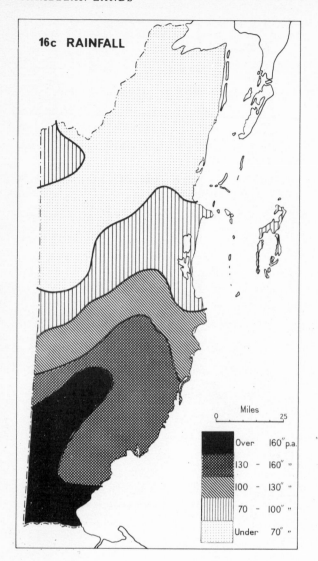

16c RAINFALL

Miles
0   25

⬛	Over 160" p.a.
	130 - 160" "
	100 - 130" "
	70 - 100" "
	Under 70" "

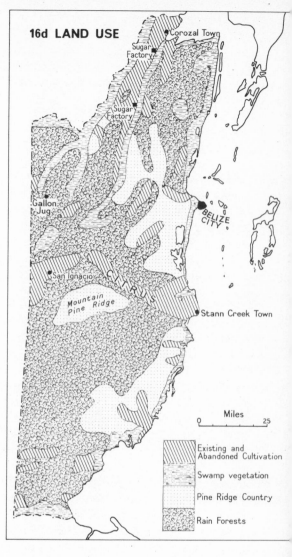

16d LAND USE

Corozal Town
Sugar Factory
Sugar Factory
Gallon Jug
BELIZE CITY
San Ignacio
Mountain Pine Ridge
Stann Creek Town
CAYES

Miles
0   25

	Existing and Abandoned Cultivation
	Swamp vegetation
	Pine Ridge Country
	Rain Forests

These are surmounted by occasional ridges such as the rugged peaks of the Coxcomb which reach 3,700 feet and are deeply dissected by river gorges. The Maya Mountains are composed of Palaeozoic sedimentary rocks, mainly sandstone and shale, with many granite intrusions which have brought minerals, including gold and tin, to the surface. Decomposition of the granite itself has produced *kaolin* or white china clay. As the deposits are so difficult of access, little is known about them and no mining operations have yet been attempted.

The Maya Mountains end so close to the sea that the coastal strip connecting the northern and southern lowlands is only about 10 miles wide. The large northern lowland is a raised limestone platform, mostly under 500 feet in height, though in the west near the Guatemalan border it rises to over 800 feet. Along the coast marine silting has created many shallow lagoons, some of which have been entirely cut off from the sea. All the principal rivers and many of their tributaries follow old fault lines and flow for long distances in a north-easterly direction parallel with the coast. They are often bordered by swamps, and in places they broaden out into lakes. The southern plain, though more limited in extent, contains a much greater variety of sedimentary rocks, which include limestone, sandstone and shale. It is crossed by many short, swift streams which radiate from the Maya Mountains.

In the coastal waters there are numerous reefs and associated sand and mangrove cays, many of which are large enough to support coconut groves and maintain fishing communities. The main reef farther offshore, extends for practically the whole length of the coast and is the second longest in the world.

CLIMATE

Belize, lying as it does on the eastern side of Yucatán between latitudes 16° N and 18° N, stands in the path of the Trade winds and therefore has similar climatic conditions to the rest of the Caribbean. Mean temperatures range from 85° F. in the hottest month to 72° F. in the coldest. On hot summer days the temperature may rise to 96° F. while in winter when a cold norther is blowing out from the United States it may fall to below 50° F. The winters are thus rather colder than elsewhere in the Caribbean.

Largely because of the location of the mountains, rainfall in Belize increases rapidly from north to south. Corozal Town, near the Mexican border, has an average of only 50 inches a year, while Punta Gorda in the south has 175 inches. In the rainy months from June to October the climate is hot and humid, though a short dry spell known locally as the Maugre Season usually occurs in August. The winter dry period which lasts in the north from December to May is long enough to suit the cultivation of sugar cane, while in the south, where it is limited to February, March and April, conditions favour tree crops such as bananas, cocoa and citrus.

Like all highlands the Maya Mountains are always a few degrees colder than the plains, and also receive more rain.

Belize was long thought to lie outside the normal hurricane belt, but in recent years all parts of the country have suffered from severe storms. A thousand lives were lost when Belize City was struck in 1931 and several hundred when it was struck again in 1961. Punta Gorda in the south, Stann Creek Town in the centre and Corozal Town in the north have also been badly damaged by hurricanes.

VEGETATION

Nearly 90% of Belize is clothed with tropical forest, the character of which varies from place to place. Rain-forest takes up the greatest area. It contains a great variety of trees. They include mahogany—the most valuable timber today—rosewood, found only on the southern plain, bulletwood, the cohune and other palms, and sapodilla from which chicle is obtained. Cedar and breadnut grow on limestone soils in both northern and southern plains. Pine forest occurs in large stands or "ridges", chiefly where there are poor sandy or gritty soils. In this case the term "ridge" has nothing to do with relief, referring instead to a region having a distinct type of vegetation. Indeed much of the pine ridge country in both northern and southern plains is perfectly flat. On the other hand pine trees grow in the highlands too. One of the most recently developed areas is the Mountain Pine Ridge lying between 1,000 and 3,000 feet on the northern flanks of the Maya Mountains. Under the pine trees grows a poor wiry grass which merges into savanna at the edge of the forest and into swamp vegetation on the lowest, most waterlogged land. Mangrove forests fringe the coast, the lower portions of the river valleys and some of the inland lagoons.

FOREST PRODUCTS

From the time of the earliest settlement up to 1960, forest products provided Belize with its chief source of income. The logwood trade begun by the original settlers lasted until the nineteenth century, by which time the colony was securely founded. Then, as a result of the discovery of synthetic dyes with a greater range of colours, exports declined and today they are negligible. The place of logwood was taken by mahogany, first for the European and later for the American market, and to a much lesser extent by cedar, used to make cigar boxes in Havana and the southern United States. At the beginning of this century there was a rapid rise in the export of chicle to satisfy the demands of chewing-gum consumers, mainly in America. For some years this proved very profitable but now that some manufacturers are using an artificial product instead of pure chicle the trade has dwindled considerably. In recent years timber cutting has been extended to the pine forests, and pine has become the second most valuable timber. In 1963 mahogany lumber accounted for 13%, and pine, cedar and rosewood for 3% of the total domestic exports of the country.

16e. Mountain Pine Ridge country.

Partly because land has always been so cheap, but also because the trees suitable for cutting are scattered throughout the forests, the people controlling the timber trade have acquired large properties. One company alone owns and leases over a million acres. Most of the lowland is now in private hands and, though Crown Lands take up over half the total area of the country, they are largely confined to the mountainous regions which have hitherto been inaccessible. In recent years, because so much of the best timber has been removed from the northern plain,

the Government has built roads to open up its own lands, which now produce the bulk of the country's mahogany. The Government has also taken in hand the tasks of controlling forest exploitation, fire prevention and reafforestation. Even so, mahogany and pine trees are being cut more quickly than they can be replaced, and unless markets can be found for other timbers the industry will soon face a serious decline.

Timber cutting mostly takes place in the dry season. At the beginning of the year gangs of labourers are transported to camps in the forest, where huts are built to accommodate them. In the case of mahogany the trees to be cut are selected by an expert woodman employed by the Government. He marks those which have reached marketable girth, and they are cut and hauled out by special tractors to the nearest road or suitable place on a river bank. Now that so little timber is left near the rivers increasing use is being made of roads built to tap the last remaining virgin stands in the country. In the richest mahogany-producing area around Gallon Jug a short railway has been laid to take logs to the New River. Here they are lashed together in large rafts which float down to Corozal Town and are then towed along the coast to Belize City, where there is a large saw-mill. Pine logs do not float, so they are cut up by small portable mills in the forest and the sawn lumber is taken out by road. Another product—resin—is extracted and exported from Big Creek farther south.

The life of the chiclero is harder than that of the forest worker, for he must travel over long distances in the forests to collect the required amount of chicle. Moreover, his work takes place in the wet season, for it is only then that the gum flows freely. On reaching the sapodilla tree he cuts zigzag gashes in its bark with a machete so that the gum trickles down to the bottom, where it is collected in a canvas bag lined with rubber. The liquid is poured into an iron pot and boiled until it thickens, when, on being emptied out, it sets as a hard block looking rather like a large loaf of bread. These blocks, stamped with the chiclero's initials, are carried into Belize City by mules. Working in this way a chiclero will supply anything from 500 to 2,000 lbs. each season.

The best chicle comes from the northern part of Belize and from the neighbouring province of Petén in Guatemala. Output has decreased in recent years, partly because cheaper synthetic substitutes are now being used in certain brands of chewing-gum and partly because the trees take a long time to recover after each tapping.

AGRICULTURE

Only a small proportion of Belize is under cultivation in any one year and, apart from the small areas of commercial crops noted below, agriculture is still mainly in the hands of the Maya and the Caribs who grow subsistence crops by traditional but very

16f. Mahogany logs at Belize City awaiting the saw-mill.

16g. Mahogany planks awaiting export.

primitive methods. The rest of the inhabitants rely almost entirely on imported produce, including canned milk, fruit and vegetables and meat, which could all be replaced by fresh foods produced at home. In 1963, food accounted for 26% of the total imports.

There can be no doubt that the present population which amounts only to about twelve per square mile is too small to expand commercial cultivation quickly. It would therefore appear that the best way of doing so would be to encourage the immigration of experienced farmers, perhaps from the West Indian islands. In practice this is no easy task. Belize does not have the money to assist settlers in opening up new lands or to sustain them for years until their crops become profitable. Besides, as can be seen from Map 16b, very few parts of the country are accessible by road. Inland transport costs are therefore high, so much so that canned and frozen fruits and vegetables shipped from America have been sold in Belize more cheaply than fresh local products. New roads are being built, but they are so expensive that progress is slow and opportunities for immigrants are still limited.

THE MAYA AND SHIFTING CULTIVATION

For many years Mayan Indians have gradually been re-entering Belize. They have built villages on both the northern and southern lowlands, for although the Government has allotted them reservations covering thousands of acres in the Toledo District, they are not restricted to them. To support themselves they burn and clear the bush and cultivate the patch of land so obtained for two or three years by which time the weed growth has become so thick that the easiest thing to do is to prepare another clearing. They therefore need at their disposal many times the area they can cultivate in any one year. Fortunately their numbers are small, some 10,000 all told, and adequate space is still available. Fortunately, too, the abandoned land or "wamil" as it is called, rapidly reverts to bush, and so soil erosion is not serious. Nevertheless, it is an inefficient and wasteful system and does nothing to improve the land. The staple crop of the Maya is maize, but they also grow rice, black beans and tobacco, and keep cattle, pigs and poultry, mainly for subsistence, though some of them do sell a little maize and meat. Small quantities of maize are even available for export. The Maya do not all live in this way, for some of them collect chicle (they form the majority of the chicleros) and others are employed on cane farms and in cutting timber.

CARIB SUBSISTENCE

Some of the descendants of the Black Caribs who first began to settle in Belize at the beginning of the nineteenth century live in coastal villages in the Stann Creek and Toledo Districts where they still carry on their old way of life. The men undertake the heavy work of burning and clearing the land but then return to their principal occupation, fishing, while the women plant, tend and reap the crops. Rice, maize, beans and root crops are grown, as well as cassava, from which starch is extracted to make bread. Before the war a factory was erected in the Stann Creek valley to refine cassava starch, but supplies were insufficient to keep it in operation.

COMMERCIAL FARMING

At various times a number of export crops have been established in Belize, but for various reasons almost all of them have enjoyed only moderate success and have then declined in value.

Sugar Cane

The sugar industry in the north was established about 1850 by Spanish refugees fleeing from an Amerindian revolt in Yucatán. With its moderate rainfall, long dry season, flat land and good soils, the area they chose was very suitable for cane cultivation. On the other hand this was the period of West Indian decline

16h, 16i. A chiclero at work. What is he doing in each case?

when Britain abandoned her preferences on colonial sugar and when the output of beet sugar in Europe was soaring. Nevertheless with the aid of some Chinese and Indian indentured labour Belize was able to satisfy local needs and at times produce a small surplus for export.

In 1936 a small but well-equipped factory was built at Pembroke Hall, near Corozal Town, to produce both white and brown sugar. It replaced a number of older, less efficient mills in the neighbourhood and encouraged cane farmers to increase their supplies. In order to give further encouragement, in 1959 the Commonwealth Sugar Agreement allotted Belize an export quota of 25,000 tons at a time when the actual exports were virtually nil. Since then this quota has been increased, an additional quota has been granted by the United States and the area under cane has grown. The Pembroke Hall factory has been enlarged and a second one has been built at Tower Hill near Orange Walk Town. In 1965 the production exceeded 35,000 tons and this is expected to triple by 1970. Using new land and modern mechanized methods the sugar industry of Belize is able to expand at a time when it is not prospering in other West Indian territories.

Coconuts and Cohune Nuts

Coconuts grow on the sandy coastal areas and cays and to a limited extent inland. In former times the industry was a valuable one but low prices in the 1930s discouraged growers from looking after their trees and from planting new ones. In recent years hurricanes and disease have also contributed to the decline in output. Most of the nuts come from the Turneffe Islands and are taken to Belize City by sailing-boats each week. Some are exported to the United States but most are converted into copra and soap mainly for local consumption.

The tall cohune palm occurs extensively throughout the rain-forest. Cohune nuts are used to make a variety of products, especially cooking oil, but the yield is not sufficient to make the task of cracking the thick hard shells and extracting the kernels very profitable. As in the case of coconuts, exports are very small.

Cocoa

At the beginning of this century cocoa was grown successfully in various parts of Belize, especially in the south. Most of the plantations were later abandoned owing to the low price of cocoa, and attention was diverted to banana cultivation. Production is now small.

Bananas

Banana exports began towards the end of the nineteenth century. Output from the Stann Creek area increased so rapidly that in 1908 the Government built a railway along the North Stann Creek Valley to carry the fruit to a shipping pier at Commerce Bight. This attracted the attention of the United Fruit Company which established large plantations there and began a regular shipping service to America. The railway was extended to serve new lands farther up the valley. Then Panama disease appeared and in fifteen years production fell from 800,000 stems a year to a tenth of that figure. The plantations were abandoned and the railway was dismantled. However, banana cultivation continued in the hands of small farmers on lands still free from the disease, a road was built in place of the railway, and exports rose again to a record total of 939,000 stems in 1937. Then the combined effects of disease and the wartime shipping shortage led to a collapse of the industry, which has never since recovered. The pier at Commerce Bight, destroyed by a hurricane in 1941, has never been rebuilt. Banana production is now negligible. Farmers in the Stann Creek area are concentrating instead on the production of citrus fruits.

Citrus

In the 1920s and 1930s grapefruit grown in the Stann Creek area were so good that they won several international awards. A thousand acres were under cultivation when the war broke out in 1939 and the shipping shortage became so acute that very little fruit could be exported. Since the war, however, the industry has expanded and orange trees have been planted in large numbers. Citrus orchards now extend as far inland as the Cayo district. Orange and grapefruit juice, grapefruit segments and essential oils are all made at a factory at Pomona in the Stann Creek Valley. They are exported together with some fresh fruit from Commerce Bight. In 1963 they accountep for almost 30% of the exports (not including re-exports).

Livestock

Although several parts of Belize are very well suited to profitable cattle and pig rearing, the livestock industry has only been developed in recent years. The Maya have always kept animals for subsistence, but as they offered very little milk, butter or meat for sale, animal products were a costly import. To eliminate this needless expense pastures and herds have been improved and extended, especially on the lowlands round San Ignacio. The number of cattle now exceeds 25,000. Even so, little fresh milk is available in Belize City.

Other Crops

Belize is self-sufficient in maize and cassava, the staple food crops of the Maya and Caribs respectively. These people also share in the production of vegetables, beans and rice. Some rice still has to be imported but enough is grown to make worth while the operation of a modern mill in Belize City. A little tobacco is grown, but the local cigarette industry relies mainly on imported leaf.

FISHING

Though Belize is within easy reach of some of the richest fishing grounds in the Caribbean, the fishing industry is small. It is mainly in the hands of the Caribs, who are skilful sailors but are restricted to the coastal waters by the size of their boats. Their catch is limited by the primitive equipment they use, and exports are very small. Some river fish are caught, mainly by the Maya. Lobsters are plentiful along the coast and there is a small export of lobsters and frozen lobster tails to the United States. A pre-war sponge fishery centred on the Turneffe lagoons has closed because of disease and the old trade in tortoiseshell has almost ceased as this commodity has been replaced by cheaper plastics.

TOURISTS

Belize has not shared in the profitable tourist industry of the northern Caribbean or of its neighbour, Mexico. A few keen fishermen visit the cays but there is little else to attract visitors for a holiday.

THE PEOPLE

People of African and mixed descent form the largest racial group in Belize, numbering some two-thirds of the total population. Next come the Maya, who make up about 17% of the total. There are three main groups of Mayas, each with their own language. As they speak Spanish rather than English as their second language, they are relatively isolated and backward. Those of the Caribs who live in the coastal districts also have their own customs and speak patois, but they are a less distinct community and some have entered the professions. There are small groups of Europeans, Indians and other peoples in the country.

Before its destruction by hurricane Hattie in 1961, Belize City contained almost 40% of the population of Belize. This was an unusually large percentage for an under-developed country with no manufacturing industries. It could partly be accounted for by the fact that there were few farmers to disperse the population throughout the country. In addition, many forest workers and their families lived in Belize City for several months a year when there was no work to be done in the forests. After the hurricane it was agreed that the site of the town had so many disadvantages that it was decided to build a new capital about 50 miles inland on the road to San Ignacio.

One of the disadvantages was that ocean-going ships had to cross the reef at a point 14 miles south of Belize City, and on reaching the town had to lie a mile or more off-shore and be loaded and unloaded by lighters. Secondly, the town itself was built on low-lying reclaimed land only a foot or two above the sea, so that drainage was difficult and pure water had to be piped 11 miles to the town. Besides, it was open to flooding during hurricanes, as happened in 1961 when the sea was driven half a mile inland. A third disadvantage was that Belize City was surrounded by a useless, insect-infested, crab-ridden swamp, across which roads had to be built at great expense.

In spite of these drawbacks people moved back to Belize City after the hurricane, and it still dominates the trade of the country. There are no ports north of it because the sea is too shallow to take any but the smallest boats. To the south there are some deep-water harbours, such as Commerce Bight, but their hinterlands are restricted by the Maya Mountains and so they cannot rival the capital in importance.

As Belize City has always handled nearly all the imports, it has become the chief distributing centre and therefore the focus of the country's road system.

It is also the banking centre and the passenger terminus for those travelling by sea or by air. Its few industries include the manufacture of cigarettes, soap and edible oils, sawn timber and wooden goods.

COMMUNICATIONS

Until recently there have been so few roads in Belize that the bulk of the traffic has had to be carried by river. Four rivers have been especially important: the New and Hondo Rivers in the north—each navigable by shallow-draught vessels for over 60 miles—the Sibun River, and the Belize—navigable to San Ignacio, a distance of 120 miles. The Belize River with an average width of 140 feet and a depth of 6 to 9 feet has always been the chief waterway of the country. It is still used to float out timber, though it has lost much of its other traffic since a road has been built from Belize City to San Ignacio.

In order to connect the chief towns, to develop existing forest and agricultural areas and to open up new ones, major and feeder roads are being constructed. However, even today Belize has only 1 mile of motorable road for every 20 square miles of territory. It is true that this compares favourably with Guyana, which has 1 mile of road to every 250 square miles, but it is much worse off than developed countries. For instance, in Barbados there are 4 miles of road to every square mile of land.

TRADE

Though the trade of Belize is small for its size, it is larger than that of any of the Commonwealth Eastern Caribbean territories, several of which have about the same population. In 1963 the total domestic exports were worth $15,300,000 and the imports amounted to about $33,000,000.[1] The United Kingdom bought most of the sugar and citrus and some of the forest products, taking in all 42% of the exports. The United States took 31% of the exports, and Jamaica took 4%, made up mainly of timber. In return, 44% of the imports came from the United States, 26% from the United Kingdom, and about 4% each from the Netherlands, Canada, Trinidad, and Jamaica.

Belize acts as an *entrepôt* for that part of Mexico near its frontier. It is ideally placed to do the same for Guatemala, but because of the disturbed political relations between the two countries this trade is very small. The total re-exports of Belize in 1963 were worth about $3,770,000.

[1] For currencies see page vi.

THINGS TO DO

1. Compare the population and the trade of Belize with that of the country in which you live.
2. Discuss the relationship between the size and the density of the population of a country and its economic development.
3. Discuss the present and probable future development of forests and agriculture in Belize.

QUESTIONS

1. Explain why Guyana and Belize are both scantily peopled and little developed. C.S.C. 1952.
2. (*a*) Compare the distance by sea from England to Valparaiso, San Francisco and Auckland by way of the Panama Canal and by way of Cape Horn. (*b*) What Caribbean imports and exports are likely to pass through the Canal?

CHAPTER SEVENTEEN

Guyana

Area (estimated): 83,000 square miles; population (1964): 638,000; density of population: between 7 and 8 per square mile

THE SOUTH AMERICAN SETTING

That part of South America which lies north of the equator is occupied almost entirely by the Republics of Colombia and Venezuela, and by Guyana, French Guiana and Surinam. Colombia has an area of 439,400 square miles and a population of 14 million, and Venezuela has an area of 352,000 square miles and a population of 6 million.

The Andes, which fork into a number of separate ranges known as cordilleras, are the source of several precious minerals, in particular emeralds, platinum, gold and silver. Between their snow-capped summits and the hot coastal plains there are several zones of cultivation. On the coastlands, the valleys and the lower slopes, bananas, sugar cane, rice and cocoa are the chief crops. Some rubber, balata, balsa wood and other forest products are also produced. Coffee, grown on the middle slopes, is the chief agricultural export of both of the Republics. Here, and higher up, there are dense clusters of population in sheltered basins, such as Bogotá, Valencia and Caracas. In addition to coffee, such crops as cotton, tobacco, maize, wheat, barley and vegetables are grown and livestock is reared. Finally, above the upper limit of cultivation there are wide expanses of poor, wind-swept grasslands where sheep and other animals are kept. Natural approaches into the mountains are provided by such valleys as the Magdalena, Cauca and Atrata. Elsewhere roads and sometimes railways have been built at great expense.

Venezuela is the world's second largest oil-producing country and the world's largest oil exporter.

8a. The South American setting.

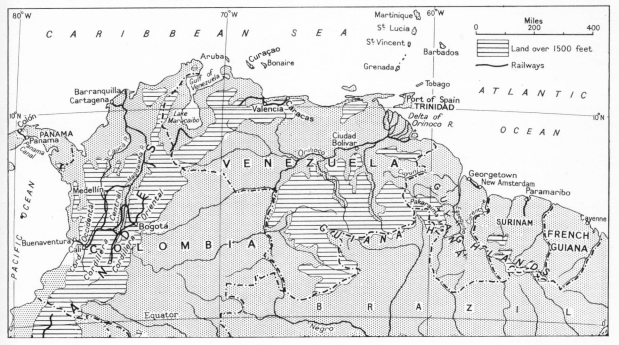

161

The main fields lie along the eastern and western shores of Lake Maracaibo and to some extent under the eastern part of the lake itself. Another smaller field, together with a pitch lake, occurs at Guanoco near the Gulf of Paria and there is a third north of Ciudad Bolivar. The bulk of the Venezuelan output is exported to Curaçao, Aruba and Trinidad for refining. Oil and its products amount to 95% of the exports of Venezuela. Colombia is a less important producer, the largest fields lying on the Venezuelan frontier near Lake Maracaibo and in the Magdalena Valley. Iron ore and coal exist in both countries and some steel is manufactured.

Large expanses of savanna occur in the interior of both countries. They are sparsely settled and little developed, the chief occupation being cattle ranching.

Most of the people of Guyana, Surinam and French Guiana live on a very narrow strip of land near the coast where they cultivate sugar, rice and a variety of other crops. Gold and diamonds are produced in small quantities in the interior. Guyana and Surinam both produce large quantities of bauxite.

DEVELOPMENT OF GUYANA

Considering its distance from Europe, its limited natural resources, the primitive life of its inhabitants and the difficulty of penetrating into the interior, the north-east shoulder of South America became known to the world at a surprisingly early date. About the beginning of the sixteenth century a legend grew up that this area was fabulously wealthy. It was said that in the heart of the forest the last Incas, safely hidden from their Spanish conquerors, had built a golden city. Many parties of Spaniards searched for it in vain, though some claimed to have seen its buildings gleaming in the distance. In 1594 Sir Walter Raleigh, believing these tales, persuaded Queen Elizabeth I to allow him to lead an English expedition to the region. Suffering cruelly from the heat and the exertion of rowing against a powerful current, he and 100 men penetrated some distance up the Orinoco River. Later, Raleigh wrote that "every stone we stooped to take up promised either gold or silver by his complexion", but with "no means but our daggers and fingers to tear them out" he was able to show on his return only a few samples of ore which most people believed he had dug up near his home in England. A second expedition to the Orinoco in the reign of

James I was even less successful and brought about Raleigh's imprisonment and execution.

Under the terms of the Treaty of Tordesillas, this part of South America lay on the borderline between Spanish and Portuguese possessions. Both these nations hesitated to colonize it, so early in the seventeenth century Dutch settlers did so instead. Rather than search for precious minerals, they established plantations along the banks of such rivers as the Essequibo, Demerara, Berbice, Corentyne, Coppename and Surinam. The ruins of one of their forts—Kykoveral—built at the junction of the Cuyuni, Mazaruni and Essequibo Rivers, is still to be seen. It is not far from Bartica.

At first tobacco and sugar cane were their chief crops but later cocoa, coffee and cotton were exported as well. But these riverside settlements did not last long. The soil, poor to begin with, gradually became exhausted and by the 1720s the estates were being abandoned. The forest crept back over them and there is scarcely a trace of them today.

The settlers had only one place to turn. Penetration farther upstream was barred, for—as you can see from Map 17b—nearly every river has a waterfall or a rapid not many miles from its mouth, which no ship could cross. The settlers were therefore forced to move down to the coastlands and develop them. This was a gigantic task. The land was so low and so flat that great areas were covered by the sea at high tide. To reclaim it a wall had to be built to keep out the sea and canals had to be dug to drain the swamps left behind. To speed up development the Dutch allowed in other people, particularly French and British settlers who, using slave labour, gradually created new plantations. With these improvements the area became an attractive prize and it changed ownership several times. In the end three of the Dutch colonies, Essequibo, Demerara and Berbice, were ceded to Britain.

The work of draining and improving the coastlands continued. Sugar cane was planted on all the new estates and sugar became by far the most valuable export. This development was still going on when the slaves were freed. So many of them left the estates to fend for themselves that in order to preserve the sugar industry other sources of population had to be found. There was a new wave of immigration, largely from India. Today people of Indian descent form

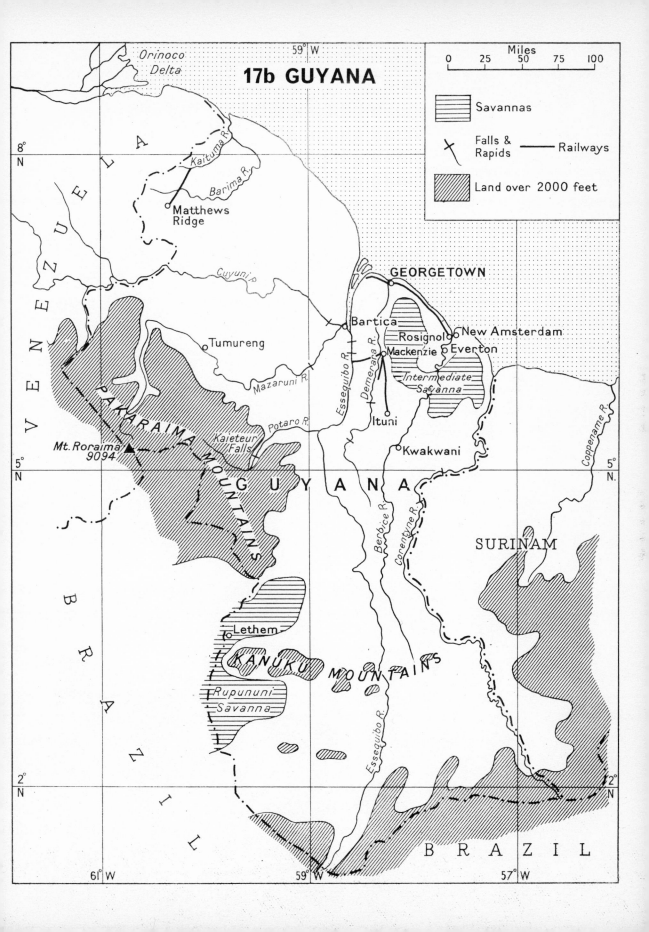

Miles
0 25 50 75 100

Savannas

Falls & Rapids — Railways

Land over 2000 feet

17b GUYANA

Orinoco Delta

8° N

Kaituma R.
Barima R.

Matthews Ridge

Cuyuni R.

VENEZUELA

Tumureng

Mazaruni R.

Essequibo R.

Potaro R.

Kaieteur Falls

Mt. Roraima 9094

PAKARAIMA MOUNTAINS

5° N

GUYANA

Demerara R.

GEORGETOWN

Bartica

Rosignol
Mackenzie   Everton

New Amsterdam

Intermediate Savanna

Ituni

Kwakwani

Berbice R.

Corentyne R.

Coppename R.

SURINAM

5° N.

BRAZIL

Lethem

KANUKU MOUNTAINS

Rupununi Savanna

Essequibo R.

2° N

BRAZIL

2° N.

61° W   59° W   57° W

about half of the total population. Many are still engaged in the sugar industry. Many others cultivate rice—the second most important crop in the country.

THE LAND

Guyana is roughly rectangular in shape, being about three times as long from north to south as it is from east to west. It may be divided into four physical regions.

(i) *The Alluvial Belt*

Along the coast there is a narrow strip of lowland at most 20 to 30 miles wide composed of thick sediments, mainly clay. Wells drilled into it provide a valuable source of pure water. In contrast with the

other regions it contains no mineral wealth, though in the north-west, near the Venezuelan frontier, drillings have been made just off-shore in the shallow sea in the hope of finding oil.

(ii) *The Sandy Lowlands*

Behind the alluvial belt there lies a region of undulating land 50 to 400 feet in height and about 100 miles wide. Originally part of the interior plateau, it was worn down to a peneplain ages ago. Then, it is believed, the action of heavy tropical rain weathered the crystalline rocks along its edge so that a narrow belt of bauxite, sometimes over 30 feet thick, was formed. Finally, as a result of a temporary submergence of the peneplain beneath the sea, deposits of

17c. Mining bauxite.

white sand were laid on top of the bauxite, covering it completely and protecting it from further erosion when the land emerged to its present level.

Bauxite is the ore from which aluminium is obtained. Alloys of this metal are used in the aircraft, packaging, food-processing and electrical industries as well as for making many other things such as the pots and pans of the kitchen. Bauxite itself is used as an abrasive and is made into fire bricks to line the inside of furnaces. Large quantities of the mineral are therefore always in demand.

At least 70 million tons of bauxite are known to exist in Guyana, the biggest deposits lying along the junction of the alluvial belt and the peneplain east of the Essèquibo River. It is worked mainly around Mackenzie on the Demerara River, at Ituni some 40 miles south, and at Kwakwani on the Berbice River.

Before the ore can be reached, the forest has to be burned or chopped down, and draglines, bulldozers or powerful hoses must strip or wash away the overburden of white sand which may be over 100 feet thick. The mineral is therefore more expensive to mine than Jamaican bauxite which lies on the surface. On the other hand it is of better quality. It is a pinkish, fairly hard, clay-like rock. The company operating at Mackenzie and the two neighbouring settlements of Wismar and Christianburg blasts it loose with dynamite and loads it into railway trucks which are hauled by diesel locomotives to the town. There the bulk of the ore is crushed, washed and dried in huge oil-fired kilns, and some is further purified by calcining it—that is, heating it to a very high temperature. The exports of calcined bauxite (which amounted to 490,000 tons in 1965) are the largest in the world. The most recent development at Mackenzie is the extraction of the pure oxide, alumina (275,000 tons were exported in 1965).

Mackenzie is a modern, well-planned settlement at the head of navigation of the Demerara River some 60 miles from the sea. Since work began there in 1916, Mackenzie, in spite of its isolation, has grown rapidly to become the second largest town in Guyana. Over 20,000 people live there, most of whom work in the factories or on the wharves loading the ships which take the bauxite and alumina abroad for manufacture into aluminium. Most of the bauxite goes to Canada, but as heavily laden vessels are unable to cross the shallow sand-bars at the mouth of the Demerara River, bauxite is taken in half-empty ships or in small vessels to Trinidad, where it is stored and transferred to large ships for the last stage of the journey. It is even more difficult to export the ore mined at Kwakwani. Barges carry it down the Berbice River to Everton, some 10 miles from the sea, where it is stored for shallow-draught freighters to take overseas.

During the war there was such a demand for aluminium to make aeroplanes that the exports of bauxite from Guyana rose from half a million tons to over 2 million tons a year. In 1965 the output was 2,873,000 tons, making the country the world's fourth largest producer.

(iii) The Pakaraima Mountains

In the west and north-west, 200 and more miles from the sea, there is a mountainous region which takes up about one-seventh of the country. It is a huge plateau about 2,000 feet high surmounted in places by steep-sided, flat-topped ranges which rise considerably higher. The highest point of all, Mount Roraima, on the frontier with Brazil and Venezuela, reaches 9,094 feet. These ranges are the source of many rivers which are renowned for their waterfalls when they reach the edge of the plateau. The best known is the Kaieteur Falls on the Potaro River, a tributary of the Essequibo. It has a sheer drop of 741 feet, nearly five times that of Niagara. The region was virtually inaccessible until the coming of air transport and even today few people live there, apart from Amerindians.

The plateau is composed mainly of ancient sandstone, with igneous and metamorphic rocks in places. It contains gold and diamonds, though not on the scale envisaged by Raleigh. Rivers have carried down both these minerals and deposited them on their beds, where they are sought for by small groups of itinerant prospectors known locally as "porknockers".

Most of the diamonds come from the Upper Mazaruni River where Tumureng is the chief collecting centre. Gold is more widespread, but the Potaro River is one of the richest sources. At present gold and diamonds form only a small fraction of the total exports, but in periods of depression in the sugar industry the number of porknockers has risen and output has increased.

Manganese ore, mined at Matthews Ridge, is taken

by rail to Port Kaituma, a shipping terminal on the Kaituma River where, like bauxite, it is shipped to Chaguaramas for re-export. It is of use in the manufacture of steel. Other minerals known to occur in various parts of the interior include columbite-tantalite—which is in demand for the manufacture of jet engines—platinum, and iron ore.

(iv) *The Southern Uplands*

The southern part of Guyana is little known. It is believed to consist largely of ancient metamorphic rocks and granite. Near the rivers the land is low and there are large swamps. Elsewhere there are some low plateaus, including the Kanuku Mountains, which reach a height of 3,000 feet in places.

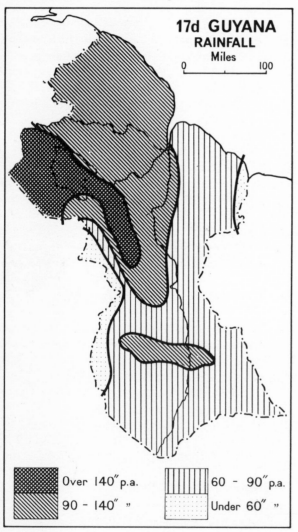

CLIMATE

In the coastal areas the humid equatorial climate is tempered by the sea breezes and Trade winds; the forest interior is very humid and oppressive, although the nights are cooler than in the coastal belt. In the savanna the climate is tropical but varies according to elevation. This is the least humid region.

Rainfall varies from about 90 inches a year on the coast to as much as 140 inches in the forest areas but drops again to about 60 inches in the savannas, where the dry seasons are more prolonged.

THE INTERIOR

From the point of view of settlement, there are only two regions in Guyana—the densely peopled coastal strip and the sparsely settled interior. A large proportion of the inhabitants of the interior are Amerindians. Some of them still live a tribal life, speaking their own dialects and preserving their own customs. They produce enough cassava, sugar, plantains and vegetables for their own needs. They also hunt silently

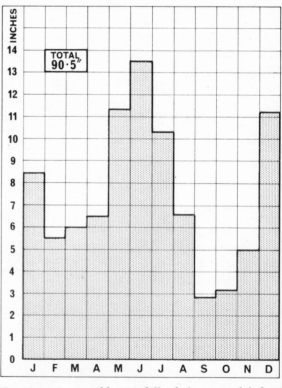

17e. *Average monthly rainfall of the coastal belt of Guyana.*

and skilfully, using bows and arrows to shoot fish in the rivers, and blowpipes with poisoned darts to kill birds and wild animals in the forests. With their blowpipes they are so accurate that they can hit a matchstick at 20 yards. Large animals die in about 10 minutes. Some of their poison, curare, is sent abroad, where it is of use in medicine.

In the early days of Dutch colonization the Amerindians suffered severely from slave raids and from European diseases. Now only a fraction of their former numbers, they have been allotted vast reservations where they can live protected from further exploitation. One of them is as large as Jamaica.

Many Amerindians have left the reservations and are employed in mining, cattle ranching and timber cutting. Others work in the forests earning a living by collecting Brazil nuts and balata, which is the congealed sap of the bulletwood tree. The balata "bleeders", as they are called, are expert not only in finding their way to the bulletwood trees, which are widely scattered, but also in the method of bleeding. This is a difficult job, for the trees are delicate and there are strict laws to prevent them from being cut down or destroyed by careless handling. The men use ladders and ropes to climb the trees and cut the bark in a herringbone pattern with a machete so that the balata trickles down to the bottom, where it is collected in bags. The milky liquid is poured into a box, when a scum soon forms on its surface. This is peeled off and hung over a stick to dry. The process is repeated until the box is empty, after which the sheets of balata are carried down to the coast for export.

Balata, unlike rubber, does not stretch, so it is used to make machine-belting, such as fan belts in cars. It is also used to insulate submarine telegraph cables and to make the casings of golf balls. Since the discovery of satisfactory substitutes the demand for balata has declined.

Different types of forest cover some 70,000 square miles of Guyana, that is, over 80% of the total area of the country. The most important type is the rainforest which occurs in the wetter lowland areas. Because of the difficulty of transporting logs, timber cutting has to take place close to the banks of navigable rivers. This restricts operations to some 14,000 square miles. At present the bulk of the logging and saw-milling takes place in the area known as the

17f, 17g. Amerindians demonstrating how to shoot fish and how to use a blowpipe.

17i. Cattle on the Rupununi savanna. The animals are of a hardy, quick-maturing breed capable of resisting heat, drought and flies. Their long legs enable them to cover large areas of grazing land.

Bartica triangle, bounded by the Essequibo and Marzaruni Rivers.

The forests contain hundreds of species of trees, but only a few are in demand. The most important is greenheart, found only in Guyana. It is used all over the world for marine construction as it does not rot in water and resists the attack of sea creatures which can destroy even steel. Amongst other trees cut are crabwood, mora and wallaba, which are used for fuel and for local building. Mora is used to make furniture, as it resembles mahogany. Wallaba has become the basis of a plyboard industry in which wood chips are mixed with resin and pressed into strong boards. These are used for a variety of purposes, including furniture-making and prefabricated houses. There are many other excellent varieties of wood which are not exported at present because they are not known abroad.

In two parts of the interior the forests give way to large expanses of grassland.

(i) The *Rupununi* savannas take up over 5,000 square miles of land in the south-west close to the Brazilian border. They are divided into two sections, a northern and a southern, by the thickly forested Kanuku Mountains, where some balata is obtained. The rainfall of these savannas is lower than elsewhere, being less than 60 inches a year in most places, and there is a dry season lasting from the beginning of October to the end of April. Three factors have hindered their development. First, during the rainy season large stretches of the savannas are flooded. Second, partly because of the long drought, the grass is of poor quality so that, although about 50,000 cattle are reared on large ranches, each animal needs over 30 acres of grazing even in the best areas. (On the best West Indian pastures a cow can be kept on less than an acre.) Third, the remoteness of the district makes marketing a problem. It has been solved by a method which contrasts with the primitive conditions of so much of the interior. The cattle are slaughtered at an abbatoir at Lethem and the refrigerated meat is sent by air to Georgetown.

Several thousand Amerindians live in the Rupununi savannas. Many of them earn a living as cattlemen, as they are expert riders. Others cultivate tobacco, cassava, corn and vegetables, burning and preparing the fields in the dry season and planting their crops when the first heavy rains arrive.

17h. Greenheart logs being transported by truck. What can you tell about the trees?

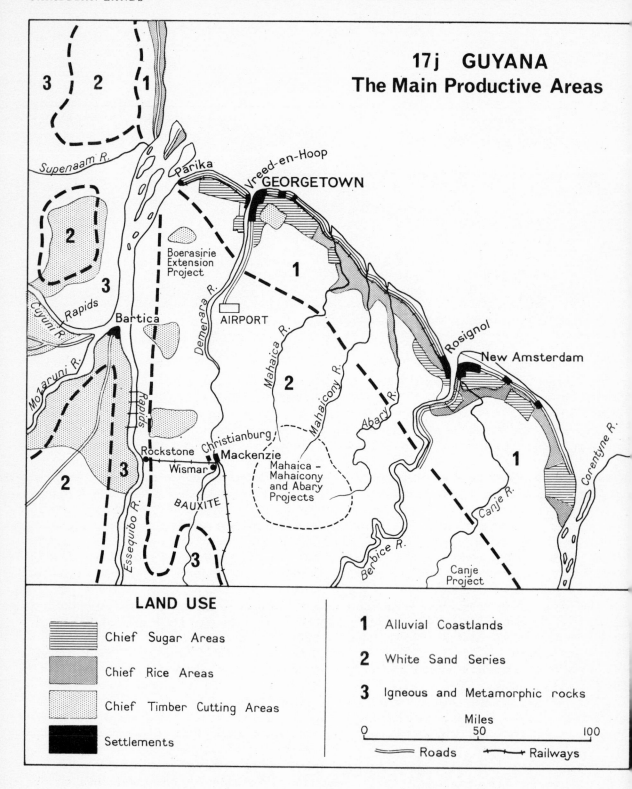

17j GUYANA
The Main Productive Areas

3 2 1

Supenaam R.

Parika

Vreed-en-Hoop

GEORGETOWN

2

3

Boerasirie
Extension
Project

Cuyuni R.

Rapids

Demerara R.

AIRPORT

1

Bartica

Mazaruni R.

Mahaica R.

Rapids

2

Mahaicony R.

Rosignol

New Amsterdam

Abary R.

Rockstone

Christianburg

Mackenzie

Corentyne R.

Wismar

3

2

Mahaica –
Mahaicony
and Abary
Projects

BAUXITE

Canje R.

1

Essequibo R.

3

Berbice R.

Canje
Project

LAND USE

Chief Sugar Areas

Chief Rice Areas

Chief Timber Cutting Areas

Settlements

1 Alluvial Coastlands

2 White Sand Series

3 Igneous and Metamorphic rocks

Miles

0   50   100

Roads   Railways

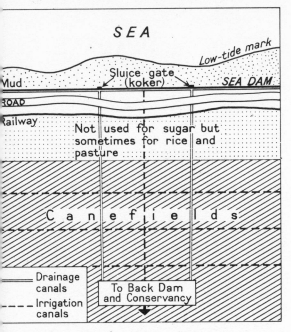

SEA

Low-tide mark

Mud · Sluice gate
(koker) · SEA DAM

ROAD

Railway

Not used for sugar but
sometimes for rice and
pasture

C a n e f i e l d s

Drainage
canals
Irrigation
canals

To Back Dam
and Conservancy

7k. Land use near the coast.

(ii) The *Intermediate* savannas lie east of the
Demerara River and extend to within a short distance
of the coast. Here the grass is of even poorer quality
than that of the Rupununi and very few cattle are
reared there.

In addition, a few patches of savanna occur on
plateau summits in the Pakaraima Mountains.

THE COASTAL FRINGE

Ever since the first successful cultivation of the
coastlands began, virtually all further settlement has
grown up there and the interior has remained almost
unaltered. However, even on the coastlands progress
has been limited, for after two centuries of effort less
than a tenth of their area has been properly drained
and cultivated. Settlement is still almost entirely confined to that section about 100 miles long and 2 to 8
miles wide between the Essequibo and Corentyne
Rivers. Even here men's efforts have often proved
fruitless, and large areas of land which were once
brought under cultivation have since been abandoned.

It is therefore a mistake to think of Guyana with
less than seven people per square mile as an obvious
home for large numbers of emigrants from the over-
crowded Commonwealth Caribbean islands. On the
cultivated land, which amounts to $1\frac{1}{2}\%$ of the total

area of the colony, the population density is 1,000 per
square mile, almost as high as that of Barbados. This
is more than agriculture can support, and the usual
features of overpopulation—poverty, bad housing
and insufficient employment—are all present.

Unfortunately it is not easy to open up new land
in Guyana in spite of the enormous area available. It
seems certain that the vast forests and savannas can
never support dense settlement, and though new land
is being opened up on the coastal strip, this is a slow
and costly process.

The difficulty of developing the coastlands has
arisen because they lie, almost everywhere, a few feet
below high tide mark and so, as we have seen, a wall
has had to be built to keep out the sea. In addition
to this all residential and cultivated areas have to be
protected from flooding by fresh water during the
frequent periods of very heavy rain. This protection is
afforded by an elaborate system of dams which collect
any flood water in large, shallow inland reservoirs or
"conservancies" as they are called. These are drained
by thousands of canals which lead either to the lower
stretches of the rivers, where drainage is possible at
all times, or to the sea, where water can be drained
away only at low tide so that for much of the time it
has to be pumped out.

It is therefore not surprising that so little land has
been brought under cultivation.

The chief crops grown are sugar cane, rice, coconuts and provisions. In addition, some cattle are
kept, mainly for dairy purposes, and there are large
numbers of poultry.

THE CROPS

Sugar

Partly because of the nature of the land and partly
because of the climate, sugar-cane cultivation in
Guyana differs in some respects from that in the
West Indian islands. The climate of the coastlands is
typically Equatorial; that is, the average temperature
is never more than $2°F$. above or below $80°F$. and,
more important, the annual rainfall is heavy, ranging
from 80 inches in Berbice to over 100 inches in
Essequibo.

Cane grows so luxuriantly in the two very rainy
periods which last from mid November to mid
February and from May to mid August that the
yield is higher than anywhere in the West Indies.

171. La Bonne Intention estate. In what way is it different from the estate shown in plate 61?

Some comparative figures for canefields per acre are Hawaii 508 tons, Guyana 220 tons, Barbados 214 tons, Jamaica 146 tons, and Cuba 77 tons. On the other hand because of the relatively few sunny days and the restricted drier periods the sucrose content of Guyanese cane is low and it takes about 20 % more cane to make each ton of sugar. This adds to its expense.

Another contrast with the West Indies is that cane is harvested twice a year—in the two relatively drier periods lasting from mid February to the end of April and from mid August to mid November. The workers therefore do not suffer as acutely from an out-of-crop season as those elsewhere.

Owing to the high cost of land reclamation and maintenance only those sugar companies with considerable capital reserves have been really successful. About 98 % of the sugar output comes from twelve large and two small estates. These estates are situated along the sea coast and a little way up the Berbice,

Demerara and Corentyne Rivers. The nature of the land has influenced their layout. They have a narrow frontage on the sea and a much greater length stretching inland. The soil, for perhaps a mile behind the sea-dam, is not suitable for sugar cane, but sometimes provides pasture or is used to grow rice. The main road, the railway and most of the settlements are also close to the sea. Then, extending perhaps as much as 7 miles inland are the estate's cane fields, which in most cases are centred around a big factory. The estate is terminated by the back-dam which separates it from the swamp or the shallow waters of the conservancy behind.

Drainage canals stretch from the back-dam where they obtain water to the sea-dam where they drain. Some irrigation canals run parallel to these while others branch off at right angles so that each field is bounded by one drainage and three irrigation canals. On some estates waterways exceed 300 miles in length and take up an eighth of the total area. As they are

7m. A punt loaded with sugar cane being hauled to the mill.

17n. Sugar cane being fed into the mill.

expensive to maintain, every possible use is made of them. For instance, irrigation canals are brought into use to flood the cane fields for a few days whenever the rainfall is inadequate. They are also used for transport during the harvest. The reaped canes are carried from the fields and stacked in steel barges. Trains of five or six of these, each carrying 5 to 6 tons of cane, are drawn to the factory by mules, oxen and tractors. Travelling along the irrigation canals the punts cross over the drainage canals by means of greenheart bridges. Again, it is common after about four harvests have been gathered to use the irrigation canals to flood the cane fields under a foot of water for a few months before replanting. This "flood-fallowing", as it is called, destroys weeds and partially restores soil fertility lost by the practice of burning the cane before it is cut instead of saving the trash for use as fertilizer.

At present sugar cane takes up about a quarter of the land under commercial crops. The annual sugar output is usually over 300,000 tons and it rose to over 334,000 tons in 1960. About 22,000 tons is retained for local consumption and the remainder is exported. The United Kingdom takes about three-quarters of the exports and the remainder goes to Canada and the United States. In 1962 sugar formed 36% of the exports, bauxite 19%, alumina 14% and rice 13%.

Now that the territory's sugar export quota has been reached it is unlikely that much new land will be brought under cane cultivation. As the output has doubled since the beginning of the century without increase in area, further improvements in yield will probably account for any extra sugar required. Any such improvement will be of great benefit to Guyana because it will lower the cost of the sugar, which is at present the most expensive in the world.

Rice

With the opening up of new land on the coast the area under rice has expanded rapidly in recent years, and the crop now occupies between two and three times as much land as sugar cane. The output in 1964 was over 155,000 tons and this can be expected to increase.

Owing to the two wet seasons it is possible to grow two rice crops a year. Because the mid-year rains last longer and are more dependable, nine-tenths of the crop is planted in April and May and reaped in late September and October. The remainder is planted in November and harvested in March.

Rice growing in Guyana is not as easy as geographical conditions might lead us to expect, and many people growing it are very poor. Some reasons for this are:

1. Some of the rice is grown on abandoned cane fields which, it is true, were originally provided with drainage and irrigation canals. But to be of any use these canals must be properly maintained all the way from the back-dam to the sea. This was possible while the land was under one management, but it is difficult to do now that it has been split into many separate holdings. Thus in spite of recent developments, about 40% of the rice is grown on land lacking proper drainage and irrigation and there are considerable losses in very wet or very dry years. In this respect it should be noted that though the coastal average is 90 inches of rain a year, totals as low as 24 inches and as high as 200 inches have been recorded.

2. Except on the new land reclamation schemes where rice plots average 15 acres and where machinery is available, most farms are between 3 and 5 acres in size. This is too small to provide the farmer with an adequate income. On the other hand a farmer's acreage is limited to the amount of land that he and his family can reap in the short time available between the crop ripening and the seed falling to the ground and spoiling. So without mechanical aids, which most of the peasants are too poor to afford, farms cannot be increased in size and the deadlock cannot be broken. It is for this reason that most rice farmers keep a few cattle and poultry or try to earn a little extra cash by working in the cane fields during the harvests.

3. Linked with this is the fact that methods of cultivating and preparing the crop are often primitive. It is still common practice for the reaped rice to be stacked on the edge of the fields, where the grain is trodden out by oxen. This operation, known as "bull-mashing", is very wasteful.

4. Another reason for the poor quality of some of the rice is that there are many small, inefficient mills in operation throughout the country.

In recent years increased rice and vegetable production and improved living conditions for farmers has been brought about by the opening of Government-

17o. Rice in Guyana.

planned land reclamation schemes. The first was the Mahaicony-Abary Rice Development Scheme which was started in the Second World War when British rice supplies were cut off by the Japanese invasion of south-east Asia. Thousands of acres of land near the mouths of the Mahaicony and Abary Rivers were reclaimed and in a few years it became, and still remains, one of the largest areas of mechanical rice production in the Commonwealth. Others are the Boerasirie Extension Project, the Canje Project, the Tapacuma Project and the Black Bush Polder on the Corentyne coast. The Government is also aiding peasants to buy machines for their farms and has built large, modern rice mills such as that at Anna Regina to ensure that the crop is properly processed. To safeguard quality all of the rice is purchased and graded by the Rice Marketing Board. For export the better grades are packed in cardboard boxes and the cheaper grades in paper bags. These projects have helped to improve conditions, but because rice sells so cheaply in the world it is not a crop to make any country prosperous. This can be seen from the fact that though rice takes up well over twice as much land as cane the value of the rice produced is only one-third that of sugar. Usually about two-thirds of the rice crop is exported, mainly to the Commonwealth Caribbean islands as Guyana is the only territory in the region with a rice surplus.

Coconuts

Most of the coconut plantations have been established on long, narrow sand reefs which stand a few feet above the level of the surrounding land. These reefs, which run parallel to the coast, are thought to be old sea beaches. About 50 million nuts are gathered each year for conversion into copra, coconut oil, margarine, lard and soap. There is seldom much left over for export and there is room for considerable expansion, as the Commonwealth Caribbean islands can no longer supply all their needs.

Other Crops

The usual West Indian food crops are grown. Production is in most cases sufficient to satisfy rural requirements and to leave a little over for sale in the towns. Coffee grows well on the better-drained soils but the output is small and most is consumed locally. There is a small area under citrus and some lime juice exported. The area under cocoa is expanding, particularly on lands owned by sugar estates. Cocoa is manufactured locally into chocolate and confectionery.

THE PEOPLE

With the rise of the coastal sugar plantations in the late seventeenth century, labour was needed and slaves were imported in such large numbers that by 1837 there were 85,000 in the country. Since then the number of Negroes has grown, partly because of immigration from Africa and from some West Indian islands but mainly by natural increase.

The first Indians landed in 1838. By 1917, when the indenture system was stopped, nearly a quarter of a million had arrived. This was over half the total who came to the Caribbean. Though many chose to return home when their contracts expired, the majority remained in Guyana as field workers on the estates or as rice cultivators on their own holdings. Since then some have entered the professions and others have become merchants in the towns.

Though the descendants of the Indian immigrants have largely overcome language and educational barriers, they are still a distinct community. Their ties with India are still strong and there are many who say they would like to return. When, after the Second World War, India became an independent nation, a party of Indians sailed from Georgetown with the

17p. *A group of children in Guyana. What races are represented here?*

intention of settling in their old homeland. They discovered, as others have done, that "back to Africa" and "back to India" movements are no panacea, as living and working conditions in the West Indies, though often hard, are usually much better than those available in most parts of Africa and Asia.

Until recently the labouring population in Guyana suffered severely from malaria, hookworm, dysentery and other diseases. Malaria has now been eradicated in the densely settled parts of the coast. This and other improvements in health services and sanitation resulted in the death-rate being halved between 1943 and 1953 and it is still going down. Population is now increasing rapidly and because the birth-rate among the Indians is higher than that of any other racial group, the proportion of Indians in the community is steadily rising. They have become the largest racial group, making up over half of the entire population.

Other races are present in small numbers only. There are several thousand people of Portuguese descent. Originally entering Guyana from Madeira and the Azores as indentured labourers like the Indians, they soon left the sugar estates. Many have become shop-owners, especially in Georgetown. The European group is very small, but, because it controls the biggest commercial interests in the country, it is still powerful.

A small group of Chinese immigrants and the Amerindians make up the rest of the population.

The population estimates for 1964 were as follows:

Indian descent	:	320,100
African descent	:	199,800
Mixed	:	76,000
Chinese	:	3,900
Portuguese	:	6,400
Other Europeans	:	2,400
Amerindians	:	29,400

THE COASTAL TOWNS

Georgetown, with its suburbs, contains about a quarter of the population of Guyana. It first grew up as a small Dutch fort protecting the settlements along the Demerara River and became a small township when the riverside estates were abandoned in favour of the coastlands and sugar became the dominant export. A capital city and a port were needed, and as Georgetown was selected to fulfil both these functions it soon became by far the most important settlement. The residential sections developed when many of the estate-owners built themselves large houses on the outskirts of the town with the money they received from the British Government at the time of the emancipation of their slaves. At the same time many of the freed slaves also left the plantations to settle in the city, and the proportion of Negroes and coloured people in Georgetown has been very high ever since.

Most of the buildings in Georgetown are made of timber obtained from the interior forests. Today, however, many of the large buildings are being made of concrete. Development has always been hampered because Georgetown lies on flat land a few feet below the level of the sea. Drainage has been the most difficult problem and the vast majority of the dwellings in Georgetown and elsewhere along the coast are raised on wood, brick or concrete piles to protect them from the damp. Many open, muddy drainage canals, or "trenches" as they are called, lead through the city to the river, but even these may flood during periods of very heavy rain. Other canals have been covered over, and trees and grass have been planted on them to provide shaded walks in the midst of busy streets, on which, owing to the flatness of the land, there are innumerable cyclists.

Georgetown, which handles practically all the country's trade except the export of bauxite and some of the sugar, has two fronts, one on the sea and the other on the Demerara River. All the wharves, or "stellings" as they are called, have been built on the river bank, for only along the river is there deep sheltered water right up to the shore. However, even the river suffers a disadvantage in that the sand-bar at its mouth has a clearance of only 18 feet at high tide, which prevents large vessels from docking at Georgetown.

Georgetown is the administrative centre and by far the most important shopping and banking town in Guyana. It has several light industries such as food processing, brewing, saw-milling, ship-building and repairing, printing and woodwork. In addition it is the centre of the fishing industry, though most of the coastal villages have a few small boats engaged in this work.

On the opposite bank of the Demerara River is the small settlement of Vreed-en-Hoop connected to Georgetown by a fairly frequent ferry service.

Other settlements on the coast vary in size from small villages to townships containing several thousand people. The inhabitants are mainly concerned with fishing and with growing food crops and rice, though they often seek employment on the sugar estates at harvest time. New Amsterdam (15,000), the third largest town in Guyana, occupies much the same position on the Berbice River as Georgetown does on the Demerara. It was founded at about the same time, but it has never rivalled Georgetown in importance as it lies on a shallower river which can take only small coastal vessels. It acts as the chief shopping centre for those people living on the eastern section of the coastlands between the Berbice and Corentyne Rivers. It is connected by ferry to Rosignol on the western side of the Berbice River. This in turn is linked with Georgetown by road and rail. Bartica (3,500) is the focus of almost all overland communication with the interior. It is a collecting centre for timber and gold and is connected to Georgetown by a regular steamer service.

COMMUNICATIONS

As one would expect, the pattern of communications in the largely undeveloped interior is completely different from that in the densely settled section of the coastlands.

In the interior a few miles of narrow-gauge railway line have been laid chiefly around Mackenzie, to

7q. Looking across the Demerara River from Georgetown. What can you tell about communications?

carry bauxite and timber down to the Demerara River. In addition, roads run from Bartica into the logging, diamond and gold-mining areas near by. Apart from these all heavy traffic is river-borne, though even river transport is not without difficulty. Unfortunately, separating the navigable stretches, the rivers have several series of rapids which are often difficult to negotiate and in the dry season, when the water is lower, it may be impossible to cross them. It is the distance upstream of the first rapid that limits the extent of the important logging areas, just as in bygone days it limited the Dutch estates. This distance varies from about 40 to 100 miles, only a fraction of the length of the rivers themselves. Punts

towed by tugs carry timber, and motor-boats are used for passenger transport. Small steamers can reach Bartica on the Essequibo to load timber, and Mackenzie on the Demerara for bauxite. Aeroplanes provide the only other link with the interior. In a couple of hours they fly to remote places which it takes weeks to reach by other means. A few are equipped to alight on the rivers but most land on airstrips which have been prepared in the interior.

There can be no doubt that development in the interior is being retarded by lack of transport. But the money needed to build communications is not available, nor is the interior potentially rich enough to claim precedence over the coastlands which are also in need of great sums of money for development.

On the coastal strip railways and roads replace rivers as means of communication. Indeed the major rivers, all over half a mile wide near their mouths, are barriers to transport, cutting up the coastlands into four distinct segments. None of them has been bridged and the only communication from bank to bank is by ferry. There are two railways. The more important one, which links Georgetown with Rosignol 60 miles away, was the first to be built in South America. The other, a narrow-gauge line, runs for 19 miles from Vreed-en-Hoop to Parika. The main roads follow these lines closely, but in addition a road runs eastwards from New Amsterdam to the Corentyne River and another runs inland from Georgetown to Atkinson airport. Only a few miles of these roads are asphalt surfaced.

The last means of communication in this area is the sea itself. As all the cultivated land lies along the sea or the lower stretches of the rivers, some of the sugar and rice is sent by small coastal vessels to Georgetown to await shipment abroad.

TRADE

Unlike almost all the Commonwealth Caribbean islands, in recent years Guyana has often had a favourable balance of trade (that is, its exports are worth more than its imports).

As Guyana has virtually no trade with its South American neighbours, its trade is directed overseas and is based on the chief port, Georgetown. In 1962 23% of the exports went to the United Kingdom, 27% went to Canada and 21% to the United States.

In return these countries provided 35%, 7% and 23% of the imports respectively.

THINGS TO DO
1. Find out the climatic and other conditions mo suited to the cultivation of rice. Make a list of th world's major rice-producing, rice-exporting an rice-importing countries.
2. Compare and contrast the sugar industry i Guyana with that of the country in which you liv
3. Draw a percentage diagram to show the popula tion of Guyana given on page 176.

QUESTIONS
1. Using headings of your own, compare Guyan with Belize and Jamaica. On balance, which c them do you think is most similar to Guyana?
2. (*a*) Show on a sketch-map the major divisions int which Guyana may be divided. (*b*) Give a account of the main occupations of the people i each of your divisions, mentioning some of th major physical difficulties under which the occupa tions are carried on. O.C.S.E.B.(O). 1965.
3. Compare the importance of agricultural, minera and forest products in Guyana.
4. Why does such a large proportion of the popula tion of Guyana live in a relatively small part of it area? C.H.S.C. 1958.
5. How far do you agree with the statement tha "Although Guyana is a large country on the map it is really a West Indian island which happens t be separated from the mainland of South Americ by eight feet of water instead of by eight miles, a is Trinidad"?

Index

179

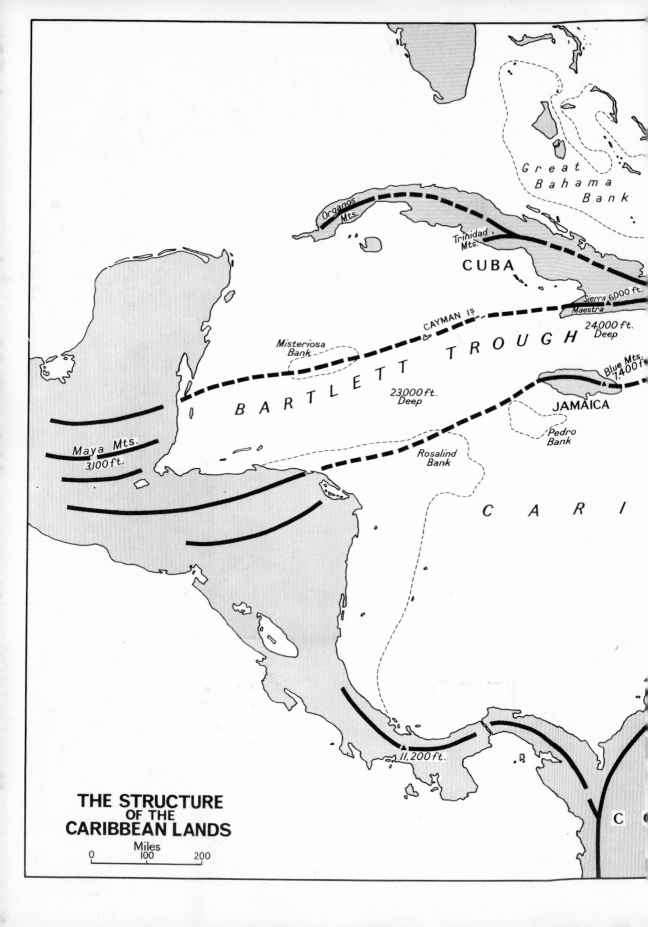

Great
Bahama
Bank

Organos
Mts.

Trinidad
Mts.

CUBA

Sierra 6000 ft.
Maestra

24,000 ft.
Deep

CAYMAN IS.

Blue Mts.
7400 f

Misteriosa
Bank

B A R L E T T   T R O U G H

JAMAICA

23,000 ft.
Deep

Pedro
Bank

Maya Mts.
3,100 ft.

Rosalind
Bank

C A R I

C

11,200 ft.

C

**THE STRUCTURE
OF THE
CARIBBEAN LANDS**

Miles

0   100   200